# LEADERSHIP FOR INNOVATION

# LEADERSHIP FOR INNOVATION

Three Essential Skill Sets for
Leading Employee-Driven Innovation

## DAVID MASUMBA

NEW YORK
LONDON • NASHVILLE • MELBOURNE • VANCOUVER

# LEADERSHIP FOR INNOVATION
## Three Essential Skill Sets for Leading Employee-Driven Innovation

© 2019 DAVID MASUMBA

All rights reserved. No portion of this book may be reproduced, stored in a retrieval system, or transmitted in any form or by any means—electronic, mechanical, photocopy, recording, scanning, or other—except for brief quotations in critical reviews or articles, without the prior written permission of the publisher.

Published in New York, New York, by Morgan James Publishing. Morgan James is a trademark of Morgan James, LLC. www.MorganJamesPublishing.com

ISBN 978-1-64279-253-9 paperback
ISBN 978-1-64279-254-6 eBook
ISBN 978-1-64279-255-3 hardcover
Library of Congress Control Number: 2018910538

**Cover Design by:**
Rachel Lopez
www.r2cdesign.com

In an effort to support local communities, raise awareness and funds, Morgan James Publishing donates a percentage of all book sales for the life of each book to Habitat for Humanity Peninsula and Greater Williamsburg.

Get involved today! Visit
www.MorganJamesBuilds.com

*To my mother, Doris, uncle J.K. and mama Eunice*

# CONTENTS

| | | |
|---|---|---|
| *Preface* | | *ix* |
| *Introduction* | | *xi* |

**PART I: INNOVATIVE THINKING SKILLS** — 1
- Chapter 1 Understanding Innovative Thinking Skills — 3
- Chapter 2 Approaches: How Do You Develop Innovative Thinking Skills? — 11
- Chapter 3 Why Is It Important for Organizational Leaders to Have Innovative Thinking Abilities in Leading Workforce Innovation? — 18

**PART II: INNOVATION ENGAGEMENT SKILLS** — 33
- Chapter 4 Definition of *Innovation Engagement Skills* — *37*
- Chapter 5 Importance of Innovation Engagement Skills — 42
- Chapter 6 Description and Expression of Innovation Engagement Initiatives — 46
- Chapter 7 Innovation Engagement Committees — 52
- Chapter 8 Application of Innovation Engagement Approaches — 55

**PART III: INNOVATION MANAGEMENT SKILLS** — 83
- Chapter 9 Ability to Engage in Innovation-Oriented Planning Activities — 101
- Chapter 10 Ability to Identify Areas for Innovation Focus — 104
- Chapter 11 Ability to Create and Implement Innovation-Performance Job Descriptions and Job Specifications — 111
- Chapter 12 Ability to Create Innovation-Challenge Questions — 114
- Chapter 13 Ability to Formulate Innovation Goals — 134
- Chapter 14 Ability to Design and Implement an Effective Management for Innovation Ideas — 156
- Chapter 15 Ability to Measure and Report Innovation Performance — 194

| | |
|---|---|
| *Summary* | *283* |
| *About the Author* | *284* |
| *Selected References* | *285* |
| *Notes* | *286* |
| *Index* | *288* |

# PREFACE

> *Ability to drive innovation in organizations is one of the top competencies required of organization leaders today.*
> —IBM Institute for Business Value

Not long ago, innovation in organizations was perceived as the responsibility of specific functional units and professionals. That's no longer the case; study after study has revealed that many organizations now perceive innovation as everyone's job, from senior leadership to the most junior employee. However, a number of studies and analysts have observed that although organizations are urging their entire workforce to get involved in driving innovation, many organizational leaders do not seem to have the skill sets required to make every employee responsible for driving innovation. So what skill sets should senior executives, managers, and supervisors possess to lead and effectively systemize innovation across all functional units of the organization?

For more than ten years, I've been engaged in innovation training and consulting, offered training programs, and interacted with organizational leaders on the topic of innovation leadership. I've also conducted reviews of a number of studies and publications related to leading workforce innovation. My experience is that most organizations and publications have a narrow perspective of the skill sets organizational leaders should possess. In many cases, the definition of these skill sets is based only on leadership-related traits and behaviors. This book contests such a narrow view point and suggests a broad perspective on skill sets for leading workforce innovation. This book is a culmination of research, experiences with clients, lessons from the practitioner world learned through various public training programs that I've conducted in different countries over the years, and my interaction with professionals at conferences and meetings. The book suggests three categories of innovation skill sets that are essential for leading employee-driven innovation: innovative thinking skills, innovation engagement skills, and innovation management skills.

# INTRODUCTION

> *Innovative companies don't just happen; they are consciously cultivated at the leadership level, and then throughout the organization.*
> —**Jeff Dyer**, Horace Beesley Professor of Strategy, Brigham Young University

**Overview**
There are five vital aspects of innovation that need to be understood from the onset. First, workforce innovation implies employee-driven innovation in which everyone in the organization is involved. In other words, employee-driven innovation aims at realizing a meaningful level of workforce engagement in advancing innovation across all functional units of an organization. The second vital aspect is that study after study has observed that in the last ten years or so, company executives across the globe have consistently ranked innovation as one of the top-priority strategies for growth, competitiveness, and survival. Third, the culture of innovation does not occur naturally; it occurs only if a climate for innovation is created. Fourth, a climate for innovation across the organization can be created only by implementing innovation-support initiatives on a continual basis. Fifth, many studies have observed that conventional management models are not effective in creating a climate for innovation in organizations. This means that there's a need for specific innovation-oriented skill sets to drive innovation across the functional units of an organization, which is where this book comes in. It will:

i. Explain what leadership for innovation entails in the context of leading employee-driven innovation

ii. Describe the three essential innovation skill sets required for leading employee-driven innovation
iii. Explain how to apply the three essential innovation skill sets to build a climate for innovation and make innovation systematic and ongoing across functional units

This introduction lays the groundwork for future chapters by providing a summary of the essence of the book, outlining the structure of the book, and defining some key phrases and terminology. The aspects covered in the chapter are as follows:
1. Premises
2. Definition of *leadership for innovation*
3. Objectives
4. Audience
5. Interpretation and derivation of the innovation skill sets
6. Innovation-performance job descriptions and job specifications
7. Meaning of making innovation "systemic"
8. Structure

## 1. Premises
The book is based on the following premises described as follows:
i. *Innovation leadership is too simplistically defined.* As is clear from my interactions with organizational leaders in various countries and from reading articles in a number of publications, many seem to have interpreted the topic of leadership for innovation in a simplistic manner. For instance, in the 2009 report *Innovation Leadership*, the North Carolina-based Center for Creative Leadership described a narrow conception of *leadership for innovation* consisting of the following aspects:
    o *Organizational encouragement:* An organizational environment where the leadership encourages followers to generate ideas
    o *Lack of organizational impediments:* A culture where barriers to innovation are identified and removed
    o *Leadership encouragement:* An environment where workforces feel a sense of freedom in making decisions about work-related projects
    o *Sufficient resources:* Workforces should be given access to resources to advance innovation across their organizations
    o *Freedom:* Innovation thrives where workforces have the freedom to decide what work to do and how to do it
    o *Challenging work:* Innovation thrives where workforces feel a sense of being challenged by their work
    o *Teamwork and collaboration:* People in innovative organizations should have open communication and support for one another's ideas across the organization

    These factors characterize a one-sided perspective that is insufficient to create the conditions for advancing innovation in organizations because, as we shall see later, the social-psychological perspective on leadership is just one of the contributions needed to develop enabling conditions for workforce innovation. In addition to the social-psychological aspects of leadership, other necessary components include "hearts-and-minds" conditions and system or structural conditions to support workforce innovation across the organization.

The joint *Leadership for Innovation* report, conducted in 2005 by the United Kingdom's Chartered Management Institute and Advanced Institute of Management Research, argues that organizational leadership can affect innovation in more complex ways than would be implied by a focus solely on inspirational leadership. However, this report presents another simplistic perspective on what constitutes leadership for innovation. The report acknowledges that there are two broad conceptions of what leaders do in relation to creating organizational conditions for innovation to thrive: leaders (1) motivate and inspire their followers and (2) design organizational contexts for innovation to thrive. The report outlines and describes various social-psychological processes (such as trait and style approaches to leadership) that leaders can apply to steer and advance innovation in organizations. However, if you take a closer look, the report does not explain how the various conventional trait and style leadership approaches can be applied in the context of instilling innovation performance in the hearts and minds of workforces. Thus, the perspective is too simplistic. In addition, the conception of leadership that the report refers to as contributing to creating enabling conditions for innovation is the "structuralist or management approach to leadership." However, the report narrows the structuralist perspective to mean the creation of effective innovation-development processes in organizations. The report does not mention creating and adopting innovation-support systems and practices, such as corporate innovation strategies, innovation-performance reports, functional-unit innovation-performance goals, workforce innovation-performance rewards, alignment of innovation-performance and talent-recruitment practices, development of innovation-performance succession-planning frameworks, and other innovation-support requirements that are critical to advancing workforce innovation across the functional units of an organization.

The position of this book in relation to these two perspectives is that it's difficult to leverage workforce innovation to drive meaningful profitability, corporate growth, and competitiveness if leaders possess a narrow perspective on innovation skill sets.

ii. *Organizations are now seeking to broaden innovation capabilities across functional units.* The conventional approach to innovation in organizations has been that innovation is the responsibility of specific functional units and professionals, yet studies have revealed that in many cases, the functional units responsible for innovation struggle to meet the organization's demands for innovation. Further, most innovative companies—such as Apple, Amazon, Google, Tesla, Microsoft, IBM, GE, 3M, Netflix, Samsung Group, Toyota, and Uber—require multiple innovation pipelines to satisfy their innovation and growth demands. Also, innovative companies are usually at risk of losing their top innovation talent. For example, according to a Forbes online publication, Apple lost about 150 innovation talent and executives to Tesla between 2008 and 2015. In order to mitigate the effect of losing innovation talent on the innovation performance of functional units, organizations are now broadening innovation capabilities across functional units and making innovation every employee's responsibility. According to a 2010 Institute for Corporate Productivity study on the topic of innovation, virtually all 641 respondents representing organizations with a thousand or more employees agreed that innovation had increased in importance across their organizations and further agreed that innovation would become more important in the next five years. In a 2012 interview with Roger Crockett, a veteran business writer and contributor to *Harvard Business Review*, on innovation and culture at Procter & Gamble, the then *CEO and chairman Bob McDonald described how innovation is perceived at* Procter & Gamble: "Innovation is perceived as the lifeblood of the company. We talk about the fact that we have five strengths. One of those strengths is innovation. We expect every employee to deliver innovation." McDonald continued, "So, whether you're the worker in a factory line, you're expected to innovate the process of making the product. Whether you're an executive assistant in a general office, you're expected to innovate that job in order to continue to improve our ability to touch and improve lives, which is our purpose."

iii. *Organizational leaders face difficulties in creating a culture of innovation.* One of the challenges that today's business leaders are facing in relation to employee-driven innovation is a lack of the right leadership skill sets needed to make innovation systemic and permanent across functional units. The 2005 *Leadership for Innovation* report by the Chartered Management Institute and Advanced Institute of Management Research, mentioned earlier, notes that leadership is required to create the right organizational climate where innovation thrives. A 2007 joint study of 293 senior executives from 17 industrial sectors across the global corporations by US-based management consulting firm, Oliver Wyman in conjunction with the Economist Intelligence Unit revealed that three out of four executives believed that an innovation strategy was critical to their company's success. However, the study revealed that fewer than half of the companies were creating a climate that fosters innovation. According to the study, the executives agreed that creating a culture of innovation across functional units was the major challenge to their leadership. The executives also agreed that the biggest obstacle was the shortage of leaders who demonstrate through their behavior that innovation is essential to business success. In the same study more than half of the respondents indicated that leaders in their companies did not establish a clear purpose and supportive climate for innovation. And the 2010 Institute for Corporate Productivity report notes that the challenge that many senior and junior organizational leaders face is that they do not have the right skill sets to lead and systemize innovation across the organization. Other reports have also revealed that in a bid to promote innovation practices across functional units of their organizations, many managers merely urge or encourage workforces, through verbal or written communications, to be innovative. My experience with managing workforces and interacting with managers across the globe is that mere encouragement of workforces to be innovative gives you zero results in terms of innovation performance from those workforces. In a 2017 study by PwC that surveyed 1,200 executives in 44 countries, one of the aspects mentioned in this report is that over the past dozen years (of conducting similar studies), the studies have consistently revealed that majority of companies are implementing operating models aimed at involving all functional units in advancing innovation. Similarly, other studies have revealed that systemizing and making innovation permanent across the functional units of an organization in a valuable way takes more than just verbal encouragement of workforces to be innovative. It requires an integrated approach that includes (1) appropriate skills and abilities of top leadership to develop the right initiatives and programs aimed at instilling emotional interest and passion for innovation in the hearts and minds of their workforces and (2) the right systems for advancing and sustaining innovation performance in the organization. It's this kind of leadership approach that many organizational leaders lack.

iv. *Current conventional management models are stacked against innovation performance.* At a conference on innovation held at Harvard Business School in 2007, panelists noted that traditional management practices have little to contribute to innovation performance. Many panelists at this conference felt that the current conventional management models are stacked against innovation performance. The obvious implication is that if organizational leaders are to meaningfully contribute to innovation performance in their organizations, they must possess the necessary innovation skills to develop and implement crosscutting innovation-support systems and practices to create a climate for innovation in their organizations.

v. *Leadership is the best predictor of innovation performance:* Studies have revealed that leadership capabilities of an organization are critical to creating a culture of innovation. For instance, in a 2008 survey of 600 hundred business executives, managers, and professionals by McKinsey & company, a global management consulting firm, respondents suggested that leadership was the best predictor of innovation performance. According to the survey, respondents who described their organizations as more innovative than other companies in its industry rated its leadership as "strong" or "very strong". However, respondents who belived that the ability of their organization to innovate was below average rated the leadership capabilities of their organization as significantly lower and, in some cases, poor. The question is, if leadership is the best predictor of innovation performance or culture of innovation in organizations, *What innovation skill sets do leaders require to execute leadership for innovation in an effective way?*

## 2. Definition of *Leadership for Innovation*

The first question on seeing the title of the book might be, *What is leadership for innovation, anyway?* This book defines *leadership for innovation* as leadership provided by individuals who possess particular innovation skill sets and the ability to execute those skill sets to build a culture of innovation in which every employee across the organization is involved in driving innovation.

## 3. Objectives
This book has four objectives:
  i. To identify and describe the three essential innovation skill sets for leading workforce innovation
  ii. To explain why the three innovation skill sets for leading workforce innovation are vital
  iii. To demonstrate how the three innovation skill sets can be developed
  iv. iv.To describe how the three innovation skill sets can be applied to execute innovation-performance duties and responsibilities across the functional units of an organization

## 4. Audience
This book has the following intended audience:
  i. Senior and midlevel managers in any sector or industry, such as pharmaceuticals, energy, financial services, computing, education services, retail, telecommunications, media services, mining, agribusiness, food services, beverage, transport and logistics, manufacturing, health services, and so forth
  ii. Individuals being developed to take up supervisory and managerial positions in their companies
  iii. Undergraduate and graduate students aspiring to work in the corporate world
  iv. Government policy makers involved in championing innovation and designing national innovation policies aimed at advancing innovation in the private sector

## 5. Interpretation and Derivation of the Innovation Skill Sets
The interpretation and derivation of the innovation skill sets involve the following aspects:

  i. **Definition of *Skills***
  Before defining *innovation skills* specifically, it is important to understand the generic meaning of the word *skills*. The general definition of *skill* is something you do or attain through training and repetition.

  ii. **Definition of *Innovation Skills***
  From the perspective of organizational functional activities, *innovation skills* can be defined as a combination of abilities that individuals can attain and apply in a particular organizational context to contribute toward advancing innovation in an organization.

  iii. **Application**
  Where and how do you apply innovation skills? The premises on which this book is based are described at the beginning of the chapter. One of those premises is that organizations are now perceiving innovation as everybody's business, from the most junior in the organization to the CEO. So in answer to the question of how and where innovation skills are applied, innovation skills are applied in every sector,

Introduction | xvii

industry, and profession and by all types of employees, irrespective of their position or level of seniority in the organization. In other words, people are not born with innovation skills; anybody and everybody can develop or attain innovation skills.

iv. **Categories of Innovation Skill Sets**
As stated earlier, this book identifies three categories or types of innovation skill sets that are essential for leading workforce innovation, namely *innovative thinking skills*, *innovation engagement skills*, and *innovation management skills*. These three categories of innovation skill sets are presented in three parts, I, II, and III respectively, with each part focusing on a particular category.

v. **Derivation of the Innovation Skill Sets**
The types of innovation skill sets on which this book is based are derived from the context of measuring or determining innovation performance. But how is innovation performance measured? Traditionally, innovation performance in organizations is measured in two contexts: *innovation inputs* and *innovation outputs*. The broad characteristics of these two contexts are discussed in detail in the final chapter of this book. In terms of how the innovation skills are derived and used to formulate the three categories of innovation skill sets on which the book is based—innovation management skills, innovation engagement skills, and innovative thinking skills—the first two of the innovation skill sets are derived from the measurement of innovation inputs, whereas the third innovation skill set is derived from the measurement of innovation outputs.

*Innovation inputs:* There are various kinds of innovation inputs or innovation-support initiatives that are usually implemented organization-wide to create a climate for innovation. Innovation inputs are characterized differently in terms of human abilities and nonhuman abilities. Some of the nonhuman abilities or capacities include research and development (R&D) spending and implementation of innovation-support technologies. However, in most cases, the climate for innovation in organizations is created by implementing specific innovation-support initiatives that are generated by direct application of human abilities or capacities. The two innovation skill sets derived from the characteristics or context of innovation inputs are outlined as follows:

- *Innovation management skills:* In a nutshell, innovation management skills involve creating and implementing organization-wide innovation-support systems, such as innovation-support strategies, innovation policies, innovation procedures, innovation plans, innovation-development processes, and workforce innovation skill-development programs.

- *Innovation engagement skills*: This innovation skill set involves the application of skills and abilities by organizational leaders to create and implement organization-wide innovation-support initiatives aimed at specifically engaging and instilling innovation in the hearts and minds of workforces.

*Innovation outputs:* The term *innovation outputs* refers to the metrics used to measure the outcome or result of implementing different forms of and approaches to innovation-support initiatives across the organization. Metrics for characterizing innovation outputs are translated in different contexts and terminologies depending on how an organization characterizes and defines the innovation output metrics. Examples of innovation outputs include innovations (developed from innovative ideas) and also the revenues generated from innovations. Thus, the generation of diverse innovative ideas by workforces that emanates from the innovative thinking abilities of workforces is also an innovative output. These abilities are normally developed over time through deliberate and specific efforts and approaches at the individual and corporate levels, such as those discussed in part I of this book. In other words, generation of innovative ideas on a continual basis by workforces does not happen naturally; it requires developing and nurturing innovative thinking abilities, which in turn influence the generation of different types and degrees of innovative ideas in the context of the functional activities of an organization. Therefore, the category of innovation skill sets derived from innovation output is innovative thinking skills. Part I demonstrates how organizational leaders can leverage their innovative thinking skills to build and lead a culture of innovation across an organization's value chain.

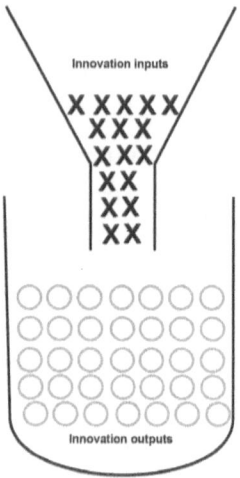

*Figure 0-1. Innovation inputs and outputs*

The simple diagram in figure 0-1 illustrates the interplay of innovation inputs and innovation outputs.

## 6. Innovation-Performance Job Descriptions and Job Specifications

It's important to understand that, like any type of skill, innovation skills are not applied in a vacuum; they are applied in job positions. So if organizational leaders are to effectively and competently apply all three types of innovation skill sets, it's vital that leaders understand the context in which each of the three innovation skill sets should be applied to lead employee-driven innovation across the organization. This is why organizational leaders should have the ability to formulate innovation-performance job descriptions and job specifications, through which leadership for innovation should be expressed or applied. Thus, this section looks at the definition and description of *innovation-performance job descriptions and job specifications*. Samples of innovation-performance job descriptions and job specifications worksheets are provided in chapter eleven.

i. **Definition:** *What are innovation-performance duties and responsibilities?*
Innovation-performance duties and responsibilities can be separated into three categories: (1) *innovative thinking–related duties and responsibilities*, (2) *innovation*

*engagement–related duties and responsibilities*, and (3) *innovation management–related duties and responsibilities*. Details on each of the three categories are as follows:

- *Innovative thinking–related duties and responsibilities:* These are duties and responsibilities that are focused on the identification of problems/needs and opportunities and the generation of innovative ideas/solutions to deal with the identified challenges, which ultimately add commercial value to the organization.

  Note that specific duties and responsibilities vary by organization and by functional unit. In terms of functional units, innovative ideas can be generated in either core or support functional units. Some of the core functional units include product design and development, manufacturing processes, market-strategy development, and customer service. Support functional units include human resources (HR), information technology (IT), procurement, finance and accounting, corporate affairs, and so forth. Also bear in mind that innovative ideas generated in support functional units are mainly for efficiency and cost-saving purposes.

- *Innovation engagement–related duties and responsibilities:* These are innovation-performance duties and responsibilities that involve the continual application of organizational assets/resources to design and implement communication initiatives in various media (i.e., various means of communication) aimed at inspiring and instilling innovation performance in the hearts and minds of workforces across functional units.

- *Innovation management–related duties and responsibilities:* These are innovation-performance duties and responsibilities that are focused on the continual design and implementation of various innovation-related systems, such as innovation-support strategies, innovation policies, innovation procedures, and innovation action plans. These contribute to creating a culture of innovation across the functional units of an organization.

ii. **Definition:** *What are innovation-performance job specifications?*
Innovation-performance job specifications are the characteristics, abilities, knowledge, and experience needed to perform duties and responsibilities related to innovation performance.

Innovation-performance job specifications are categorized into three types: *innovative thinking, innovation engagement,* and *innovation management.* Brief details on each of the three abilities are as follows:

- *Innovative thinking job specifications:* These are the characteristics, knowledge, abilities, and experience required to perform innovative thinking–related duties and responsibilities.
- *Innovation engagement job specifications:* These are the characteristics, knowledge, abilities, and experience required to perform innovation engagement–related duties and responsibilities.

o *Innovation management job specifications*: These are the characteristics, knowledge, abilities, and experience required to perform innovation management–related duties and responsibilities.

iii. Worksheets

The creation of worksheets for innovation-performance job descriptions and job specifications is covered in chapter 11.

## 7. Meaning of Making Innovation "Systemic"

Making innovation "systemic" means ensuring that innovation is made a permanent organizational habit across all the functional units of an organization by continually building different contexts of organizational capabilities for supporting a culture of innovation across the organization. Such capabilities include the following:

i. Innovation-promotion initiatives for inspiring and instilling innovation in the hearts and minds of workforces

ii. Continual implementation of programs aimed at enhancing the innovative thinking abilities of workforces

iii. Continual implementation of organization-wide innovation systems, such as functional and corporate innovation-support strategies, innovation-support policies, and innovation-support procedures

Making innovation systemic means that the top leadership of an organization must ensure that each functional unit plays a key role within the context of its functional activities to

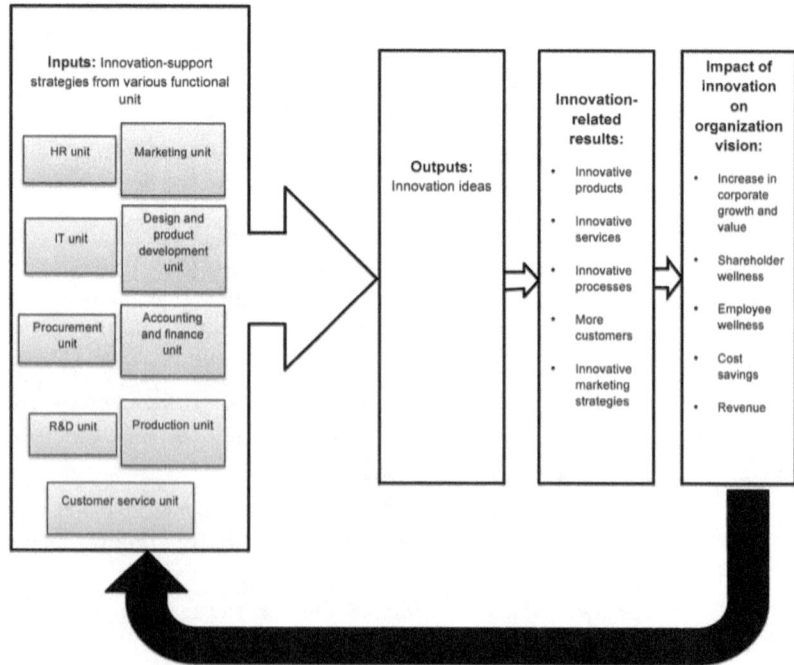

*Figure 0-2. Functional units play a vital role in implementing support strategies for advancing innovation across the organization*

develop strategies and initiatives that lead to the continual flow of diverse innovative ideas, ultimately resulting in growth in terms of product offerings, revenue, and market share.

## 8. Structure

This section provides an overview of the book's main themes and outlines how the structure of the book is presented. Figure 0-2 illustrates the role that functional units play in advancing innovation across an organization.

The implication of the diagram in figure 0-2 is that leaders across functional units should lead their functional units with purpose to play a key role in contributing to making innovation systemic across the organization. This can be accomplished by undertaking innovation-support initiatives aimed at advancing innovation in their respective functional units. However, making innovation systemic is not easy. Although there are innovation titans—such as Alphabet, Apple, Amazon, IBM, GE, Procter & Gamble, BMW, and Microsoft—that have succeeded in making innovation systemic, many companies, as indicated earlier, still face difficulties in systemizing innovation across functional units. That is why the essence of this book is the provision of innovation skill sets that organizational leaders can build and apply to make innovation systemic across an organization's functional units. The skill sets, as stated earlier, are innovative thinking skills, innovation engage-ment skills, and innovation management skills. The importance of each of the three skill sets can be likened to three pieces of a puzzle, in which each piece, as illustrated in figure 0-3, plays a vital role in holding the puzzle together.

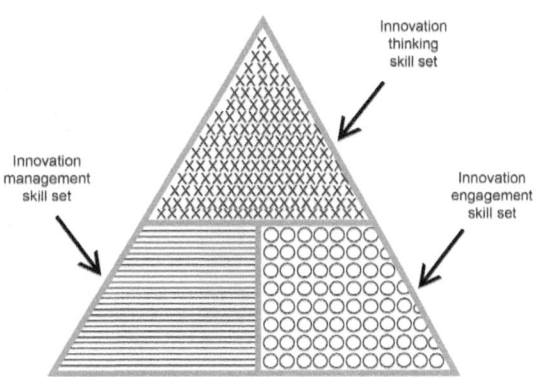

*Figure 0-3. Innovation skill sets*

What this means is that each of the three categories or types of innovation skill sets is essential in creating a culture of innovation across the organization. The implication is that without one of the skill sets, the ability to lead innovation across functional units will be impeded. The three types of innovation skill sets are presented in parts I, II, and III. Each part describes, in detail, what each innovation skill set entails in relation to leading workforce innovation, and how to develop and apply or express each of the essential innovation skill sets. The next subsection briefly outlines each of the three parts.

### Structure

Brief summaries of each of the three parts are as follows:

- ❖ **PART I:** The first category of innovation skill set is innovative thinking skills. This section focuses on how organizational leaders can translate their innovative thinking abilities into instruments that inspire workforces to develop innovative thinking abilities of their own. Part I comprises the following topics:

- o Aspects that make up innovative thinking skills
- o How to develop innovative thinking skills
- o Why innovative thinking skills are important for leading workforce innovation in organizations

❖ **PART II:** The second category of innovation skill sets is innovation engagement skills. This innovation skill set is based on the following two aspects:
- o First, because innovative thinking skills can be attained or learned by workforces, one of the vital roles of organizational leaders is exhibiting leadership approaches and styles that inspire and educate workforces across functional units to develop innovative abilities. The tools in this chapter are aimed at helping leaders achieve that objective.
- o Second, in large part, innovation is a "hearts-and-minds" concept that requires instilling the value of innovation in workforces and engaging them in innovation on a continual basis, meaning that it is vital for organizational leaders to possess skills for engaging workforces if the workforces are to own the process of advancing innovation across the organization. In other words, if an organization desires to make innovation everyone's job, from the CEO to the most junior staffer, organizational leaders require skills to inspire and instill innovation in the hearts and minds of workforces, as well as tools to educate workforces about several aspects and concepts of innovation, especially that the term *innovation* is grossly misunderstood in organizations.

Thus, part II describes what innovation engagement skills entail and how organizational leaders can consistently develop and apply approaches and techniques for realizing employee engagement in advancing innovation across the organization.

❖ **PART III:** The third category of innovation skill sets essential for leading workforce innovation is innovation management skills. The basis for innovation management skills is that inspiring workforces alone is not enough to create a climate for workforce innovation and make innovation habitual across functional units. Therefore, organizational leaders need to build innovation-support systems across all the functional units of the organization. This is where innovation management skills come into play because they are needed for building various innovation systems across functional units. Thus, part III describes some examples of innovation management skills and how these skills are applied to drive workforce innovation.

# PART I
# INNOVATIVE THINKING SKILLS

**Overview**

Part I covers the first of the three categories of innovation skill sets essential for leading workforce innovation: innovative thinking skills. This part looks at what the skill set entails and how to translate the skills into instruments of inspiring and leading workforces to develop innovative thinking abilities so that they can contribute to building a culture of innovation across the organization. Part I is structured in three chapters, as follows:

- Chapter 1: Understanding Innovative Thinking Skills
- Chapter 2: Approaches: How Do You Develop Innovative Thinking Skills?
- Chapter 3: Why Is It Important for Organizational Leaders to Have Innovative Thinking Abilities in Leading Workforce Innovation?

## CHAPTER 1
# UNDERSTANDING INNOVATIVE THINKING SKILLS

This chapter will cover the following concepts: (1) the definition of *innovative thinking skills*, (2) the importance of understanding what innovative thinking skills entail, (3) the interpretation and expression of innovative thinking skills, and (4) the expression of innovative thinking skills in the context of support functional units.

### 1. The Definition of *Innovative Thinking Skills*

To understand what innovative thinking skills are, it's important to first define pertinent terms. We begin with the definition of an *innovative person*. According to literature on innovation, an innovative person is one who possesses abilities and characteristics that drive innovative performance. The next question would then be, *What is innovative performance?* An understanding of what innovative performance entails is necessary to interpret or understand what innovative thinking skills are. Thus, in order to understand what innovative performance is, it's important to first establish the meaning of *innovation*. This book defines *innovation* as a process that involves the following:

# 4 | LEADERSHIP FOR INNOVATION

- i. Identifying a problem or need (i.e. within a particular customer/market segment or the organizational system)
- ii. Generating an innovative idea never seen on the market before to fix the identified problem/need
- iv. Converting the innovative solution into monetary value (i.e. in terms of increased revenue or cost reduction)
- iii. Transforming the innovative idea (through an established process) into a solution not seen on the market before

*Figure 1-1. Definition of innovation*

This definition of *innovation* forms the basis for interpreting what innovative performance is. You can see that the first and second parts are an expression of innovative performance. Therefore, *innovative performance* can be defined as an expression of innovative thinking skills and abilities in response to a need or problem in the particular context of an organization's functional activity. Take a look at the following story.

> A senior executive at IBM contributed to building a Life Sciences Unit at the company. Anne Robertson (not her real name) was in charge of a unit she had built from scratch to its current status of more than two thousand employees. Robertson learned that her mother had developed complications during a health treatment when she reacted adversely to a particular medication. Although Anne's mother's records were updated to warn doctors not to repeat the treatment, just three days later, another doctor missed that warning and gave her the very same medicine. Robertson was shocked when she found out how common and widespread the problem was in US hospitals. According to reports, more than one hundred thousand people die every year in US hospitals because of medical errors such as incorrect medication, incorrect dosage, inefficient diagnostics, duplicated procedures, operations on the wrong side of the body, and so forth, and the problem has been going on for many years. Robertson started thinking about how IBM could solve the problem in an innovative way or in a way not seen on the market before. Today, IBM's Life Sciences Unit manufactures and supplies IT systems that are helping hospitals manage their patient data more effectively.

This IBM story illustrates the connection between noticing a *problem* and generating an *innovative idea*, which, in essence, is an expression of innovative performance. Having described the meaning of *innovation* and how it's linked to the meaning of *innovative performance*, it's clear now that the interpretation of innovative thinking skills is based on the meanings of the terms innovation and innovative performance. That being said, innovative thinking skills are defined as a process that involves two aspects:
i. The ability to identify *problems*, *needs*, and *challenges*
ii. The ability to turn the problems and needs into *innovative opportunities* by generating *innovative ideas* or *solutions* (i.e., solutions not seen on the market before) to fix the identified problems or needs

## 2. The Importance of Understanding What Innovative Thinking Skills Entail
Why is it important for leaders to understand what innovative thinking skills entail?
  i. Innovative thinking is now a crosscutting practice in organizations. According to a number of studies, it's widely believed across industries (e.g., manufacturing, technology, financial, hospitality, health, aviation, auto, retail) that innovation is a predictor of growth and profitability. Thus, in an effort to scale innovation performance across all functional units, many organizations are adopting the practice of making innovation every employee's business. The introduction to this book cites a 2010 study by the US-based Institute for Corporate Productivity on the topic of innovation in which virtually all 641 respondents representing organizations with a thousand or more employees agreed that innovation had increased in importance across their organizations and further predicted that innovation would become even more important in coming years. In order to scale the practice of innovative thinking across the organization, one vital aspect that the top leadership has to clarify and instill in the hearts and minds of workforces is that innovative thinking is not an area reserved for specific persons or functional units. That is, innovative thinking is a skill that all employees can attain or develop, irrespective of their level in the organizational structure or the functional unit under which they fall. This fact is backed by numerous studies. To instill this message in the hearts and minds of workforces and influence or drive innovative thinking practices across functional units, first and foremost, it is important for organizational leaders to understand what innovative thinking skills entail. Further, the message can be leveraged by leadership as a motivational instrument for rallying the workforces to contribute toward generating diverse innovative ideas and to help build a culture of innovation across all the functional units of the organization.
  ii. Understanding what innovative thinking entails helps leaders to interpret how innovative thinking skills are expressed. According to the *Human Capital Trends—2012* report by Deloitte LLP, many companies are now defining *innovation* broadly to include such aspects as services, processes, business models, communication, and cost-structure improvements across the enterprise. Similarly, in an article published in the online innovation management magazine *InnovationManagement.se*, Jean-Philippe Deschamps, a renowned innovation expert and professor at Switzerland's prestigious IMD management school, observed that one of the key roles of management in governing innovation is to ensure that *innovation* is defined very broadly across the organization. Thus, understanding innovative thinking skills helps leaders to interpret how innovative thinking skills are applied and expressed across the various components of an organization's value chain such as research and development, design, manufacturing, sales, marketing, IT, procurement, distribution, HR, finance and accounting.

## 3. The Interpretation and Expression of Innovative Thinking Skills
This section illustrates how innovative thinking skills can be expressed and interpreted.

Here is an example of how innovative thinking skills can be expressed and interpreted in the context of each of the functional units of DM Personal Care Products, a fictitious company that manufactures a variety of personal care products.

*Step 1:* Identify core and support functional units of DM Personal Care Products. Let's assume the company has the following functional units:

*Core functional units*
- Product-development unit, with the following segments:
  - Body-lotions segment
  - Skin-cleansing segment
  - Hair-care segment
  - Hand-washing segment
- Manufacturing-processes department (the manufacturing-processes department comprises the same segments as the product-development unit)
- Marketing department, with the following units:
  - Pricing unit
  - Product-promotion unit
  - Product-delivery unit
  - New-markets unit
  - Packaging unit
- Customer service department

*Support functional units*
- Procurement department
- HR department
- Finance and accounting department
- IT department
- Corporate affairs department

*Step 2*: Create worksheets for interpreting innovative thinking skills in the context of the identified core and support functional units.

Worksheets 1-1 through 1-5 illustrate how to interpret innovative thinking skills in the context of the identified business segments and functional units.

Worksheets 1-1 through 1-4 cover the interpretation of innovative thinking skills for *core functional units*. Worksheet 1-5, introduced in the following subsection, is for *support functional units*.

Understanding Innovative Thinking Skills | 7

Worksheet 1-1. Interpretation of innovative thinking skills in the product-development functional unit

| Product categories and segments | How do you define or express innovative thinking skills in the context of the product-development functional unit? |
|---|---|
| Body lotions | Innovative thinking skills in the context of the product-development functional unit would be interpreted as the ability to do the following:<br>• Identify problems and needs relative to the product categories and segments of the product-development functional unit<br>• Turn the problems and needs into innovation opportunities by generating new product ideas or solutions (i.e., product solutions not seen on the market before) to fix the identified problems or needs |
| Skin cleansing | |
| Hair care | |
| Hand washing | |

Worksheet 1-2. Interpretation of innovative thinking skills in the manufacturing-processes functional unit

| Manufacturing-processes categories | How do you interpret or express innovative thinking skills in the context of the manufacturing-processes functional unit? |
|---|---|
| Body lotions | Innovative thinking skills in the context of the manufacturing-processes functional unit would be interpreted as the ability to do the following:<br>• Identify problems and needs relative to the four product categories of the manufacturing-processes unit by use of appropriate techniques<br>• Turn the problems and needs into innovation opportunities by generating new manufacturing-processes ideas or solutions (i.e., manufacturing-processes solutions not seen on the market before) to fix the identified problems or needs |
| Skin cleansing | |
| Hair care | |
| Hand washing | |

Worksheet 1-3. Interpretation of innovative thinking skills in the marketing functional unit

| Marketing components | How do you interpret or express innovative thinking skills in the context of the marketing functional unit? |
|---|---|
| Pricing unit | Innovative thinking skills in the context of the pricing unit would be defined or expressed as the ability to do the following:<br>• Identify a *pricing opportunity* within the pricing principles of the company's business model<br>• Generate innovative pricing ideas (i.e., not seen on the market before) |

| | |
|---|---|
| Product-promotion unit | Innovative thinking skills in the context of the product-promotion unit would be defined or expressed as the ability to do the following:<br>• Identify a *product-promotion opportunity*, either in a completely new market or in a customer segment within the existing market, for the organization's existing products or services<br>• Generate an *innovative product-promotion strategy* (i.e., not implemented by the organization or competitors before) |
| Product-delivery unit | Innovative thinking skills in the context of the product-delivery unit would be interpreted as the ability to do the following:<br>• Identify *problems* or *needs* within the product-delivery unit<br>• Generate an *innovative product-delivery idea* (i.e., not implemented by the organization or competitors before) |
| New-markets unit | Innovative thinking skills in the context of the new-markets unit would be defined or expressed as the ability to do the following:<br>• Identify a *market opportunity*, in either a completely new market or a customer segment within the existing market, not served by competitors or the organization's existing products or services<br>• Generate an *innovative new-markets strategy* (i.e., not implemented by the organization or competitors before) |
| Packaging unit | Innovative thinking skills in the context of the packaging unit would be interpreted as the ability to do the following:<br>• Identify *problems* or *needs* within the packaging unit<br>• Generate an *innovative packaging idea* (i.e., not implemented by the organization or competitors before) |

Worksheet 1-4. Interpretation of innovative thinking
skills in the customer service functional unit

| Functional unit | How do you interpret or express innovative thinking skills in the context of the customer service functional unit? |
|---|---|
| Customer service | Innovative thinking skills in the context of the customer service functional unit would be interpreted as the ability to do the following:<br>• Identify a *problem* or *need* within the customer service unit or segments<br>• Generate *innovative customer service ideas* (i.e., not implemented by the organization or competitors before) |

## 4. The Expression of Innovative Thinking Skills in the Context of Support Functional Units

As noted earlier, the support functional units of DM Personal Care Products include the following:

o   HR department
o   IT department
o   Procurement
o   Finance and accounting department
o   Corporate affairs department

It is important for organizational leaders to understand that the context of innovative thinking skills in support functional units involves the ability to generate cost-saving innovative ideas. Worksheet 1-5 provides an example of how to interpret and express innovative thinking skills in the context of the previously listed support functional units of DM Personal Care Products. The leadership must ensure that workforces understand that innovative thinking skills in the context of the organization's support functional units are expressed in the context of cost-saving and efficiency purposes.

Worksheet 1-5. Innovative thinking skills
in the context of support functional units

| Support functional units | How do you interpret or manifest innovative thinking skills in the context of support functional units and cost savings? |
|---|---|
| Human resources (HR) | Innovative thinking skills in the context of innovative HR cost-saving ideas would be interpreted as the ability to do the following:<br>• Identify a *cost-saving opportunity* within the organization's HR functional components<br>• Generate *innovative cost-saving ideas* in the context of HR practices |

| Information technology (IT) | Innovative thinking skills in the context of innovative IT cost-saving ideas would be interpreted as the ability to do the following:<br>• Identify a *cost-saving opportunity* within the organization's IT functional components<br>• Generate *innovative cost-saving ideas* in the context of IT practices |
|---|---|
| Procurement | Innovative thinking skills in the context of innovative procurement cost-saving ideas would be interpreted as the ability to do the following:<br>• Identify a *cost-saving opportunity* within the organization's procurement functional components<br>• Generate *innovative cost-saving ideas* in the context of procurement practices |
| Finance and accounting | Innovative thinking skills in the context of innovative accounting cost-saving ideas would be interpreted as the ability to do the following:<br>• Identify a *cost-saving opportunity* within the organization's accounting functional components<br>• Generate *innovative cost-saving ideas* in the context of accounting practices |
| Corporate affairs | Innovative thinking skills in the context of innovative corporate affairs cost-saving ideas would be interpreted as the ability to do the following:<br>• Identify a *cost-saving opportunity* within the organization's corporate affairs functional components<br>• Generate *innovative cost-saving ideas* in the context of corporate affairs practices |

## CHAPTER 2
# APPROACHES: HOW DO YOU DEVELOP INNOVATIVE THINKING SKILLS?

*Studies have shown that innovation is close to 80 percent learned and acquired.*
—**Hal Gregersen**, Executive Director of the MIT Leadership Center

This chapter considers how innovative thinking skills can be developed. At the innovation training events that I have conducted, I'm usually asked questions such as the following: What are the characteristics of innovative people? How do you develop innovative thinking skills? On most occasions, these questions would begin on a low note but end up in a very passionate discussion among training delegates. Opinions would usually range from innovative thinking being an inborn attribute to it being an attainable ability. The long-held view of experts in the fields of psychology and innovation is that humans have billions of brain cells and great creative capacity. Implying that, generally, people have an amazing potential for innovative thinking; however, most people do not automatically have the ability to tap into the brain's creative and innovative potential. The question is, then, *what approaches can be applied to develop innovative thinking skills and the ability to tap into innovative potential?* To answer this question, this section looks at two aspects: (1) the importance of understanding approaches that organizational leaders can use to foster the development of innovative thinking skills and (2) examples of approaches for building innovative thinking skills.

## 1. The Importance of Understanding Approaches that Organizational Leaders Can Use to Foster the Development of Innovative Thinking Skills

Why is it important for organizational leaders to understand approaches that can be applied to build innovative thinking skills? The point made so far in this section is that every person in an organization has the potential to build innovative thinking abilities and to innovate in the context of the organization's functional activities. That said, it's important for organizational leaders to understand approaches for developing innovative thinking skills so that they are able to enact strategies and programs aimed at motivating, inspiring, and supporting workforces to attain innovative thinking abilities and contribute to the goals of the organization for functional-unit and corporate innovation.

## 2. Examples of Approaches for Building Innovative Thinking Skills

What are some of the approaches to building innovative thinking skills? Numerous studies have been conducted—and many suggestions and opinions offered—on the various approaches that innovative entrepreneurs use to develop or improve their innovative thinking skills. One of these studies is a CNN six-year-long innovation research project conducted by professors from Harvard Business School, INSEAD, and Brigham Young University and published in 2009. The CNN study, which included more than three thousand executives and five hundred innovative entrepreneurs, identified six skills and characteristics that enhance innovative thinking abilities and separate the so-called blue-sky innovators from the rest: *associating, questioning, observing, experimenting, networking,* and *discovering.* Some of the CEOs and entrepreneurs who score high in these abilities include Michael Dell, Michael Lazaridis, and Pierre Omidyar. The following subsection looks at how these six skills can be applied.

### *Application of the Study Findings*

The main focus of this section is not to reproduce the findings of the aforementioned study but to use the findings as a basis for suggesting approaches and techniques that can be applied to develop some of the characteristics of innovative people cited in the study. An outline of the characteristics and how to develop them follows:

i. *Associating:* The CNN study found that associating was one of the characteristics of innovative entrepreneurs. According to the dictionary definition, *associating* means "to combine, to interlace, to intertwine, to bring into relation, or to connect." In the context of innovative thinking, how is the characteristic of associating developed so that it can be leveraged to contribute to innovative thinking abilities? Organizational leaders can utilize various resources and communication techniques to urge and encourage workforces to regularly use the power of imagination to link associations and connections between unrelated things to generate ideas to solve a problem. In other words, leaders can urge workforces to be regularly engaged in the practice of interlacing and intertwining ideas from different areas or fields to solve a particular problem. Many inventions and innovations have been developed by connecting ideas from very different fields to solve a problem. For instance, ideas that were developed for computers have been used in cell phones. Products that were meant to solve a particular problem have serendipitously solved other problems. For instance,

## Approaches: How Do You Develop Innovative Thinking Skills? | 13

at the time of writing this book, I was also working on my small invention called the CT Holder. When I was putting together ideas for this small kitchen device, I found myself "importing" an idea that had been used on a device in a very different context for my kitchen device invention.

ii. *Questioning:* The second characteristic or ability revealed in the study was questioning. The dictionary definition of *questioning* is "an expression of inquiry, asking and showing curiosity with the view of obtaining answers and insight." In the context of innovation, questioning could be interpreted as a mental activity that involves showing curiosity, examining, and asking questions to explore an issue for the purpose of obtaining particular insight with the view of finding an innovative solution by generating an innovative idea. In terms of how one can build the characteristic of questioning, leaders should use various communication techniques to regularly encourage workforces to build habits and practices that involve showing curiosity, examining, and asking questions to explore insights. Leaders should also help workforces by creating capacity-building programs and tools aimed at enhancing the innovation-related questioning abilities of their workforces. Some of the training programs could focus on things like how to formulate and use simple questions that challenge common practices by asking "Why?" or "Why not?" or "What if?"

Chapter 12 (in part III of the book) provides an innovation-related questioning tool called *innovation-challenge questions*. The innovation-challenge questions, as we shall see later, are pinpointing exploratory questions formulated to reveal specific organizational or community problems, needs, and business opportunities that require innovative solutions.

Over the years, I have developed the practice of bouncing off what-if questions to myself. I practice what-ifs on any challenge requiring a solution, ranging from simple to difficult challenges and situations. For example, when I was putting together various ideas for my simple kitchen device invention, the CT Holder, I would generate tons of what-ifs for each component of the device. I also use a lot of what-ifs when developing frameworks, visual illustrations, and case studies and when working on tasks for my books and innovation training proposals and consulting engagements.

iii. *Observing:* According to the 2009 CNN study by the Harvard Business School, INSEAD, and Brigham Young University professors, observation is a key tendency of innovative people. According to the dictionary definition, observing is the action or process of watching something or someone carefully in order to gain information. In the context of idea generation, observing can be interpreted as an *action* or *process* that involves watching what people actually do or what events take place during a situation for the purpose of gaining information to develop a solution. For example, my CT Holder idea is a direct product of observation. I generated the idea after observing, for many years, that no product had been developed to deal with a simple (but frustrating) challenge that people experience when undertaking the activity whose problem the CT Holder is designed to fix. Since the device is yet to be patented (at the time of writing this book), I cannot disclose more details than this.

In the organizational context, the question is, *How can organizational leaders help workforces build or enhance their observation abilities?* Let's look at some of the basic aspects that need to be understood. First is the basic fact that all people have *observation abilities* that they apply on a daily basis in every aspect of life. Second, according to studies, people begin acquiring observation skills from childhood through various activities. Third, people's observation abilities tend to be influenced by the level of emotional interest and passion for a particular hobby, academic or professional specialty, and any activity that earns them a livelihood. For instance, police officers have very good observational skills for anything related to their work (e.g police officers must learn to observe facial expressions or tone of voice), soccer players have a high degree of observational skills for their game, and fishermen and farmers tend to develop very good observational skills for their occupations. The bottom line is that the strength of our observational skills is skewed toward the areas that we have passion for and an emotional interest in, as well as professional specialties and occupational concentrations. No matter the type of observational skills that one is skewed toward, there are ways to improve observational skills, which in turn has the potential to enhance one's innovative thinking skills.

In terms of how organizational leaders can help their workforces to build the characteristic of observation, leaders can use various communication techniques to regularly encourage workforces to develop or enhance their observation abilities. Leaders can also help through capacity-building programs and tools aimed at enhancing the innovation-related observation abilities of workforces. The following are some of the general techniques that can be used to build or enhance one's observation skills:

o   Practice the attitude of observing things around you whenever you can
o   Observe with curiosity, and ask yourself questions about the things that you observe.
o   Practice the attitude of watching and paying attention to what people around you are doing, and look for particular details to ask yourself questions about
o   Eliminate distractions each time you are intently observing and asking questions about something
o   Use various test-your-observation-skills aids, such as games, puzzles, and visual illustrations
o   Develop the attitude of asking yourself questions when watching a sports game, movie, or television show

iv. *Experimenting:* The fourth characteristic identified by the aforementioned 2009 CNN study is that innovative entrepreneurs regularly try out new ideas in various forms. According to the dictionary definition, experimenting is a test or trial-and-error procedure carried out with the purpose of establishing the validity of a hypothesis. In the context of the generation of innovative ideas, the connection is that, normally, before an innovative product or service solution is launched on the market, experimenting with a prototype takes place to establish the innovation's efficiency and effectiveness. Whether small or large, complex or simple, one of the common factors in all the products and services offered in the various industry sectors—such as food, fashion, electronics, aircraft, books, furniture, and transportation—is that they undergo an experimentation or prototype procedure before they are finally adopted for use. The purpose of experimentation is to ensure that the product, service, process, or other innovation fulfills the purpose for which it was invented and developed, as well as to ensure that the product or service meets regulatory requirements. And because experimentation processes usually involve a lot of thinking, analysis, tweaking, and generation of ideas to improve the product or service under consideration, the process has the potential to enhance one's creativity and innovative thinking ability. That being said, *What is the role of organizational leaders in helping workforces to leverage the practice of experimenting to enhance their innovative thinking abilities?* First, because experiments and prototypes are a test or trial procedure, they provide an opportunity for generating ideas; leaders can use various communication techniques to regularly instill the benefits of conducting experiments to enhance one's innovative thinking abilities in the hearts and minds of the workforces.

Second, leaders should constantly inform their workforces about some of the approaches and techniques that one can engage in to practice with experiments and prototypes, and where possible, the organization should provide resources with information on experimenting activities. For example, a simple approach to experimenting is to use easily accessible materials, such as paper and duct tape, to illustrate an idea. I've used paper and duct tape to illustrate and fine-tune simple innovative product ideas. Another example of an experimenting activity is to disassemble and reassemble items, thinking through how and why each of the components was developed and included. Such items could include toys, furniture, simple electronic gadgets, and so forth. For example, I never used to like buying furniture from IKEA because of the hassle of assembling and dissembling involved, which is sometimes very frustrating, but through experimenting, I have gradually developed an interest in dissembling and assembling stuff, which often leads to new ideas. Other experimentation approaches can take place in the kitchen—for example, tweaking recipes and developing recipe experiments or prototypes. I love this too. I like mixing ingredients and coming up with something new—sometimes my inventions taste good, and sometimes they don't; it's the spirit of experimentation that's important. There are a lot of examples of renowned entrepreneurs and innovators who leveraged their attribute of experimentation to enhance their innovative thinking abilities. For instance, according to the online magazine called *Biography*, at the age of fifteen, intrigued by the expanding world of computers and gadgetry, Michael Dell purchased an early Apple computer for the strict purpose of taking it apart to see how it worked. This is one of the noticeable innovative traits that Michael Dell had when he was growing up: taking stuff apart and reassembling it. Leaders can also help through capacity-building programs and tools aimed at enhancing the innovation-related experimenting abilities of their workforces.

v. *Networking:* The fifth attribute of highly innovative people identified in the 2009 study is networking. The dictionary definition of *networking* is that it is a supportive system of sharing information and services among individuals and groups having a common interest. Numerous analysts on the subject of networking and innovation have suggested that individuals and firms that do not formally or informally exchange knowledge limit their knowledge base and ultimately reduce their opportunities for enhancing innovative thinking abilities. It's important to know that whether at the individual or institutional level, network relationships play a vital role in advancing innovative thinking abilities. How? For instance, there are many types of innovations—for example, product innovations, process innovations, customer service innovations, marketing innovations, procurement innovations—that resulted from ideas that were originally generated from network relationships with customers, suppliers, professional associations, trade conventions, faith-based conventions, political conventions, and so forth. That being said, *What is the role of leaders in helping workforces to develop networking attributes?* First, leaders can use various communication techniques to regularly instill the benefits of networking to enhance one's innovative thinking abilities in the hearts and minds of workforces. Second, leaders should constantly inform their workforces about networking approaches and strategies and leverage networking events to enhance innovative thinking and the generation of innovative ideas. Organizational leaders can create illustrations or models of how various networking relationships or events can be leveraged to enhance innovative thinking abilities—for instance, an illustration could include suggestions for how professional associations, customer conventions, supplier conventions, entertainment events, faith-based networks, and community-based networks can be leveraged to enhance innovative thinking abilities. Leaders should also provide their workforces with information on some of the guidelines for effective networking. For instance, leaders should emphasize diversity. "Like minds think alike," the saying goes; therefore, diversity can foster innovation rather than the status quo. Organizational leaders should ensure that workforces understand how diversity is a factor when it comes to networking, and they should give specific suggestions to workforces on how to make use of diversity at networking events. For instance, one suggestion is that individuals should attempt to meet and establish relationships with people who have demographic characteristics different from their own, for example, in terms of age, gender, race, profession, work experience, or geographical area. Leaders can also help through capacity-building programs and tools aimed at educating workforces about networking and how to leverage it to enhance innovative thinking abilities.

vi. *Envisioning:* The sixth and last characteristic of innovative people identified in the 2009 CNN study is envisioning. Great innovators have also been referred to as great *visionaries.* For example, the late Steve Jobs, the chairman and cofounder of Apple, Inc., who pioneered the personal computer industry and changed the way people think about technology, is referred to as one of the greatest innovators and visionaries of modern times. In the organizational context, envisioning is the ability

# Approaches: How Do You Develop Innovative Thinking Skills? | 17

to understand, predict, or picture key aspects of market (local or global) trends or patterns that affect the organization's business trends.

So in terms of innovative thinking, *What is the role of organizational leaders in helping workforces to develop envisioning attributes?* First, leaders can use various communication techniques to regularly instill the importance of the power of having a *vision* to enhance one's innovative thinking abilities in the hearts and minds of workforces. Second, leaders should constantly inform their workforces about some of the techniques that can be used to build envisioning attributes to enhance innovative thinking abilities. Some tips for enhancing envisioning attributes are as follows:

o Develop the tendency of randomly envisioning perspectives, trends, and future scenarios in various industry sectors, such as telecommunications, computing, automobiles, aviation, railway, food, fashion, film, music, cosmetics, books, banking, insurance, and hospitality
o Read the corporate visions and strategies of companies across industry sectors Read autobiographies of renowned innovators and visionaries
o Explore the profiles and backgrounds of various innovations and discoveries
o Develop a habit of creating market-trend databases on particular industry sectors

## CHAPTER 3
# WHY IS IT IMPORTANT FOR ORGANIZATIONAL LEADERS TO HAVE INNOVATIVE THINKING ABILITIES IN LEADING WORKFORCE INNOVATION?

*Example is not the main thing in influencing others. It is the only thing.*
—**Albert Schweitzer**, French-German Theologian

Chapters 1 and 2 covered the elements of innovative thinking skills and how they can be developed. This chapter focuses on why it is important for organizational leaders to possess innovative thinking abilities in leading workforce innovation. According to the old and common cliché in leadership, "Leadership is by example." The application of this adage is that for a leader to expect a particular behavior from followers, the leader must be seen to exhibit the same, or even better, behavior that he or she expects from followers. Studies in leadership by example, also referred to as *leadership role modeling*, have revealed that in most cases, followers will demonstrate a particular behavior demanded of them by their leaders only if they see their leaders displaying a similar behavior. In other words, followers learn through emulation or imitation. For instance, if you, as a leader, emphasize the behavior of good time management to your teams, you must lead by excelling in observing task deadlines so that your followers can emulate you. Similarly, if you champion a culture of cost saving, you've got to lead by example by being the first one stay on budget. In simple terms, you cannot champion a behavior or culture that you don't exhibit yourself and expect your followers to adopt it. One of the most widely quoted aphorisms of Mahatma Gandhi is as follows: "What we do and what we say must be in alignment." So in a basic sense, the essence of leadership by example is about setting standards in collaboration with followers and, in turn, leading followers in embracing and exhibiting the set standards.

In innovative thinking practices, the principle of role modeling is critical. Organizational leaders have to be seen to be contributing to the generation of innovative ideas and not just evangelizing innovation to their followers. Leaders who model desired behaviors undoubtedly have much more of an effect on workforces in terms of enhancing their innovative thinking abilities than leaders who merely persuade or encourage their teams to be innovative without them, the leaders, being seen to be innovative. Does this imply that organizational leaders must be top innovators in their organizations or teams? Not at all; the point is that they must be seen to reflect, to a meaningful degree, what they're encouraging their workforces to do. They must be seen to be innovators or possess meaningful innovative thinking abilities.

At a seminar presentation, one attendee asked me whether noninnovative individuals in organizations should not be appointed as leaders. My response was that every organization has attributes and guidelines on which leadership-appointment decisions are based. However, for any organization that calls itself an innovation company and has adopted innovation as a core strategy for its long-term growth and competitiveness, it is vitally important that organizational leaders at different echelons of the organization exhibit meaningful degrees of innovative thinking ability.

Thus, this chapter will cover three aspects: (1) the importance of innovative thinking abilities in leading innovation in organizations, (2) translating innovative thinking abilities into instruments for advancing innovation, and (3) examples of leaders who have leveraged their innovative attributes to drive innovation.

## 1. The Importance of Innovative Thinking Abilities in Leading Innovation in Organizations

Why is it important for organizational leaders to possess innovative thinking abilities in leading innovation? Three reasons are foremost:
i. *It can have a potential radiant effect on the innovative thinking of followers.* As emphasized at the beginning of this chapter, it's vital that leaders are not seen by their followers to be mere rhetorical champions of innovation; instead, they must be seen to be contributing toward the innovation performance of the organization through the generation of various types and degrees of innovative ideas. When leaders are seen to be contributing to the generation of innovative ideas, such behavior by the leaders can potentially inspire workforces to build innovative thinking abilities, which will result in the generation of innovative ideas in the context of the organization's business model, thereby contributing to meeting the functional and corporate innovation goals of the organization. This chapter opened with a quote by Albert Schweitzer, a French-German theologian who died while serving as a missionary in the West-Central African country of Gabon at the age of ninety in 1965. Schweitzer repeatedly said, "Example is not the main

thing in influencing others. It is the only thing." This quotation underscores why leadership role modeling is such a vital aspect when leading people. In terms of leading workforce innovation, research shows that nothing encourages and builds innovative abilities in followers like leadership role models in innovative thinking abilities. Many studies have established the relationship between the innovation-role-modeling behavior of leaders and the innovation performance of their followers. For instance, studies suggest that if a leader takes risks by acting in ways that are outside conventional norms, he or she makes a visual statement to followers that risk-taking is encouraged, and followers are thus influenced to be more comfortable with taking risks; risk-taking is a major attribute of innovative thinkers. For example, in a 2012 survey conducted by Kuczmarski & Associates, a US innovation consulting firm, out of the eighty-seven US-based companies sampled, the study revealed that 62 percent of the successful firms had their CEOs actively involved in contributing to the pipeline of innovative ideas, compared with only 30 percent of the unsuccessful firms.

A study conducted in 2011 by Innovation Excellence, a US-based innovation consulting and research firm, looked at differences between companies with high versus low innovation premiums and found that senior leadership's innovative skills made a serious difference. According to the study, CEOs of *high-innovation-premium* companies scored at the 88th percentile in terms of innovative abilities. By comparison, CEOs of average companies scored only at the 62nd percentile. The study also found that innovative leaders spent approximately 31 percent of their time actively engaged in *innovation-centered activities*, compared with only 15 percent by leaders of less innovative companies. "Doubling the time a senior leader personally invests in getting new ideas typically delivers significant returns," the report indicated. Another study observed that practicing leaders and managers interested in promoting creativity in their followers must accurately assess whether followers perceive them as role models for creativity.

ii. *The innovative thinking skills of leaders can potentially be leveraged to attract and retain top innovation talent.* As discussed previously, organizational leaders contribute to advancing innovation in their organizations by exhibiting different types of and approaches to innovation abilities, such as innovative thinking abilities, innovation engagement abilities, and innovation management abilities. In terms of innovative thinking abilities, there is evidence that leaders with strong innovative thinking attributes tend to attract and retain top innovation talent.

Studies have revealed that one of the reasons why many innovative companies have been successful at innovation-led growth over a long period is because these companies—such as Alphabet, Apple, Amazon, Tesla, Microsoft, and GE—are driven by innovative leaders who have a strong passion for innovation and also have strong innovative thinking abilities. Such a reputation is a magnet for the attraction and retention of innovation talent who, in most cases, want to join a company or stick around longer so that they can learn unique skills on how to lead innovative companies from their top innovative leaders. In an interview with CNBC, Chief Financial Officer Ruth Purat hinted that innovation-based leadership was one of the reasons she joined Alphabet in 2015 (then Google). Between 2008 and 2015, Tesla hired more than 150 top innovation individuals.And according to media reports, a number of these talents with unique innovation skills attribute their joining Tesla to the CEO's unique innovative thinking abilities and his passion for and emotional interest in innovation, which some of the workforces liken to attributes of the late Steve Jobs.

iii. *Innovative leaders tend to generate innovation mantras.* Leaders who possess innovative thinking attributes tend to have the knack for innovation mantras, which are vital for engaging and instilling innovation in the hearts and minds of workforces. During my research on how innovative leaders leverage their innovative attributes to lead innovation across the organization, one aspect that I discovered is that most leaders with strong innovative thinking attributes not only tend to lead innovation through the generation of innovative ideas (by example), but they also understand that innovation in organizations does not occur naturally; they know that an organization must have the right climate for innovation to thrive. With that in mind, these leaders have a knack for regularly formulating a variety of innovation-motivating slogans and catchphrases for instilling innovation in the hearts and minds of their workforces. They regularly use innovation-motivating slogans to emphasize the importance of innovation to the company's growth and competitiveness and also to evangelize to their workforces about innovation being every employee's responsibility. These leaders also ensure that the company has no perceived obstacles to innovation by regularly implementing crosscutting innovation-support systems.

Here are some examples of innovation quotes or mantras from top corporate leaders:

- *"Innovation distinguishes between a leader and a follower." —Steve Jobs*
- *"The cure for Apple is not cost cutting. The cure for Apple is to innovate its way out of its current predicament." —Steve Jobs*
- *"Some people see innovation as change, but we have never really seen it like that. It's understanding things and making them better." —Tim Cook*
- *"An innovative opportunity is missed by most people because its dressed in overalls and looks like work." —Thomas Edison*
- *"I believe innovation is the most powerful force for change in the world. People who are pessimistic about the future tend to extrapolate from the present in a straight line. But innovation fundamentally shifts the trajectory of development." —Bill Gates*
- *"The biggest risk is not taking any risk." —Mark Zuckerberg*
- *"When you innovate you've got to be prepared for anyone telling you you're nuts." —Larry Ellison*
- *"If what you're doing is not seen by some people as science fiction, probably it is not transformative enough." —Sergey Brin*
- *"Solving big problems is easier than solving little problems." —Sergey Brin*
- *"If you're not failing, you're not innovating." —Elon Musk*
- *"Great companies are built on great products." —Elon Musk*
- *"Our industry does not respect tradition. It only respects innovation." —Satya Nadella*

o   *"Innovation in today's world is the best and only way to really win and the best to grow organically, and succeed on a sustained basis." —A.G. Lafley*

## 2. Translating Innovative Thinking Abilities into Instruments for Advancing Innovation

In addition to the natural radiant effect that the innovative thinking of organizational leaders has on motivating followers to build innovative thinking abilities, leaders can also use their innovative thinking abilities and attributes to contribute to instilling the spirit of innovative thinking in the hearts and minds of workforces. How? There are a number of approaches and techniques that organizational leaders can apply to translate their innovative thinking abilities into instruments for motivating their followers. The following are a few examples:

i. *Share stories:* Leaders can use different contexts of innovative thinking–related stories to encourage and contribute to helping their followers build innovative thinking attributes. For example, leaders can share stories on particular activities they undertake that help them generate innovative ideas, such as jogging on a trail, working out at a gym, driving on a highway, or taking a shower. Other stories could include how many of their ideas were rejected or the number of times they tried and failed before they came up with an effective innovative idea; leaders could also describe how they mentored particular individuals, helping them to become top innovators.

ii. *Show visual illustrations:* Leaders can use simple visual illustrations, such as selfies of themselves doing activities that help them stimulate innovative ideas.

iii. *Display patent certificates:* Have you heard about or seen organizational leaders displaying their academic credentials in their offices? This is ill-advised because academic certificates do not drive the growth of an organization; it's ideas that do. Particularly, it's innovative ideas that drive organizational growth, progress, and survival. As a symbol on which organization survival and progress depend, leaders can display their patent certificates and awards in their offices to motivate workforces to build innovative thinking abilities.

iv. *Talk about innovative thinking attributes:* Innovative thinking is not a natural characteristic but a talent or ability that emanates from particular attributes that are developed over time. Organizational leaders can use their innovative thinking abilities by chatting with followers about their (the leaders') strongest innovative thinking attributes or characteristics and how they developed them and how long it took them to do so. Examples of innovative thinking attributes include envisioning, observing, networking, experimenting, questioning, and associating, among many others.

## 3. Examples of Leaders Who Have Leveraged Their Innovative Attributes to Drive Innovation

Annually, a number of leading business publications list rankings of the most innovative companies, for instance, *Forbes* magazine's "World's Most Innovative Companies," Strategy&'s "Global Innovation 1000," and Fast Company's "Most Innovative Companies."

Innovative Thinking Abilities | 23

These rankings cover a wide range of companies across industries. Besides the annual rankings of the most innovative companies, lists of the most innovative CEOs are occasionally released by some business publications. What is interesting with these rankings is that if you take a closer look at the lists of the most innovative companies, you are likely to notice that they have one thing in common: usually, the top leadership of such companies tends to have strong innovative thinking abilities. From Henry Ford (the man who altered the course of the auto industry) to Conrad Hilton (the man who transformed and internationalized the American hospitality industry) to Thomas Edison (the cofounder of General Electric) to Juan Trippe (the founder of the defunct Pan American World Airways, commonly referred to as Pan Am), founders and leaders of innovative companies, both small and large, have in most cases tended to have strong innovative thinking abilities. Evidence shows that one of the differences between large noninnovative corporations and the most innovative corporations is that in the latter, the top leadership is deeply involved in generating innovative ideas. "In interviews with dozens of senior executives of large organizations," one report revealed, "we found that in most cases they did not feel personally responsible for coming up with innovations. They only felt responsible to 'facilitate the innovation process' and make sure someone in the company was doing it. But in the world's most innovative companies senior leaders like Jeff Bezos (Amazon), Marc Benioff (Salesforce.com), A. G. Lafley (Procter & Gamble) and the late Steve Jobs (Apple) didn't just delegate innovation; their own hands were deep in the process."

The following are some examples of modern-day corporations whose growth and innovation performance have been influenced by the innovative thinking abilities of their top leadership:

i. *Apple, Inc.'s Steve Jobs:* The late Steve Jobs is globally referred to as a once-in-a-lifetime, exceptionally innovative, and visionary corporate leader of modern times who transformed technology, media, and retailing through his innovation leadership approaches and innovative thinking abilities. According to the literature, all the companies that Steve Jobs founded and led—from his initial stint at the then named Apple Computers, which he cofounded with Steve Wozniak in 1970; to Pixar Animation, which he cofounded in 1986; to NeXt Corporation, which he founded in 1988; up until his return to Apple in 1997—Steve Jobs inspired his followers through his leadership-for-innovation approach and, more effectively, through his innovative thinking abilities. When Steve Jobs returned to Apple in 1997, the company that he had cofounded was struggling to survive, and on day one, Steve Jobs declared that he was going to lead the transformation of Apple Computers by instilling innovation practices in all functional aspects of the organization. He immediately adopted the catchphrase "Think differently" as the company's innovation-motivating slogan. Over the years, using his slogan of "Think differently," Steve Jobs instilled the culture of innovation in the hearts and minds of his executives and followers, and through his practice of leading innovation by example, he imprinted innovative thinking behavior in his top executives; through the admiration that the executives had for Jobs's innovative ingenuity, this radiant effect also cascaded down to the rank-and-file staff, who were inspired to push their innovative thinking to limitless heights. The impact of Steve Jobs's innovation leadership by example on Apple's growth and industry dominance is common knowledge. Jobs died on October 5, 2011. According to records, at the time of his death, Jobs had more than three hundred patents.

ii. *Alphabet's Larry Page and Sergey Brin:* Through their exceptional and unique innovative thinking abilities, Larry Page and Sergey Brin founded a company in their dorm room at Stanford University in California—a company that has now become one of the most innovative search engines of modern times. In the first exhibition of their exceptional innovative thinking skills, Larry Page and Sergey Brin filed their first patent for a page-rank algorithm while studying at Stanford. Since Google's incorporation in 1998 (it is now a subsidiary of Alphabet), the founders have, through their exceptional innovative abilities, continued to influence innovation across all structures of the company. To ensure that innovation was enshrined and sustained as a culture, from the very beginning, Page and Brin initiated policies that were aimed at creating conditions that would continually advance and sustain innovation across Google. For instance, they had to hire proven corporate leaders with innovative abilities to ensure a radiant effect on the rest of the workforce. In a presentation at the Innovation at Google conference in March 2011 in San Francisco, Patrick Copeland, the senior engineering director at Google (who is very passionate about innovation and who was hired from Microsoft), revealed that Google has a recruitment mechanism called "Spot the Innovators," which the company uses to look for people with a track record of innovation. And in an interview reported in *Think Quarterly* (a Google newsletter that covers the company's innovation activities), the company's senior vice president explained how Google has managed to sustain its innovation culture, saying, "Nurturing a culture for innovation has been key to the company's success. As we have grown to over 26,000 employees in more than 60 offices, we've worked hard to maintain the unique spirit of innovation that characterized Google way back when I joined as employee #16."

Over the years, innovation has been credited as a reason for Google's success in being one of the most admired workplaces in the world.

iii. *IBM:* Ranked as one of the most innovative companies by media organizations that conduct innovation performance surveys across the globe, with an understanding of the impact of innovative leaders on championing innovation across an organization, IBM is one of the multinational corporations that has invested heavily in both R&D and in the innovation leadership capabilities of its executives. According to company reports, one of the aspects of IBM's innovation culture is that all individuals holding leadership positions contribute to championing innovation within their functional contexts by exhibiting satisfactory levels of innovative thinking abilities and also by contributing to setting conditions that support and encourage innovative thinking in teams because the company understands that passion and emotional interest for innovation must begin with the top leadership. In a farewell statement to the company in January 2012, Samuel Palmisano, IBM's former chairman, president, and CEO, described how innovation values have transformed and steered the company to what it is today: "In my view, the defining value that IBM has provided over the years has been the way we think, from the top leadership through to every employee. Today, as in the past, when people turn to our company, I believe they are looking for how IBMers approach problems, as well as for the types of problems we choose to approach—we have over the years chosen to define success as bringing to the world innovations that make a lasting difference." As a result of the company's massive integrated investments in innovation performance, IBM continues to record sustained growth, and for the first time in the company's history, it recorded revenues topping $100 billion in 2011. It was also ranked as the seventh most valuable company in the world in 2011, and according to the literature, IBM was the leading investor in innovation that year, with R&D expenses of more than $6 billion. Additionally, according to information from the US Patent and Trademark Office (USPTO), IBM continues to hold the number-one rank in terms of patents, which it has done for eighteen consecutive years, with a record 5,896 patents in 2011, becoming the first company to break the 5,000-patent mark in a single year. Following the retirement of Samuel Palmisano at the beginning of 2012, the company tapped another innovation guru, one of the most influential and exceptionally innovative brains at IBM, Ginni Rometty, as Palmisano's replacement. Innovation analysts say she is more than capable of continuing with the exceptional corporate innovation capabilities developed and sustained under the leadership of Palmisano. Rometty is credited with spearheading IBM's growth strategy, which is anchored on innovation in cloud computing and analytics businesses. According to one company statement: "Rometty's recognition and influence go beyond IBM borders because her influence has been recognized globally. She has been named to *Fortune* magazine's 50 Most Powerful Women in Business for eight consecutive years, ranking #1 for 2012, she was also named in the 50 Most Influential People list of *Bloomberg Markets* magazine in September 2012. Other publications in which she appeared as most influential include *Forbes* and *Time* magazines."

iv. *Dell Inc.'s Michael Dell:* Although Michael Dell may not be as technologically savvy and innovatively gifted as Steve Jobs, his excellent level of innovative thinking abilities and innovation leadership attributes have propelled the company to be one of the biggest PC makers of the modern era. From the time he established the company, Michael Dell anchored his business idea and entrepreneurial spirit on innovation performance. According to records, after establishing his company in 1984, steering the company through growth stages, and later becoming the youngest CEO of a Fortune 500 company, Michael Dell realized that to compete in the brutal PC market, he needed a radical innovative idea for reaching customers. He then came up with an innovative market strategy for bypassing the middlemen and selling directly to customers. For twenty years, Dell Inc. has been following this direct build-to-order sales model. The company's longtime market-strategy model involves customers planning their own configuration of the product and placing orders directly with the company through the phone or on Dell's website. To date, Michael Dell continues to influence innovation performance by continually adopting practices aimed at advancing and sustaining innovation across the company. According to company publications, some of the practices include R&D efforts that now span various locations around the world and recruitment of highly innovative talent for top leadership positions in the company, with some of the executives having more than thirty patents under their belts. Another Dell initiative developed under Michael Dell's influence and aimed at fostering innovation is a program called Dell Fellows, which recognizes staff for their contributions to innovation. In addition, Dell's Inventor of the Year is an annual program that involves honoring outstanding inventors among Dell employees.

v. *Amazon's Jeffrey Bezos:* Jeff Bezos, who won the *Economist* magazine's Innovation Award, has instilled a culture of innovation in his executives and employees across all functional units of Amazon. Leading by example in championing innovative thinking skills, Bezos ensures that every manager possesses innovative thinking abilities, and he routinely checks innovation goals for his managers. According to company records, Bezos poses one common question to new hires, especially managers. He asks them whether they have ever invented or innovated anything. Under Bezos's guidance, Amazon has grown from an online book merchant to a massive online retailer of a wide variety of products. And through his exceptional innovative thinking abilities and innovation leadership skills, Bezos guided Amazon to be the first company to invent an e-reader, the Kindle. Bezos continues to leverage his innovative thinking attributes to inspire his teams to expand the company's device offerings beyond the Kindle. In 2016, for example, Amazon launched the voice-activated Echo device.

vi. *Starbucks's Howard Schultz:* Founded in the 1980s, Starbucks became a household name in the 1990s, with Howard Schultz as CEO throughout the decade. In 2000, Howard Schultz stepped down as CEO. According to media reports, eight years after Schultz left, and amid a global financial crisis, Starbucks began faltering, and this prompted the founder to return to the company as CEO. In his presentation to the London Business Conference in May 2011, Schultz revealed that when he returned to Starbucks in 2008, he discovered that the company had forgotten about the meaningful innovation practices on which Starbucks had been anchored since its establishment in the 1980s, and he noted that since his return, he had been championing innovation to get the company back on its innovation-performance footing. He did so by initiating a number of innovative business decisions and ideas and by creating conditions that inspire and encourage innovative thinking and innovation leadership across the company's functional units. He has also empowered Starbucks teams to regularly challenge the status quo.

vii. *Procter & Gamble's Alan George Lafley:* As part of the top leadership at Procter & Gamble (P&G), Lafley ingrained innovation as a core practice and business strategy across all functional units and divisions. Lafley led P&G for two separate periods, from 2000 to 2010 and again from 2013 to 2015. In 2015, he stepped down as CEO of P&G but was maintained as its executive chairman, eventually retiring in June 2016. Viewed as one of the best chairmen and CEOs in P&G's history, Lafley accomplished what he did through a focus on innovation and the consumer. According to company records, when Lafley became P&G's president and CEO in 2000, the company had ten different billion-dollar brands. When he retired from his position as chairman, president, and CEO in 2010, the company's portfolio had grown to twenty-three different billion-dollar brands, with additions like Gillette, Old Spice, Tide, Charmin, Pampers, and Duracell. The company's market capitalization more than doubled, making P&G one of the five most valuable companies in the United States and among the ten most valuable companies in the world. Lafley's innovative business abilities and innovation leadership practices (such as making innovation everybody's business at P&G) have been credited as reasons for the company's success in the last decade. Speaking at an innovation conference in Palm Springs, Florida, in November 2011 organized by Ernst & Young, Lafley described his involvement in the innovation processes at P&G: "The biggest decision we made was to move to an open innovation platform. The problem at P&G in 2000 was not that we weren't inventive. The problem with us was that we weren't turning that invention into innovation that created customers that benefitted customers, that created value for customers or a better experience for customers, and that's all I wanted to do." Lafley continued, "So, P&G innovations have become so successful and a part of people's daily lives because the company innovates its brands with the customer in mind 100 percent of the time. I'm a big believer in pushing the idea, the innovation, and the technology in front of the prospective customer very early in the process. I learned this working with a lot of very good design shops. We used to spend way too much time and way too much money designing and engineering pretty ornate prototypes. This pushed us to prototype very quickly and prototype very crudely. Consumers are smart. You just want them to get the idea."

At the same conference in Palm Springs, Chris Thoen, former director of innovation and knowledge management at P&G, shared his insights into how innovation and consumer focus have been the keys to P&G's success: "The drive and focus on innovation Lafley instilled in the company during his time there is now one of the most important aspects of the organization's business. Lafley instilled in the hearts and minds of staff the belief that innovation is the way for a sustainable competitive advantage and business growth. Everyone in the organization breathes innovation in and out every day. At Procter & Gamble, innovation is seen as the cornerstone to develop the best possible products for consumers everywhere in the world. Innovation has been a great game changer at P&G, especially over the past 10 years." In 2010, Lafley received the Edison Achievement Award in recognition for his contribution to innovation leadership practices.

viii. *Microsoft's Bill Gates:* From the time Microsoft was founded in 1976 until he relinquished his active involvement with the company in May 2014, Bill Gates's ingenuity, innovative thinking attributes, and innovation leadership abilities were responsible for building one of the most highly profitable and valuable companies of the modern era. Microsoft was ranked the sixth most valuable company in the world by *Forbes* in 2011. Known for his shrewd and "tough-love" kind of leadership style, Bill Gates played a center-stage role in consistently advancing innovation management in all functional aspects of Microsoft. Besides his CEO position, Gates was also the company's chief software architect, a position he used to manifest his amazing and rare technological ingenuity and innovative thinking abilities, which also constantly inspired and influenced his executives to build their innovative thinking attributes and innovation leadership competencies. As a result of the strong innovation practices that Gates's leadership ingrained in Microsoft over the years, the company has managed to deal with the multiple large-scale challenges of competitors that the software giant constantly faces across its different product platforms. Additionally, his successors have continued to steer the company's innovation culture through leading by example—that is, by leveraging the innovative thinking skills and attributes that continue to drive and sustain Microsoft's innovation practices. According to company reports, the software giant invests around $9 billion a year in innovation-support and R&D activities and registers an average of three thousand patents a year.

ix. *Microsoft's Satya Nadella:* When Satya Nadella, referred to as the "innovation driver," was appointed as Microsoft's CEO, taking over the position from Steve Ballmer, the company was not doing well in the area of expanding its product offerings, and this contributed to the company lagging behind in terms of competitiveness against its industry peers. The company's flagship product platform, Windows, was facing hard times from the rise of the iPhone and Android platforms, and Microsoft stock was not performing as expected. For instance, according to company records, in 2007, Microsoft market capitalization was four times that of Apple and 25 percent more than that of Google. But when Nadella took over as CEO in February 2014, market capitalization was about 35 percent smaller than Apple and about 45 percent smaller than Google. The third CEO in the approximately forty-year history of Microsoft, Nadella was appointed CEO on February 4, 2014, according to company publications, specifically to drive innovation across all business groups of the company. One company news release reads, "Nadella has taken over from Steve Ballmer to prioritize three things, innovation, innovation, innovation." After his appointment, Nadella immediately implemented his well-thought-out innovation-engagement strategies. For instance, he sent an email to the company's more than 135,000 employees in which he emphasized innovation. "We need to prioritize innovation," he wrote. He also stated, "Our industry does not respect tradition. It only respects innovation." In his vision-promotion video aimed at Microsoft's workforces, he mentions the word *innovation* many times, stating that his leadership would remove any obstacles to innovation so that innovative thinking could thrive across all business groups of the company. Before his appointment as CEO, Nadella held various positions across the company's business groups. In most of the functional divisions where he served, he initiated innovative ideas that contributed to the transformation of the company's product platforms. For instance, according to company records, Nadella led the transformation of Microsoft's business and technology practices from client services to the cloud infrastructure. And soon after Nadella's announcement as CEO, Microsoft founder and former CEO Bill Gates spoke glowingly about Nadella's innovation talents in a video message to Microsoft staffers, stating that Nadella had steered innovation-led growth in the various business groups in which Nadella had served. Gates also said that Microsoft had a long history of innovation and that the appointment of Nadella was part of the company's next chapter of expanded product innovation and growth.

At the time of writing this book, Nadella has already served as CEO for three years; although Microsoft is not yet completely out of the woods, multiple independent and company reports suggest that Nadella's approach of leveraging his innovative thinking attributes and innovation leadership and management style to transform various business groups of Microsoft seems to be steering the company in the right direction. For example, a company release states that Nadella has provided strong, consistent vision and execution on the company's mobile-first and cloud-first strategy and has continued to effectively guide the transformation of the company's culture to focus on broadening the its product platforms through innovation.

x. *Tesla's Elon Musk:* The cofounder of PayPal, SpaceX, and Tesla Motors, Elon Musk is one of the most respected innovative brains of today's world and has transformed every business he has ventured into, such as electronic payments, electric cars, and commercial spaceflight. Musk was born and raised in South Africa. According to media reports, he studied physics and later business in the United States, then went on to enroll in a PhD program at Stanford University in California, but like many highly innovative entrepreneurs have done, he decided to drop out of the PhD program to pursue his entrepreneurial interests. Musk launched a highly innovative online mapping and directory service that later became known as PayPal. He later sold the company and used the money to fund some of his new business ventures, including Tesla, a company that manufactures electric cars, and SpaceX, a commercial spaceflight company. The manner in which Musk has successfully steered his business ventures reflects his ability to leverage his innovative thinking attributes and his strong emotional interest and passion for innovation. For instance, consider Tesla: within a short period, the company has recorded tremendous growth under Musk's innovation-led leadership style, with ambitious targets such as producing five hundred thousand vehicles in 2018. Like most highly innovative leaders, Musk leverages his innovative thinking attributes as instruments of inspiring innovation across all functional units and divisions of the two companies (Tesla and SpaceX) that he manages as CEO by regularly formulating innovation-motivating slogans and catchphrases, which, as mentioned earlier, are an effective approach for instilling the spirit of innovation in the hearts and minds of workforces.

xi. *3M's George Buckley and Inge Thulin:* A $20 billion global technology company with leading positions in the electronics, telecommunications, industrial, consumer and office products, health care, and safety industries, among others, 3M has been in existence for more than one hundred years and is regarded as one of the most innovative companies in the world. In an interview with the *Economist* magazine in March 2011, and in a presentation to the Global Leadership Summit at London Business School on May 25, 2011, former chairman, president, and CEO George Buckley explained why 3M has managed to remain innovative for so long. Buckley (CEO from December 2005 to February 2012) cited a number of reasons; one is that the company has had a long practice of having each generation of leaders pass along the leadership-for-innovation values to successive leaders. And the second reason is that 3M has had strong innovation-support practices aimed at continually developing and strengthening the capabilities of innovation talent, such as innovative thinking abilities and innovation leadership competencies. George Buckley's successor, Inge Thulin, days after taking office in February 2012, made a public statement to the media that he would continue with former CEO George Buckley's priorities for innovation. And in a presentation to shareholders on November 8, 2012, at company headquarters in Saint Paul, Minnesota, Thulin reiterated his and the company's commitment to innovation: "Innovation is at the center of our plan, so it is essential that we strengthen our commitment to R&D," said Thulin. "I am confident that 3M innovation, along with world-class talent, strong R&D and manufacturing capabilities, unparalleled global reach, and our unrelenting focus on operational excellence, will drive future success for our company and our shareholders."

xii. *Marc Benioff:* Benioff is the founder, chairman, and CEO of Salesforce, a cloud-computing company founded in 1999. According to media reports, (such as *The New York Times*, December II, 2011) Benioff is credited as being one of the early players in revolutionizing the software industry by using the internet to revamp the way software programs are designed and distributed. Media reports also indicate that Benioff was personally involved in coming up with the idea for Chatter, social networking software for businesses that is a mix of Facebook and Twitter. Chatter helps folks in his company network better by letting them efficiently connect with others and see what work is being done and what ideas others are generating across the company. Chatter represents Benioff's idea for how to help others be better networkers. All Salesforce employees (management and nonmanagement alike), according to the company literature, get at least two days of innovation training each year to help them maximize their contributions to company-wide innovation processes. Additionally, Benioff's skill as an innovator has helped Salesforce generate a high innovation premium.

xiii. *Fabrizio Freda:* Freda is the president and CEO of Estée Lauder Companies Inc. He was appointed on July 1, 2009, to succeed William P. Lauder. According to company and media reports, Freda excels at challenging the status quo by listening, observing, and "playing the outsider." After arriving at Estée Lauder, according to media reports, he spent six months on a "listening tour," zigzagging across Lauder's worldwide operations in 140 countries. In a statement to the media, Freda said he uses the power of listening to generate innovative ideas. "I strongly believe in the power of listening," says Freda. Listening, he says, helps him connect the dots. "The way my thinking and creativity goes, is listening, connecting and creating," according to Forbes online magazine, posted on September 5, 2012.

xiv. *Facebook's Mark Zuckerberg:* Zuckerberg is the CEO of Facebook. He cofounded Facebook, now the world's largest social network, based in Palo Alto, California, when he was twenty. An NBC News article notes, "Zuckerberg's great innovation was to understand that people would rather see one another online than look at third-party content. People would rather see friends and family than news or search engine results." Zuckerberg faced strong competition when he entered the social networking business. For example, Myspace was by far the largest social network in the world. It was owned by and had the backing of one of the world's largest media companies—Rupert Murdoch's News Corp. However, through his innovative abilities, Zuckerberg managed to build the world's largest social network and created the largest advertising platform in the United States by convincing major marketers that social networks are advertising-friendly, not platforms for the ridicule and attack of large companies. Over the years, Zuckerberg has built a strong culture of innovation, partly through his innovation leadership behavior, which creates conditions that inspire Facebook teams to generate innovative ideas. In an interview with a Silicon Valley media outlet, CIO Digital Magazine, Tim Campos, Facebook's chief information officer, described how the culture of innovation has been instilled in the hearts and minds of Facebook employees. "Facebook is all about innovation," says Campos. "To be the best, we need to innovate. And for people to innovate, they need the freedom to make mistakes—it's part of the learning process."

xv. *Netflix's Reed Hastings:* Hastings cofounded Netflix in 1998 in Los Gatos, California, to offer flat-rate rental-by-mail DVDs to customers in the United States. Hastings's innovative idea was that it would be more convenient for people who watch DVDs at home to receive them at home. Since founding the company, Hastings has expanded the company's services through various other innovative ideas. For instance, according to company reports, as broadband technology developed and became widespread in 2004 and 2005, Netflix used it to launch a business that allowed consumers to stream premium content from Netflix servers to their PCs. The service was upgraded two years later so that the films and TV shows could be streamed straight to televisions. Hastings has also set up deals to license content directly from studios, which poses a major threat to cable TV and telecom fiber-to-the-home businesses. Hastings changed the infrastructure models for video rental, video-delivery systems, and premium-content access, all within just thirteen years. Over the years, as the company grew, it began getting noticed for its innovative management practices. According to the literature, Netflix shares shot up 1,000 percent in five years as a result of the company's innovation-driven growth. And to date, the company has amassed a collection of one hundred thousand titles and more than twenty million subscribers.

xvi. *MassDevice.com report:* In June 2011, MassDevice.com, a network of manufacturers of medical devices, released a report listing the five most innovative CEOs in the medical device industry. The report also outlines how the top five CEOs were leading by example—that is, how the leaders, through their innovative thinking attributes, were encouraging and influencing their followers to be innovative.

*Bottom line*

It's important for organizational leaders to possess innovative thinking abilities in leading workforce innovation for a number of reasons. First, leaders can utilize their innovative thinking skills to build employee engagement in advancing innovation across the organization. This chapter opened with a quote from Albert Schweitzer, and it's fitting to repeat this vital point: "Example is not the main thing in influencing others. It is the only thing." This means that leaders must translate their innovative thinking attributes into instruments for influencing innovation practices across the organization. The second reason is that leaders can potentially leverage their innovative thinking skills to attract and retain top innovation talent. Third is that leaders who possess innovative thinking attributes tend to have a knack for formulating innovation-motivating slogans and catchphrases, which are vital for instilling innovation in the hearts and minds of workforces. Chapter 3 also provided examples of corporate leaders with strong innovative thinking attributes who have leveraged these attributes to build workforce engagement in advancing innovation across functional units.

# PART II
# INNOVATION ENGAGEMENT SKILLS

*Innovation is a mind-set that should pervade the whole organization.*
—**Professor Jean-Philippe Deschamps**,
International Management Development, Switzerland

## Overview

Unless workforces are engaged in innovation, the organization's efforts to scale innovation throughout the whole company will remain a rhetorical exercise. Thus, the second category of innovation skill sets that is essential for leading workforces is innovation engagement skills. Part II covers *what* these skills entail and *how* to apply them.

There's lots of evidence across industries—namely pharmaceuticals, financial services, computing, education services, retail, telecommunications, mining, agribusiness, food services, beverages, transport and logistics, energy, manufacturing, and health services—on the power of innovation to transform organizations. There's also a lot of evidence on what lack of innovation in organizations can result in. Later, we'll cover in detail the significance of innovation in an organization and how the leadership can harness innovation to drive sustainable growth. As stated before, harnessing innovation to benefit the organization in meaningful ways involves the implementation of many dimensions of and approaches to innovation-support initiatives and activities on an ongoing basis. One such dimension is innovation engagement, which involves helping workforces across the organization build passion for, emotional interest in, and commitment to advancing innovation. Part II opens with a quote from Professor Jean-Philippe Deschamps: "Innovation is a mind-set that should pervade the whole organization." Sentiments indicating that innovation is a hearts-

and-minds process have been expressed by many innovation experts and analysts. However, one aspect rarely emphasized is the issue of tools for instilling and maintaining innovation so that it is pervasive in the hearts and minds of workforces. It is important to understand that pervasiveness of innovation in the hearts and minds of workforces is not a natural occurrence; it requires consistent implementation of programs, activities, and approaches aimed at building workforce engagement in advancing innovation across functional units. This is not easy. It is a challenging task that requires specific abilities for securing employee engagement in innovation. However, most organizations tend not to build such capabilities. Instead, there is just an occasional mention of the term *innovation* by the leadership and occasional encouragement of workforces to contribute innovative ideas. Usually, this takes place at company meetings, or a few lines on how innovation is considered a vital practice in the organization might be included in the organization's performance reports. The casual and ordinary approach to engaging workforces in advancing innovation is, in large part, one of the reasons why most companies struggle to build a sustainable culture of innovation across functional units.

To scale innovation in a meaningful way, there must be recognition and appreciation by the top leadership that pervasiveness of innovation in the hearts and minds of workforces involves a great deal of work that requires consistent implementation of specific hearts-and-minds programs, approaches, and techniques. The leadership should also understand that if innovation is meaningfully instilled in and engaged by workforces, everyone in the organization will own the process of advancing innovation, and they will invest their passion, emotional interest, and commitment to contribute toward harnessing innovation (through generation of ideas) to drive organizational growth. Thus, the basis for innovation engagement skills is twofold:

i. Innovation is largely an issue of mind-set and attitude, which means that to build a culture of innovation, organizational leaders must possess skills for engaging workforces' passion, emotional interest, and commitment to advance innovation across the organization.

ii. One of the premises on which this book is anchored is that organizations now perceive innovation as everyone's job, from the CEO to the most junior staffer. However, innovation does not occur naturally; leaders need skills to implement a variety of programs and activities aimed at educating workforces about different aspects and concepts of innovation—especially the fact that innovation is grossly misinterpreted in many organizations.

To realize a meaningful level of workforce engagement in innovation, organizational leaders need to possess the ability to consistently develop and implement programs, approaches, and techniques for educating workforces about various aspects and concepts of innovation across functional units and, most importantly, the ability to instill innovation in the hearts and minds of workforces. This is where the innovation engagement skill set comes into play.

**Structure of This Section**

Part II is divided into the following five chapters:

- Chapter 4: Definition of *Innovation Engagement Skills*
- Chapter 5: Importance of Innovation Engagement Skills
- Chapter 6: Description and Expression of Innovation Engagement Initiatives
- Chapter 7: Innovation Engagement Committees
- Chapter 8: Application of Innovation Engagement Approaches

## CHAPTER 4
# DEFINITION OF *INNOVATION ENGAGEMENT SKILLS*

This chapter covers the following aspects:
1. Context of definition
2. Informative and inspirational styles: What do the two styles entail?

**1. Context of Definition**
As noted earlier, the innovation engagement skill set is a hearts-and-minds ability, and *innovation engagement skills* is defined as follows: the ability by organizational leaders to consistently educate workforces about different aspects of innovation through *informative* and *inspirational* styles using different communication approaches and techniques for the following purposes:
  i. To change misconceptions that workforces may have about innovation by explaining whose responsibility it is to innovate and that innovative thinking skills can be attained or learned by anybody
  ii. To secure workforces' belief in innovation as a driver of revenues, growth, competitiveness, and personal career development
  iii. To secure employee buy-in and engagement (i.e., passion, emotional interest, and commitment) in advancing innovation across the organization's value chain and business model
  iv. To secure workforces' desire to contribute toward various innovation-support strategies for advancing innovation across the organization

The following list outlines some of the dimensions and aims of innovation engagement skills:

i. To regularly educate and inspire workforces (e.g., at meetings, conferences, or retreats; in brochures, articles, and newsletters) in terms of what the vision of the company is for the next three to five years and why innovation is vital to realizing that vision

ii. To regularly articulate and convey to workforces across the organization (through different types of messages and visual illustrations) that innovative thinking skills can be attained or learned by anybody

iii. To regularly articulate and communicate various innovation-support initiatives—such as innovation strategies, innovation policies/procedures/plans, innovation goals, and innovation targets—implemented by the company to advance innovation across the organization, such as the following:
   o Functional-unit innovation strategies
   o Functional-unit innovation goals
   o Corporate innovation goals
   o Innovation-talent-recruitment policies
   o Workforce innovation-performance-evaluation policies
   o Innovation-talent-succession-planning policies
   o A framework for reporting functional-unit innovation performance
   o A framework for reporting corporate innovation performance
   o A framework for assessing and managing organization-wide innovation ideas
   o A framework for formulating organization-wide innovation-challenge questions

iv. To regularly articulate and communicate types and degrees of innovations launched or implemented by various functional units of the organization

v. To regularly articulate and communicate (in simple and clear terms) the innovation performance of the company in each functional unit or division and in terms of the organization as a whole

vi. To regularly educate workforces about various aspects of innovation, such as the following:
   o The meaning of *innovation* in the context of the company's value chain and business model
   o What the concept of *types of innovation* entails in the context of the company's business model and functional units
   o What the concept of *innovation degree* entails
   o The significance of innovation in terms of the growth and competitiveness of the company and also in terms of career advancement of the workforces

vii. To regularly formulate innovation-motivating slogans, catchphrases, and visual illustrations aimed at contributing toward instilling innovation performance in the hearts and minds of workforces

viii. To regularly create techniques to effectively communicate innovation-motivating slogans, catchphrases, and visual illustrations aimed at instilling innovation performance in the hearts and minds of workforces

ix. To regularly exhibit fit-for-purpose attitudes, language, and actions aimed at contributing toward creating an organizational climate that encourages innovative thinking across the organization
x. To apply many of the other available approaches aimed at inspiring workforces to build innovative-performance competencies

## 2. Informative and Inspirational Styles: What Do the Two Styles Entail?

As noted, *innovation engagement skills* refers to the ability of organizational leaders to educate workforces about different aspects of innovation through informative and inspirational styles using different communication approaches and techniques, with the aim of changing misconceptions about innovation and also helping workforces to build and unlock passion for, emotional interest in, and commitment to advancing innovation in the organization. The immediate question would then be, *What do informative and inspirational styles of fostering innovation engagement in the hearts and minds of workforces entail?* Although the gist of both styles centers on educating workforces about various aspects of innovation and instilling passion for and emotional interest in innovation in the hearts and minds of workforces, the difference between the two styles is made clear by the following descriptions of each:

i. *Informative style*: This style involves instilling innovation in the hearts and minds of workforces by informing them (through various communication options) on a regular basis about the innovation-support systems—such as innovation strategies, innovation policies, innovation procedures, innovation goals, and innovation plans—that the organization intends to implement or has implemented to advance innovation across the organization. It also involves crosscutting communication by leadership about the innovation performance of various functional units or divisions of the organization and the organization as a whole.

ii. *Inspirational style:* This style involves the constant use of innovation-motivating slogans, catchphrases, and visual illustrations to instill passion for and emotional interest in innovation in the hearts and minds of workforces. The inspirational style aims to achieve two things: (1) to influence workforces to believe in and understand wholeheartedly the importance of innovation to the competitiveness and growth of the organization and also to their career advancement and (2) to instill in the hearts and minds of the workforces a can-do attitude regarding the development of innovative thinking abilities. How is this done? By regularly communicating to workforces the inspirational message that nobody is born with innovative thinking abilities—rather, they're attained, and anybody can learn innovative thinking skills.

### Example

From a nonbusiness perspective, one illustration that gives a good depiction of the use or characterization of the informative and inspirational styles is a comparison of speeches by two former US presidents, Bill Clinton and Barack Obama, at the Democratic National Convention (DNC) in September 2012. These two leaders delivered their speeches on different days; both were great speeches, but they had different styles. Clinton delivered his speech on Wednesday, September 5, and Obama delivered his on Thursday, September 6. What is interesting about the speeches is how the two leaders rallied the huge audience at the venue and the viewers across the US to reelect President Obama.

In his speech, Clinton made a case for President Obama by constantly quoting qualitative and quantitative data on what President Obama had achieved during his first four-year term. In his speech, Clinton articulated the following points:

i. What Obama's economic recovery policies had achieved
ii. Obama's plans for advancing innovation across sectors
iii. The number of jobs created by the Obama administration, including the number of manufacturing jobs, which had been low for the previous decade
iv. Obama's national educational policies, which focused on preparing young people for twenty-first-century jobs and student loan reforms
v. Obama's energy-sector policies
vi. The five-point benefits of Obama's health-care insurance reforms, including clarifications on some of Obama's health-care policies, such as the savings created by Obama's Medicare plan
vii. Medicare and Medicaid policy contrasts between Obama and the then Republican presidential nominee, Governor Mitt Romney
viii. Highlights of Obama's debt-reduction plan versus Romney's plan

Thus, Clinton's approach would be considered an informative style. In contrast, President Obama made the case for his reelection to the DNC audience and the American voters through the constant use of motivational and catchphrases centered on words and phrases such as *hope, change, aspirations, opportunity for all, the American dream*, and *the unwavering character of Americans*. Some examples of the motivational phrases in Obama's DNC speech are as follows:

i. "With hope, American problems can be solved."
ii. "America can make it as long as we don't waver."
iii. "You have the choice to go backward or move forward with me."
iv. "You can choose the right future for America."
v. "You can choose leadership that is proven and tested."
vi. "Our efforts must not waver."
vii. "Change must be defined by the hopes and aspirations of the people."

*Application of Informative and Inspirational Styles*

The question is, *How are informative and inspirational styles applied to instill innovation in the hearts and minds of workforces?* An application of the informative and inspirational styles in the context of championing innovative thinking to create a culture of innovation is as follows:

i. *Informative style*: The informative style can be applied with the following actions:
    o Explaining and articulating how innovation is linked to the overall corporate strategy of the organization
    o Articulating functional-unit innovation-performance goals and targets
    o Explaining and articulating how the innovation-performance goals of each functional unit are aligned with the functional-unit strategy

- o Explaining and articulating how innovation strategies are being implemented across functional units
- o Articulating other innovation-related systems and practices, such as innovation-idea-development procedures, innovation-challenge questions, and various strategies and policies for innovation talent (e.g., innovation talent-recruitment policies, innovation-performance reward policies, talent-diversity policies, innovation talent-succession planning)
- o Articulating the number of innovation ideas generated, innovation ideas undergoing development, and innovations launched by various functional units
- o Articulating and explaining the frameworks for innovation-performance reporting that the organization has adopted
- o Articulating the impact of innovation on the performance of the company over a given period

ii. *Inspirational style:* In the context of leading workforce innovation, the inspirational style is applied through the use of innovation-motivating slogans, catchphrases, and visual illustrations focused on various aspects of innovation, such as the following:
- o Articulating and illustrating how innovation is critical to realizing the organization's vision
- o Articulating innovation-motivating slogans, catchphrases, and visual illustrations that regularly remind workforces about their potential to generate innovative ideas
- o Constantly articulating how innovation performance can drive the organization to greater heights, including examples of companies that have used innovation to transform their business model and achieve unprecedented growth
- o Articulating and illustrating how innovation can propel the careers of workforces to greater heights

# CHAPTER 5
# IMPORTANCE OF INNOVATION ENGAGEMENT SKILLS

Chapter 5 looks at why it's vital for organizational leaders to possess innovation engagement skills in leading workforce innovation. The following are three reasons:

i. *The need to inspire workforces to believe that innovative thinking abilities can be attained:* One of the challenges that organizational leaders face in leading workforce innovation is that many workforces tend to hold low expectations of themselves when it comes to generating innovative ideas. This attitude of low expectations is often compounded by the belief—espoused by many organizations over the years—that innovation is the responsibility of specific functional units and professionals. Since the current trend in organizations is to make innovation every employee's responsibility, organizational leaders now have a responsibility to change the thinking of workforces about innovation by continually instilling in them the fact that nobody has exclusive rights to innovative thinking abilities based on their inborn capabilities or current job positions and that anybody can attain innovative thinking abilities and generate innovative ideas. However, with innovation leadership still being an uncommon and somewhat unnatural competency for many organizational leaders, unfreezing the workforce thinking or attitude of "I can't generate innovative ideas" can be a daunting task. The good news, though, is that it's doable—with the appropriate skills, specific tools, and tact. As stated in chapter 4, the purpose of innovation engagement skills is to equip organizational leaders with tools and approaches that can effectively change the misconceptions that workforces have about innovation and educate workforces that innovative thinking skills can be developed by anybody, irrespective of status in the organization or type of profession.

ii. *Organizational leaders need hearts-and-minds skills to champion innovation across the organization*: The introduction of this book outlined four premises on which this book is anchored. One of the premises is that many organizations are now adopting the practice of making innovation every employee's business. However, it was also stated that many organizational leaders have no ability to formulate tools for communicating or publicizing innovation systems and innovation practices across the organization. When it comes to championing innovation across the organization, it must be understood that instilling innovation in the hearts and minds of workforces is not an easy task, and without the right skills, it's almost impossible to educate workforces about and instill in them the various aspects of innovation.

Experts on strategy execution have observed that many organizations are good at strategy formulation; however, when it comes to strategy execution, most of the organizations don't cut it. Many analysts in strategy implementation have indicated that one of the weaknesses many organizations have, which in many cases accounts for poor strategy execution, is organizational leaders' lack of skills to create effective initiatives to instill the organization's strategy in the hearts and minds of workforces. *Harvard Business Review* termed the process of instilling the organizational vision and strategy in the hearts and minds of the workforce *strategy communication* and observed that it's one of the challenges that organizational leaders are faced with when it comes to strategy execution. As a result, because the workforces, who are key stakeholders in strategy execution, do not wholeheartedly own and are not emotionally invested in the organization's vision and corporate strategy, the result is a negative impact on the strategy-execution process. In fact, an often-quoted *Fortune* magazine study published in 1999 found that 70 percent of CEO failures came not as a result of poor strategy but the inability to execute strategy. And in one of their publications, the architects of the Balanced Scorecard approach (a framework for strategy development and execution), Robert S. Kaplan and David P. Norton, revealed that one of the key barriers to strategy execution is a lack of understanding of company strategy by workforces; they also noted that 85 percent of executive teams spend less than one hour per month discussing strategy. In his most recent (2013) book, *Playing to Win: How Strategy Really Works*, former P&G CEO A. G. Lafley states that because strategy is formulated at all levels of the organization, to be successful, it needs to be communicated at all levels as well. Lafley emphasizes that the members of management must communicate their strategies to the whole company. Lafley warns that the challenge, though, is to find simple, clear, and compelling ways to communicate organizational strategies across functional units. "A massive binder or thick PowerPoint deck won't do for the organization. Thus, it's important to think explicitly about the core of the strategy and the best way to communicate its essence broadly and clearly," writes Lafley.

In his book *Balanced Scorecard Diagnostics: Maintaining Performance*, Paul Niven notes, "Regardless of the forum or field of endeavor, at the end of the day, true success resides in the power manifested by hearts and minds." This underscores the importance of communicating and publicizing innovation throughout the organization. But as stated earlier, instilling innovation in the hearts and minds of workforces is difficult without appropriate skills; for this reason, it is important for organizational leaders to possess the necessary skills and competencies to design and implement a wide range of innovation engagement initiatives (using both informative and inspirational styles) that are effective in building passion for, emotional interest in, and commitment to innovation in workforces, which will consequently result in consistent generation of innovative ideas and achievement of innovation goals across the organization.

iii. *Organizational leaders need to possess the ability to thoughtfully formulate creative, compelling, and inspiring innovation catchphrases:* In my experiences as a trainer and consultant and through my interactions in the practitioner world, I've seen many organizations use traditional techniques to try to inspire the desired workforce behavior, such as displaying phrases aimed at communicating the values, mission, or vision of the organization to workforces; these posters are usually displayed in particular locations around the offices or hallways. The posters often bear common phrases, such as those highlighted here in figure 5-1.

| Company X | Company Y |
|---|---|
| **Our core values**<br>• Customer satisfaction<br>• Mutual respect<br>• Teamwork<br>• Sense of urgency | **Our core values**<br>• Commitment<br>• Innovation<br>• Honesty<br>• Customer service<br>• Trust |

What is interesting about this practice is that the majority of the organizational leaders do not even bother to ask themselves how effective the phrases they have inscribed on the posters have been in motivating the desired behavior. In fact, in most cases, the general organizational behavior fails to reflect the inscribed organizational values. For instance, a number of organizations will include or display on the poster a phrase such as "Innovation is our core value," yet the majority of the leadership and the workforces do not even understand what *innovation* means in the context of the company's nature of business. Additionally, the company may not even have put in place the necessary crosscutting innovation-support systems and practices, yet the poster proclaims, "Innovation is our core value."

The point from the foregoing is that, irrespective of the size and type of organization, leaders cannot just proclaim phrases that are not thoughtfully generated, that are uncreative, and that are not compelling or inspiring and hope to instill the inscribed values and practices in the hearts and minds of workforces. In reality, the effect is likely to be zero in terms of instilling the intended message. Thus, the phrases should be thoughtfully generated, should be compelling and motivating, and must be applied using a variety of approaches and techniques in a creative and effective manner. In other words, the approaches and techniques used should be well thought out, persuasive, creative, and ultimately effective in terms of instilling various aspects of innovation messages in workforces so that they are able to translate the messages into habitual innovation-related behavior.

So, in part, innovation engagement skills are meant to equip organizational leaders with knowledge of the importance of crafting persuasive, creative, simple, and inspiring hearts-and-minds innovation messages. They also equip leaders with some techniques for using innovation concepts to formulate persuasive and simple innovation-related messages, with the desired effect being to help workforces build passion for and emotional interest in innovation.

## CHAPTER 6
# DESCRIPTION AND EXPRESSION OF INNOVATION ENGAGEMENT INITIATIVES

The purpose of this chapter is twofold: (1) to describe what innovation engagement initiatives are and (2) to outline techniques for and approaches to innovation engagement initiatives. Chapter 6 comprises the following aspects:

1. Definition
2. Approaches to expressing innovation engagement initiatives

**1. Definition**
The term *innovation engagement initiatives* refers to an integrated range of informative and inspirational styles and organizational activities through which innovation engagement skills are expressed to instill innovation in the hearts and minds of workforces.

Stated differently, innovation engagement initiatives involve development and implementation of different kinds of programs and activities, on a regular basis, for the following purposes:
  i. Educating workforces about what various aspects and concepts of innovation entail
  ii. Inspiring and instilling innovation in the hearts and minds of workforces so that workforces are meaningfully engaged in terms of building passion for, commitment to, and emotional interest in advancing innovation across the organization
  iii. Publicizing the various innovation-support strategies and systems implemented or intended to be implemented by the organization

# Description and Expression of Innovation Engagement Initiatives | 47

iv. Educating workforces about the significance of innovation to achieving corporate growth and long-term competitiveness of the organization, the impact of innovation on the economic well-being of communities, and the influence of innovation on the career development of workforces

In chapter 4 we gave detailed examples of dimensions and aims of innovation engagement initiatives and activities, you can refer to these for a more elaborate description of the meaning of innovation engagement initiatives.

## 2. Approaches to Expressing Innovation Engagement Initiatives

There are two approaches to expressing innovation engagement initiatives:
i. Use of innovation-motivating slogans and catchphrases
ii. Use of visual illustrations

Details of the two approaches follow.

i. **Use of Innovation-Motivating Slogans and Catchphrases**

As mentioned a number of times, instilling innovation in the hearts and minds of workforces is not easy because it requires the application of different forms of approaches and techniques. Whatever the technique that you use, it has to be creative and have a high chance of effectiveness. One of the techniques is harnessing the power of motivational slogans. Great slogans are memorable, and they captivate people's emotional interest and passion in relation to the intended context or purpose. Thus, innovation-motivating slogans are one of the effective techniques for instilling innovation engagement in the hearts and minds of workforces throughout the organization.

However, inasmuch as motivation slogans have a great deal of impact, that impact is dependent on, among other aspects, the quality of the slogans and catchphrases and the techniques used to communicate them across the organization. For this reason, it's important for the organizational leadership to create innovation engagement committees so that the committees can be tasked with focusing on specific innovation engagement initiatives and activities. Modalities for establishing committees are outlined later in part III. Once established, these committees should also be oriented to a number of pertinent aspects, such as how to formulate and publicize innovation-motivating slogans. The orientation can be done through seminars or workshops. The following are some of the characteristics of good innovation-motivating slogans:

o *Use simple and emotionally connecting language:* Innovation-motivating slogans should be written in simple, creative language and should have the potential to stimulate an emotional connection in the hearts of workforces. An example of an innovation-motivating catchphrase with less of an emotional effect could be written as follows:

"Lack of innovation weakens the competitiveness of our company."

On the other hand, the following innovation catchphrase will potentially have a stronger emotional effect on the hearts and minds of workforces than the first one:

"Lack of innovation creates a laid-back culture, laid-back products, and a laid-back company. And a laid-back company cannot be competitive!"

- *Workforces should be able to form pictures or images from the message:* You should ensure that workforces are able to form visual images from the innovation-motivating slogans. Remember, because slogans consist only of words, without visual illustrations, innovation-motivating slogans should allow workforces to create visual images from the words used. Here is an example:

    "Our company lives on ocean waves: without innovation, we're tossed!"

- *Reflect the context of the message used:* Ensure that you create innovation-motivating slogans that reflect the context of the intended innovation message that you are trying to communicate. For instance, slogans centered on the connection between innovation and the organizational vision, revenues, profits, competitiveness, career development, and so forth should clearly reflect this context.

- *Use impacting language:* Innovation-motivating slogans are intended to enculturate various aspects of innovation in the hearts and minds of workforces. Ensure that the language expressed in the slogans enables workforces to ingrain the intended aspects of innovation in their hearts and minds. For example:

    "Innovation is the sailboat of the vision of our company."

- *Illuminate benefits in simple and creative terms:* If you are trying to communicate the benefits of innovation, ensure that the innovation-motivating slogans make clear, in simple and creative ways, the benefits of innovation to the company, communities, and workforces.

*Examples of Channels for Communicating Innovation-Motivating Slogans*

You could have well-crafted innovation-motivating slogans and catchphrases, but if you have no effective techniques or channels through which to communicate, convey, or publicize them across the organization, the intended purpose of the slogans will not be realized. Thus, the teams responsible for creating innovation engagement slogans should use a great deal of resources, commitment, and creativity when suggesting techniques or channels for publicizing innovation-motivating slogans across the organization. The starting point should be for the top leadership (through an ad hoc committee) to come up with guidelines on the kind of engagement techniques or channels that would be acceptable to the organization. One of the guidelines, for example, could be that innovation engagement committees are required to periodically submit to the top leadership proposals for innovation engagement techniques or channels, and the top leadership of the organization would then give guidance on which techniques or channels would be suitable and adaptable to the organization's cultural settings, ability to fund, and ability to implement and adopt. Some examples of techniques or channels that could be used to communicate innovation-motivating slogans and catchphrases across the organization include the following:

- Innovation-motivating posters
- Innovation-motivating slogans on pens
- Innovation-motivating slogans on mouse pads
- Innovation-motivating slogans on mugs

Description and Expression of Innovation Engagement Initiatives | 49

- Innovation-motivating slogans on water bottles
- Innovation-motivating slogans on bags
- Innovation-motivating slogans on birthday and Christmas cards
- Innovation-motivating slogans on T-shirts
- Innovation-motivating slogans on company uniforms
- Innovation-motivating slogans on calendars
- Innovation-motivating slogans on hats
- Innovation-motivating slogans for computer screensavers

ii. **Use of Visual Illustrations**

In addition to innovation-motivating slogans and catchphrases, the second technique for communicating or publicizing innovation engagement messages is the use of visual illustrations to educate workforces about innovation.

What does promotion of innovation through visual illustration mean? It is a technique that involves the use of simple visual art, pictures, or any type of drawing to communicate a particular context of innovation to workforces with the intention of (1) educating workforces about a specific aspect of innovation; (2) instilling the message of the importance of innovation to the company, communities, and workforces in the hearts and minds of those workforces; and (3) instilling the spirit of innovative thinking in the hearts and minds of workforces.

The following are some of the aspects of innovation that can be communicated across functional units with the use of visual illustrations:

o The meaning of *innovation*
o The significance of innovation to the organization, communities, and the career development of the workforces, thereby stimulating emotional interest and passion for innovation performance in those workforces
o Dimensions of innovation (types and degrees of innovation)
o Innovation strategies, innovation policies, innovation procedures, and innovation practices across the organization

*Importance of Visual Illustration*

The use of visual illustration as one of the effective techniques for educating workforces about aspects of innovation and instilling the importance of innovation in the hearts and minds of those workforces is based on the idea that visual communication has a greater power to inform, educate, persuade, captivate, and motivate people to get involved and support a particular cause. Numerous studies have been conducted on the impact of visual illustrations on productivity. For instance, a study by the University of St. Gallen in Switzerland showed high productivity in managers who used a lot of visual illustration techniques to communicate various organizational activities to workforces compared with managers who did not use visual illustration techniques.

*Types of Visual Illustration Techniques*

A number of techniques can be applied to communicate or promote visual messages about innovation across the organization. Some of these techniques include the use of signs, pictures, drawings, graphic designs, and electronic resources, such as monitors displaying different kinds of innovation-related visual illustrations These aspects can be used in different forms to depict, convey, or communicate a particular context of innovation. Some of the contexts of innovation that can be conveyed or communicated across the organization include the following:

- o  Visual illustrations on the connection between innovation and increases in revenues and profits, growth, competitiveness, and career development for workforces
- o  Visual illustrations on the meaning of *innovation*
- o  Visual illustrations on the significance of innovation
- o  Visual illustrations on types of innovation in the context of the organization's business model
- o  Visual illustrations on the meaning of *innovation degree* (radical innovations and incremental innovations)
- o  Visual illustrations on various external trends driving the need to advance and sustain innovation performance in the company
- o  Visual illustrations about the company's innovation vision
- o  Visual illustrations of functional-unit and corporate innovation goals and targets
- o  Visual illustrations of the company's innovation policies and practices, such as the following:
  - • Funding for innovation R&D
  - • Innovation skills development
  - • Rewards and recognition policies
  - • Innovation performance measurements and reporting framework
  - • Innovation performance succession planning
  - • The innovation-idea development process
  - • The innovation-idea submission process
  - • Innovation strategies

*Other Approaches*

Other approaches that can be used to promote innovation and engage workforces across the organization include the following:

- o  Regularly record the CEO's innovation statements in video and audio formats, making sure they are publicized and accessible to all workforces
- o  Regularly translate some of the CEO's statements on innovation into innovation slogans and catchphrases
- o  Create a documentary about innovation in the company that can be accessed by all the workforces
- o  Introduce an innovation newsletter to be circulated to all workforces
- o  Initiate monthly "innovation town hall" meetings to be addressed by the CEO
- o  Organize departmental meetings on innovation to be addressed by heads of departments and other senior managers
- o  Establish an "Innovation Day" where various activities are conducted as a way of indicating to workforces the importance that the company attaches to innovation performance

## Description and Expression of Innovation Engagement Initiatives | 51

- o   Introduce innovation-performance awards to be given to individuals and teams
- o   Circulate to workforces reports on how the organization has performed in terms of innovation performance against competitors over a particular period of time
- o   Circulate to workforces information about innovation-support policies and systems
- o   Circulate to workforces stories on how innovation has contributed to making some companies great
- o   Arrange visitations or internships for staff to highly innovative companies

## CHAPTER 7
# INNOVATION ENGAGEMENT COMMITTEES

As stated earlier, undertaking innovation engagement campaigns across functional units not only requires the continual formulation of various innovation initiatives and activities, but it also involves the application of a variety of creative approaches, techniques, and channels for communicating innovation-related messages. To build the capability for the continual formulation of diverse innovation-promotion initiatives and techniques to convey innovation-related messages across functional units, it's important for the top leadership to create innovation-promotion committees whose role should be to regularly formulate, implement, and evaluate innovation engagement initiatives and communication techniques or channels across the organization. Thus, chapter 7 covers the following topics relating to the creation of innovation engagement committees: (1) aspects to consider and (2) creating action plans for innovation engagement activities.

**1. Aspects to Consider**
The following are some of the aspects to consider when creating innovation engagement committees:
  i. Innovation engagement committees should comprise staff from various functional units to enhance diversity in terms of abilities and ideas for promoting innovation across the organization.
  ii. The number of innovation engagement committees should be determined by the size of the organization and geographical spread of the company (i.e., locations or branches).

Innovation Engagement Committees | 53

Table 7–1. Example of Committees for creating specific innovation messages

| Committee for educating workforces on the meaning of innovation | Committee for promoting the significance of innovation | Committee for educating workforces on types of innovation | Committee for educating workforces on innovation degree | Committee for promoting connection between organizational vision and innovation |
|---|---|---|---|---|
| **This committee would focus on formulating** catchphrases, visual illustrations, motivational slogans, seminars, articles, stories, and so forth to educate workforces on what innovation is and some innovative thinking techniques that workforces can use to enhance their ability to generate innovative ideas. | **This committee would focus on formulating** catchphrases, visual illustrations, motivational slogans, seminars, and articles on various trends in the business environment and sharing stories on how innovation can drive the growth of the company and has steered growth or competitiveness in other companies. | **This committee would focus on formulating** catchphrases, visual illustrations, motivational slogans, seminars, articles, stories, and so forth to educate workforces on the types of innovation in relation to the organization's business model. | **This committee would focus on formulating** catchphrases, motivational slogans, articles, stories, visual illustrations, and so forth to educate workforces about innovation degree. | **This committee would focus on formulating** catchphrases, visual illustrations, motivational slogans, articles, stories, and so forth to constantly communicate how critical innovation performance is to meeting the performance goals of different functional units of the company and realizing the organizational vision. |

iii. Organizational leaders should come up with guidelines for innovation engagement approaches and techniques so that committees do not develop overly expensive engagement techniques or techniques that do not mesh well with the values and practices of the organization.
iv. To come up with effective innovation engagement initiatives and communication techniques or channels, committees should focus on the specific contexts of the messages on which innovation engagement activities will be centered. For instance, you could have a committee responsible for creating messages (slogans or catchphrases) focused on certain aspects of innovation, such as the alignment of the organizational vision to innovation, drivers of innovation, meaning of *innovation*, significance of innovation, and dimensions of innovation. Some examples of committees that focus on the specific contexts of innovation messages are highlighted in table 7-1 to the right.
v. Once constituted, each committee should come up with a list of responsibilities to be approved by the top leadership of the organization.
vi. Once the list of responsibilities is approved, the next step is for the innovation-promotion committees to begin their respective activities. The first step is for each committee to submit its action plan to an ad hoc committee created to ensure that all committees are up and running. The creation of action plans is addressed in the next section.

## 2. Creating Action Plans for Innovation Engagement Activities

Each of the innovation engagement committees (IECs) should understand how to create action plans for educating workforces about specific aspects of innovation. Here are some examples of things to include or take into account:

o A simple and clear title of the overall task in relation to educating workforces about innovation
o An objective statement of the overall task of educating workforces about different aspects of innovation
o Elements to operationalize different aspects of the action plan, such as the following:
- *What:* Specific activity to be conducted in relation to the overall task of educating workforces about different aspects of innovation
- *Who:* Name of a person or team to perform the specific activity in relation to the overall objective
- *When:* Time frame for conducting each activity
- *Resources:* What is needed to conduct each activity to achieve the intended purpose of the specific activity
- *Output:* Expected outcome from each of the earmarked activities for implementation. Again, the expected outcomes of each activity should be related to the overall task of educating workforces about innovation and instilling innovation in the hearts and minds of workforces.

## CHAPTER 8
# APPLICATION OF INNOVATION ENGAGEMENT APPROACHES

To effectively execute an organization-wide innovation engagement process, leaders can leverage basic innovation terms, specific innovation concepts, and general innovation aspects to instill innovation in the hearts and minds of workforces across the organization. Chapter 8 looks at how organizational leaders can apply their innovation engagement skills, abilities, and various resources to educate all workforces and instill in their hearts and minds the basic innovation terms, specific innovation concepts, and some vital aspects of innovation. Examples of important elements of innovation that workforces need to be educated about and have instilled in their hearts and minds include the following; (1) connection between innovation and organizational vision, (2) significance of innovation, (3) meaning of innovation, and (4) dimensions of innovation. Summaries of each of these aspects are as follows:

**1. Connection between Innovation and Organizational Vision**
Realizing the organizational vision is the single most important reason why many organizations pursue innovation, and because of this, the connection between innovation and realizing the organizational vision is one of the aspects of innovation that leaders should use their innovation engagement skills to instill in the hearts and minds of workforces. When creating innovation engagement messages that focus on the connection between innovation and realizing the organizational vision, it is important to distinguish between *organizational vision* and *corporate strategy*. This is because innovation is a form of strategy,

and according to a number of publications, many organizational leaders seem to have difficulties in educating workforces about how an organizational vision differs from a corporate strategy. What is an organizational vision? This book defines *organizational vision* as a picture expressed in a statement form of what the organization should be like after a specific period. In other words, it's an expression of a vision for the organization's future. On the other hand, a strategy is *what will get the company from where it is now to where it wants to be after the specified period.* In other words, strategy is how a company intends to realize its vision. Stated differently, vision answers the question, *What do we want our organization to be like in the next three to five years?* Strategy answers the question, *How are we going to get there?*

*Illustration*
Assume you are a member of an organization's leadership team and want to create various innovation engagement messages aimed at educating workforces about the connection between innovation and realizing the organization's vision. Specific steps in the process are as follows:

i. Outline the vision perspectives of the organization. What does this mean? Usually, companies have different perspectives on how to formulate their visions. Some companies have a one-sentence vision statement, whereas others take a multidimensional approach in which the organizational vision is expressed from more than one perspective, such as two, three, or four vision perspectives focusing on core concepts. For example, one company's organizational vision might consist of the following four vision perspectives:
   o *Market share:* Takes into account what the company intends to be like in relation to market share within a defined time frame
   o *Market leadership:* Outlines the company's vision to be a market leader in a particular industry over a specified period
   o *Revenue vision:* Outlines the financial vision of the company over a specified period. In other words, how much revenue does the company intend to generate in the next three to five years?
   o *Shareholder-value vision:* Outlines the desired percentage of growth in dividends over a specified period
ii. Formulate vision-focused innovation slogans, catchphrases, and visual illustrations that reflect the company vision. These should have the potential to instill passion for and emotional interest in innovation in the hearts and minds of workforces.
iii. Identify techniques, channels, or methods for communicating the messages reflected in the vision-focused innovation slogans, catchphrases, and visual illustrations across the organization.

## 2. Significance of Innovation
Remember that one of this book's premises is that innovation has become critical to the vibrancy of any organization or industry. Because of the significance of innovation, organizations are now implementing innovation practices to build a climate that allows everybody in the organization to get involved in advancing innovation. The ultimate reason

## Application of Innovation Engagement Approaches | 57

for implementing innovation practices is to contribute to achieving organizational growth and efficiency-related goals, eventually leading to the realization of the organizational vision. In other words, innovation brings about new products, new services, new markets, efficient processes, cost savings, revenue generation, competitiveness, enhanced customer experience, realized investor expectations, and solutions for community problems—and a whole lot of other things. From these highlighted aspects, you can see that innovation touches the core existence of an enterprise, and that is why it is often said that innovation is a predictor of the profitability, growth, competitiveness, and survival of an organization. Given the importance of innovation, leaders should be able to leverage different contexts of the significance of innovation to instill innovation in the hearts and minds of workforces across the organization. This can be done by formulating effective messages through slogans, catchphrases, and visual illustrations that are focused on different aspects of the significance of innovation.

When creating messages on the significance of innovation, it is also important to formulate drivers of innovation. The drivers of innovation are innovation-related phrases and visual illustrations that depict various factors influencing the organization to make innovation every employee's business and that communicate why the organization has made innovation a permanent practice across functional units. Details on drivers of innovation are provided later in this section.

The following examples depicting the significance of innovation can be used to create concise innovation-related statements, slogans, catchphrases, and visual illustrations on why innovation is important:

i. One study compared the overall financial results of the most innovative group of companies with those that are not very innovative. According to the study, the results were clear. The most innovative companies outperformed their industry peers on three different indicators of financial success: revenue growth; earnings before interest, tax, depreciation, and amortization (EBITDA) as a percentage of revenue; and market capitalization growth. The study also compared the financial results of "highly innovation-coherent" companies in the Global Innovation 1000 to those of less innovation-coherent companies within the Global Innovation 1000 group (innovation coherence is the extent of aligning innovation strategy to corporate strategy) and found that the profit margins of companies ranked in the top third in terms of degree of innovation coherence were 22 percent higher on average than those of companies in the bottom two-thirds (not highly innovation coherent) and that the highly innovation-coherent companies also achieved 18 percent greater market capitalization growth. Additionally, the December 15, 2017, issue of *Fortune* magazine listed the most valuable companies, by market capitalization, as Apple, Google, Microsoft, Amazon, and Facebook. Perhaps not coincidentally, these companies were ranked among the ten most innovative companies in the world according to Boston Consulting Group's innovation survey report of 2016.

ii. A 2011 study by PriceWaterhouseCoopers (PwC) involving 1,201 business leaders in sixty-nine countries revealed that innovation is a strategic focal point for CEOs and that innovation is ranked as a high priority in every industry; the study further noted that 78 percent of the CEOs reported expecting product innovation to generate "significant" new revenue opportunities for their companies in the next three years.

iii. A 2010 study by Harris Interactive, an international marketing consulting company, revealed that 95 percent of the Fortune 1000 executives surveyed indicated innovation performance as critical to the future growth of their companies.

iv. A study conducted in 2009 by Frost & Sullivan, a business research and consulting firm, which involved 157 CEOs across the European Union, revealed that 85 percent of the respondents indicated that there is increasing need for innovation to withstand the ever-intensifying competitive environment in their sectors.

v. A survey conducted by the Confederation of British Industry (CBI), which was partly aimed at exploring the link between innovation and revenues, profits, competitiveness, reputation, and growth, revealed that 93 percent of the executives awarded a score of at least seven out of ten when asked to rate the importance of innovation to their companies' success. The survey further revealed that, on average, companies in Britain spend 12 percent of their turnover on investing in innovation.

vi. In a 2010 global innovation survey by McKinsey & Company, 84 percent of executives said innovation was *extremely* or *very important* to their companies' growth strategies and that without innovation, their companies would struggle to grow. Similar sentiments were expressed by the US-based Institute for Corporate Productivity Report in 2011: "Indeed, the corporate landscape is littered with the abandoned hulls of once storied organizations that no longer exist, in large part due to their failure to innovate."

Such information can be expressed in different forms of innovation-related statements, slogans/catchphrases, and visual illustrations and then conveyed to workforces in various ways.

*Educate Workforces on How Innovation Benefits Them*

It is important for the leadership to bear in mind that employees have the inherent desire to contribute toward realizing the innovation potential of the company, and at the same time, they also want to maximize their individual benefits as they contribute toward innovation performance. So in addition to understanding that innovation is a critical strategy for increasing revenues and enhancing competitiveness and growth, workforces need to see how their involvement in innovation performance benefits their career development and economic well-being. This is vital because it's often said that people have an inherent need to believe in something when they are convinced that there is something in it for them. And once they establish that there is something for them, they will "own it" and invest incredible amounts of energy and dedication to bring about its fruition. And the opposite is also the case: if workforces are not convinced there's something in it for them, they will likely exhibit unsupportive behavior toward championing innovation. How might such behavior be manifest? Workforces may display a number of anti-innovation attitudes, such as the following:

- Being indifferent to all the innovation-support initiatives that the company is implementing

- Withholding their innovative ideas
- Exploring other options to develop their ideas, such as licensing them
- Leaving the company and developing their innovative ideas elsewhere

Thus, it's important to create effective messages in the form of innovation-related slogans, catchphrases, and visual illustrations focused on how innovation directly benefits workforces.

*Educating Workforces about the Drivers of Innovation*

There are numerous internal and external factors that influence organizations to implement innovation strategies on an ongoing basis and create a culture of innovation. Figure 8-1 gives some examples of these factors:

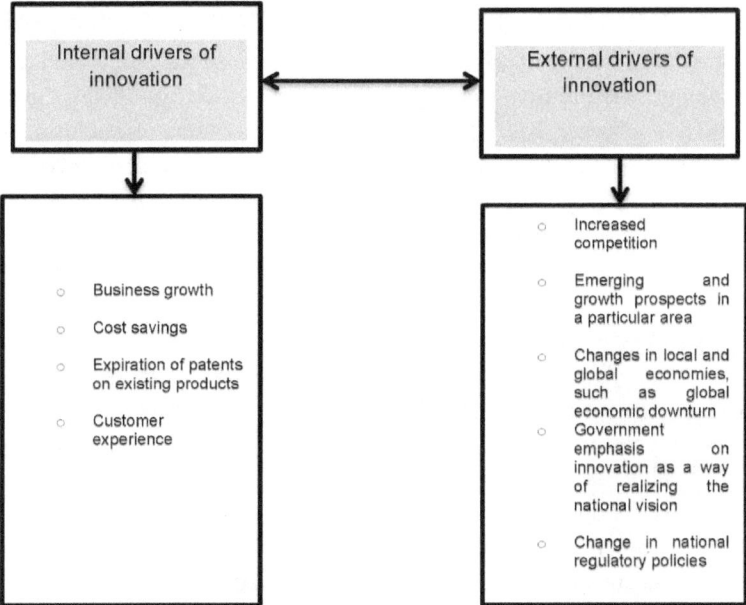

As part of the process for championing innovation across the organization, it is important for the leadership to inform and educate workforces about the factors that have necessitated the company to adopt a culture of innovation. This can be done by formulating effective messages through catchphrases, visual illustrations, and written summaries on the specific internal and external factors that are driving the culture of innovation across the organization. Examples of internal and external factors that influence organizations to adopt a culture of innovation include the following:

o *Internal innovation drivers*
- *Business growth:* In October 2011, when Virginia "Ginni" Rometty became IBM's CEO, revenues had been flat for almost six years. Her immediate goal was to boost IBM's growth through innovation in nontraditional areas.
- *Cost savings:* When Joseph Jimenez took over as CEO for the Swiss drug maker Novartis, one of his reform themes was implementing cost-saving innovation strategies across the organization.

- *Expiration of patents for existing products:* When Ian Read took charge as CEO of Pfizer, a giant drug-manufacturing company, in 2010, one of the major aspects revealed during the company's restructuring strategy exercise was that the patent expiration of Lipitor, the company's blockbuster cholesterol pill that accounted for 16 percent of Pfizer's sales, was due in 2011. As a result, Lipitor's sales were expected to fall by two-thirds by 2013, two years after the expiration. This meant the company needed to invest in innovation research to develop alternative products to mitigate the effect of Lipitor's patent expiration.

o  External innovation drivers
- *Increased competition:* In an address to Nokia employees in March 2011, Stephen Elop, who had recently been appointed as CEO, outlined the themes of his strategy. Elop disclosed that despite the 450 million phones the company sold in 2010, 402 million more than Apple, almost everything Nokia had done since 2007 was wrong. Elop told the audience that Apple and Google had changed the industry from a handset focus to a software focus, and Symbian, Nokia's software, had fallen too far to have any hope of catching up with the competition from Apple and Google. Days later, Elop announced that as part of his strategy, he was discontinuing Symbian. A few months later, he formed a technical team whose task was to develop a replacement for Symbian and also innovate a product that would compete against top players in the smartphone area.
- *Emerging growth prospects in a particular area:*
    - *Artificial intelligence and machine learning*: In the wake of predictions and general discourse on how artificial intelligence (AI) is transforming how people live and work, there is increasing prominence placed on investment in AI-related innovation research and innovation-skills development across sectors, such as financial services, computing, health care, transportation, manufacturing, retailing, telecom, and government agencies, among others. In PwC's 20th CEO Survey of 2017, AI and machine learning were noted as areas that will have a significant impact in many sectors over the next twenty years. Many companies are investing heavily in AI. For instance, Facebook is working on building the best AI lab in the world. In a statement on Facebook's Vision 2026, released on February 18, 2017, CEO Mark Zuckerberg indicated that the execution strategy for Facebook's vision will heavily rely on investing in innovation research in AI. Other companies investing heavily in AI-related innovations include Amazon, Google, Honeywell, Boeing, and Rope Technologies.
    - *Financial technology ("fintech"):* This is one of the hottest emerging and growing spaces in financial services. The growth potential is driving a lot of investment in innovative fintech services and solutions and innovation-skills development by corporations like IBM, Cisco, Accenture, Microsoft, Deloitte, Siemens, PwC, Oracle, Wipro Technology, and so

forth. There are also a lot of start-ups in the fintech field, especially in Silicon Valley.
- *Renewable energy:* Because of increased environmental awareness across the globe, renewable energy is being viewed as a huge opportunity for innovation by companies in the auto and technology industries, such as Tesla, Siemens, Philips, Samsung, and Panasonic. For instance, global investment in renewable energy in 2016 was estimated at $285.9 billion, representing an increase of about 640 percent since 2003. In July 2016, Tesla Motors opened a $5 billion "Gigafactory" for manufacturing lithium-ion batteries. It's the biggest factory in the world, about the size of 262 NFL football fields. Under its vision for an eco-friendly future, Panasonic's Corporate Division for Energy Solution Business has designed a global strategy for smart cities. Among the goals of the division is to develop, design, and implement innovative smart-city services and products across the globe, such as the Tianjin Eco-city project in China, the Punggol project in Singapore, and the Indian Delhi–Mumbai Industrial Corridor (DMIC) Project.

- *Economic downturn:* In 2008, the world's largest steel company, ArcelorMittal, was hit by the global financial crisis and economic downturn. In 2011, the company reported that the three years of weak steel demand had put downward pressure on the company's earnings and profits, and in a company statement in 2011, ArcelorMittal's CEO, Lakshmi Mittal, said his company was embracing innovation strategies to keep up with the dark market environment.
- *Change in national regulatory policies:* For example, following the 2008–2009 financial crisis, the Obama administration restructured the financial regulatory framework to deal with some of the factors that led to the financial crisis.
- *Government's emphasis on innovation as a way of realizing the national vision:* Examples of governmental emphasis on innovation include the following:
  - The Obama administration's energy innovation vision was "to lead the world in clean energy technology." This vision was intended to motivate private-sector investment in clean energy–technology innovations because of government support in terms of incentives and political will.
  - On December 15, 2008, during a press conference in Chicago, the then president-elect Barack Obama made a passionate statement on innovation, stating that innovation would be the cornerstone for realizing the goals of his administration's Economic Recovery Plan.
  - In April 2009, the Obama administration unveiled its long-term economic plan. The plan was anchored on five pillars, and each of the five pillars, according to President Obama, would be propelled by innovation.
  - On August 5, 2009, President Obama launched his administration's National Innovation Strategy, noting, "History should be our guide. The United States led the world's economies in the 20th century because we led the world in innovation. Today, the competition is keener; the

challenge is tougher; and that is why innovation is more important than ever. It is the key to good, new jobs for the 21st century. That's how we will ensure a high quality of life for this generation and future generations. With these investments, we're planting the seeds of progress for our country, and good-paying, private-sector jobs for the American people."

The point is that the leadership should, on a continual basis, leverage various internal and external innovation drivers in different forms (e.g., summary statements, catchphrases, and creative visual illustrations) to instill the importance of innovation across the organization.

## 3. Meaning of *Innovation*

By its nature, a culture of innovation is not easy to create in an organization. But it is even harder for the leadership to get all workforces across the organization engaged in the innovation process of the company if the workforces do not even understand what innovation means in the context of the company's value chain and business model. How would individuals get engaged in a process if, to start with, they do not even understand its meaning? For this reason, it's important to ensure that workforces understand the meaning of *innovation* and how the meaning relates to the organization's value chain and business model.

There are numerous definitions of *innovation*, and some of them can be misleading. I often come across definitions of *innovation* such as "generation of new ideas," "a new product," or "the act of introducing something new." Certainly, these definitions capture some aspects of what innovation is. However, if such definitions are adopted, institutionalized, and ingrained in the hearts and minds of everybody in the organization, the company risks instilling a partial meaning of *innovation* in the hearts and minds of workforces, with the accompanying risk of being bombarded with lots of ideas generated from across the organization that may not truly be innovative because they are based on a partial meaning. Thus, a full and applicable meaning of *innovation* has to be formulated.

That said, this book defines *innovation* as *a process that involves identifying a problem or need, generating a new idea that has not been seen on the market before, turning the idea into a solution to address the identified need, and then converting the solution into monetary value.* Thus, the definition of *innovation* is segmented into the following four aspects, as noted in chapter 1:

i. Identifying a problem or need (e.g., within a particular customer/market segment or the organizational system)

ii. Generating an innovative idea never seen on the market before to fix the identified problem/need

iv. Converting the solution into monetary value (e.g., in terms of increased revenue or cost reduction)

iii. Transforming the innovative idea (through an established process) into a solution not seen on the market before

The following story illustrates the connection between identification of a problem, generation of an innovative idea (solution), and monetary value: According to multiple reports, there is a huge demand for English-language learning in China. Parents in China spend more than $15 billion a year on children's English-language learning. Further, there are eighteen million new babies born in China every year but only twenty-seven thousand qualified English teachers from Canada and the US resident in China. To illustrate the extent of the problem, in Beijing alone, there are more than one million elementary school kids, meaning that twenty-seven thousand teachers is not even enough for Beijing.

> Ann Young, a Beijing-based teacher, saw an opportunity for an innovative idea. She formed a company to offer English-learning services across China in an innovative way. Upward English-4-Kids (not real name) is a Beijing-based company that contracts about 30,000 instructors in Canada and the US and matches them with about 230,000 Chinese kids for one-on-one video tutorials in English. The teachers offer online tutorials from anywhere in Canada and the US. In 2017, Upward English-4-Kids generated more than $800 million in revenue, up from $400 million in 2016.

### *Institutionalizing and Educating Workforces about the Meaning of Innovation*
We have so far defined *innovation* in a generic sense; however, workforces can easily relate to the company's innovation practices if, among other things, the meaning of *innovation* is translated to fit the context of the organization's value chain. In other words, an inability to translate the meaning of *innovation* to fit the context of the organization's value chain can potentially hinder the ability to instill innovation in the hearts and minds of workforces and thereby impede the organization's efforts to build a culture of innovation. This is because, naturally, workforces will more readily take part in the application of a concept if they can easily understand and resonate with it, both in terms of what it entails and also its relevance to the functional activities of the organization. And once they understand the concept, they'll buy into it and contribute to its furtherance. Thus, to make it easy for workforces to understand the meaning of *innovation* and to instill innovation in the hearts and minds of workforces so that they can build passion for and emotional interest in innovation, it's necessary to translate the meaning of *innovation* to fit the context of the organization's value chain. For instance, if an organization has adopted a concept such as solar innovation, culinary innovation, audit innovation, banking innovation, financial innovation, artificial-intelligence innovation, insurance innovation, or health innovation, the leadership should make an effort to interpret the meanings of innovation concepts in a detailed form that fits the context of the organization's business model. For example, brochures could be used to outline and communicate the interpretation and context of the innovation concepts.

### *Example*
Let's assume you are tasked with creating definitions of *innovation* in the context of the various functional units (value chain) of DM Personal Care Products, the fictitious company introduced earlier, for the purpose of enabling workforces to relate to the innovation practices of the company.

# 64 | LEADERSHIP FOR INNOVATION

First, identify the core and support (back-office) functional units of DM Personal Care Products, outlined as follows:

*Core functional units*
- Product-development unit, with the following segments:
  - Body-lotions segment
  - Skin-cleansing segment
  - Hair-care segment
  - Hand-washing segment
- Manufacturing-processes department (the manufacturing-processes department comprises the same segments as the product-development unit)
- Marketing department, with the following units:
  - Pricing unit
  - Product-promotion unit
  - Product-delivery unit
  - New-markets unit
  - Packaging unit
- Customer service department

*Support functional units*
- Procurement department
- HR department
- Finance and accounting department
- IT department
- Corporate affairs department

Second, create tables for translating the meaning of *innovation* in the context of the functional units of the company, as shown in worksheets 8-1 through 8-5. Worksheets 8-1 through 8-4 apply to the company's core functional units, and worksheet 8-5 applies to support functional units.

Worksheet 8-1. Definition of product innovation

| | Product-development unit | |
|---|---|---|
| Product category | Type of innovation | Definition of *innovation* in the context of the functional activities of the product-development unit |

| | | |
|---|---|---|
| Body lotions | Product innovation | An example of the definition of *innovation* in the context of this unit would be as follows:<br>1. Identifying problems/needs/gaps within the personal care market<br>2. Generating innovative product ideas (i.e., ideas never seen in the personal care space before)<br>3. Turning the innovative ideas (through an established process) into solutions (not seen by customers or the market before) to deal with the particular needs/gaps identified in the personal care space<br>4. Converting the product solutions into commercial value (i.e., in terms of customer attraction and retention, revenue, competitiveness, and growth) |
| Skin cleansing | Product innovation | |
| Hair care | Product innovation | |
| Hand washing | Product innovation | |

# 66 | LEADERSHIP FOR INNOVATION

Worksheet 8-2. Definition of manufacturing-processes innovation

| Manufacturing-processes department | | |
|---|---|---|
| **Product category** | **Type of Innovation** | **Definition of *innovation* in the context of the manufacturing processes of the four product categories** |
| Body lotions | Manufacturing-process innovation | An example of the definition of *innovation* in the context of the manufacturing processes would be as follows:<br>1. Identifying *problems* or *needs* within the manufacturing processes for the four categories of personal care products<br>2. Generating particular innovative ideas for the manufacturing processes (i.e., ideas never seen before in the manufacturing processes of personal care products) in the following categories:<br>　o Body lotions<br>　o Skin cleansing<br>　o Hair care<br>　o Hand washing<br>3. Turning the innovative ideas (through an established process) into solutions to deal with the particular need or problem identified in any of the manufacturing processes of the four personal-care-product categories<br>4. Converting the manufacturing-processes solutions into commercial value (e.g., in terms of cost savings or enhanced efficiency through an increase in production levels in a reduced time period) |
| Skin cleansing | Manufacturing-process innovation | |
| Hair care | Manufacturing-process innovation | |
| Hand washing | Manufacturing-process innovation | |

## Application of Innovation Engagement Approaches | 67

Worksheet 8-3. Definition of marketing innovation

| Marketing Department | | |
|---|---|---|
| Unit | Type of innovation *(Note: Innovations under this category could be referred to generally as marketing-strategy innovations or specifically by aligning innovation to the particular segment, as done here.)* | Definition of *innovation* in the context of the marketing functional unit |
| Pricing | Pricing innovations | Identification of a pricing opportunity, then generation of an innovative pricing idea, which is then converted (through an established innovation-development process) into a price innovation that contributes monetary value to the organization |
| Product promotion | Product-promotion innovations | Identification of a product-promotion need or problem, then generation of an innovative product-promotion idea, which is then converted (through an established product-promotion innovation-development process) into a product-promotion innovation that contributes monetary value to the organization |
| Product delivery (*often a stand-alone unit in large corporations*) | Product-delivery innovations | Identification of a need or problem within the product-delivery unit, then generation of an innovative product-delivery idea, which is then converted (through an innovation-development process) into a product-delivery-process innovation that contributes monetary value to the organization |
| New markets | Innovative ideas for new markets | Identification of a market opportunity, either in a new market (e.g., a new geographical location) or a new customer segment within the existing market not served by competitors' or the organization's existing products or services, then generation of an innovative market-strategy idea, which is then converted (through a new-market strategy) into a new market for existing products that contributes monetary value to the organization |

| Packaging | Packaging innovations | Identification of a need or problem within the packaging unit, then generation of an innovative product-packaging idea, which is then converted (through an innovation-development process) into a product-packaging innovation that contributes monetary value to the organization |

Worksheet 8-4. Definition of customer service innovation

| Customer Service Department | | |
|---|---|---|
| **Customer service component** | **Type of innovation** *(Note: Innovations under this category could be referred to as customer service innovations.)* | **Definition of *innovation* in the context of customer service** |
| Customer service | Customer service innovation | Identification of a need or problem within the customer service unit or segment, then generation of an innovative customer service idea, which is then converted (through an innovation-development process) into a customer service innovation that contributes monetary value to the organization |

Recall that the support functional units of DM Personal Care Products include the following:

❖ Procurement department
❖ HR department
❖ Finance and accounting department
❖ IT department
❖ Corporate affairs department

Worksheet 8-5 provides an example of how you can translate the meaning of *innovation* in the context of cost savings in these support functional units. As stated before, the context of innovation ideas generated in support functional units is usually focused on efficiency or cost savings within the context of a particular support functional unit. Thus, the meaning of *innovation* in the support functional units outlined in worksheet 8-5 is phrased in the context of cost savings.

Worksheet 8-5. Definition of innovation in support functional units

| Translating the meaning of innovation in the context of support functional units | |
|---|---|
| **Support unit** | **Definition of *innovation* in the context of support functional units** |
| Procurement | Identification of a cost-saving opportunity in the procurement functional unit of the organization, then generation of a procurement cost-saving innovative idea, which is then converted (through an innovation-development process) into a procurement cost-saving innovation |
| Human resources (HR) | Identification of a cost-saving opportunity within the organization's HR functional components, then generation of a cost-saving innovative idea in the context of HR practice, which is then converted (through an innovation-development process) into an HR-practice cost-saving innovation |
| Finance and accounting | Identification of a cost-saving opportunity within the organization's finance and accounting functional components, then generation of a cost-saving innovative idea in the context of finance and accounting practices, which is then converted (through an innovation-development process) into an accounting-practice cost-saving innovation |
| Information technology (IT) | Identification of an IT-related cost-saving opportunity in any of the functional units of the organization, then generation of an IT-related cost-saving innovative idea in the context of the particular practices of the functional unit, which is then converted (through an innovation-development process) into an IT cost-saving innovation |
| Corporate affairs | Identification of cost-saving opportunities within the organization's corporate affairs functional components, then generation of a cost-saving innovative idea in the context of corporate affairs practices, which is then converted (through an established innovation-development process) into a cost-saving innovation in corporate affairs |

## 4. Dimensions of Innovation

Remember, it is difficult for workforces to relate to the company's call for advancing a culture of innovation if the innovation practices have not been translated to fit the context of the company's value chain and business segments. We have so far discussed the meaning of *innovation* and how the meaning can be translated to fit the context of the organization's value chain. The second vital concept of innovation is *dimensions of innovation*. Integral to establishing the innovation practices on which the organization's culture of innovation is anchored is ensuring that an organization has a clear interpretation of the dimensionality of innovation in relation to its value chain and business model. Remember that a culture of innovation constitutes various innovation practices that are translated to fit the context of the organization's systems and business model, and one of the concepts of innovation through which an organization expresses its innovation practices is dimensions of innovation. Thus, this section covers the meaning of *dimensions of innovation* and how the meaning can be translated to fit the context of the company's value chain and business model for easy understanding by workforces. The section has covered two aspects; *definition of dimensions of innovation* and *description of types of innovation and innovation degree*. Details of these are as follows:

i. **Definition of Dimensions of Innovation**

   Innovation occurs in different organizational contexts, and these contexts are what we've referred to as dimensions of innovation. The term *dimensions of innovation* refers to ways in which innovation occurs in the context of an organization's value chain and business model. In other words, because innovation occurs in different contexts of organizational activities, *dimensions of innovation* is a term that describes the different ways in which innovation occurs (i.e., *where*) and the degree of change or newness that innovation entails (i.e., *how*).

   *Example of How to Illustrate the Dimensions of Innovation*
   A number of illustrations can be used to describe the dimensionality of innovation. One simple example would be a basket containing a mixture of fruits and veggies of different types, colors, and sizes. How does the basket of veggies and fruits relate to the dimensionality of innovation? Three relations can be highlighted:
   - *Variety of fruits and veggies:* This relates to the fact that innovation occurs in the different contexts of the various functional activities and business segments of an organization.
   - *Each fruit or veggie has a name:* This relates to the fact that there are different kinds of innovation and that every innovation has a name in the context of a particular aspect of the organization's business model, functional activity, or business segment.
   - *Each fruit or veggie has a different nutritional value:* This relates to the fact that every innovation idea is different in terms of the magnitude of newness or extent of inherent impact (i.e., an innovative idea can either be radical or incremental).

   In a nutshell, *dimensions of innovation* is a term that describes two related innovation concepts: *types of innovation* and *innovation degree*, as illustrated in the following simple diagram:

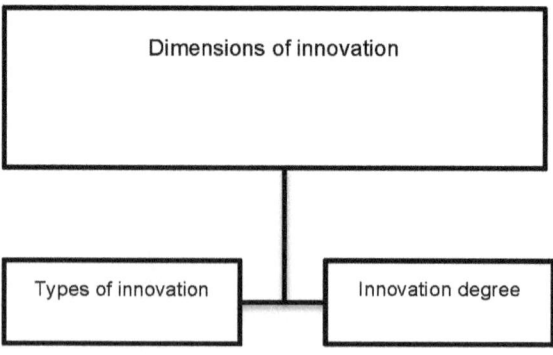

ii. **Description of Types of Innovation and Innovation Degree**
   o **Types of Innovation**

   What does the term *types of innovation* mean? Recall that *dimensions of innovation* is a concept used to describe two aspects of innovation: *where* innovation occurs and *how* innovation occurs. The term *types of innovation* relates to where innovation occurs or the context in which innovation occurs in the organization's value chain or functional activities. Innovation occurs in a variety of functional activities across the organization's value chain. For instance, there are innovation ideas (or innovations) in different contexts of products depending on the nature of an organization's product platforms. There are also process innovation ideas depending on the nature of an organization, marketing innovations, customer service innovations, and a whole host of service innovations. Further, types of innovation normally reflect the context of an organization's value chain and business model. For instance, a financial institution such as a bank would contextualize its types of innovation according to the value chain and business model. Such innovations in a bank would generally be referred to as bank innovations, and the innovations would then be further categorized according to the segments in the bank's value chain. For example, innovations or innovation ideas generated in a payment functional unit of the bank would be specified as payment innovations, and in the bank's money-transfer division, they would be contextualized as money-transfer innovations; in the retail-banking division, innovations would be referred to as retail-banking innovations. In the restaurant industry, innovations are generally translated as culinary innovations, and similarly, innovations or innovation ideas generated in the insurance industry would be contextualized according to the value chain and business model of the insurance company. For an insurance company, such as Farmers Insurance, with business segments that include home insurance, auto insurance, life insurance, and business insurance and that also offers claims and agent services, the categories of types of innovation would be contextualized or translated as home-insurance innovations, auto-insurance innovations, life-insurance innovations, business-insurance innovations and claim-process innovations.

   Some examples of common types of innovations and their characteristics are as follows:
   - *Product innovations:* Product innovations are in a tangible form, such as auto parts, phones, computers, IT accessories, building materials, heavy equipment, wood materials, furniture, clothes, foodstuffs, drinks, lotions, soaps, and so forth. As stated earlier, types of innovation can be broadened to specifically reflect the organization's value chain and business model. For example, a meat-processing company could describe types of innovation according to the product segments, such as pork-product innovations, beef-product innovations, chicken-product innovations, and so forth.

- *Service innovations:* Service innovations are in an intangible form. The following are some of the areas in which service innovations are generated or implemented: health-care services, financial services, insurance services, travel services, hotel services, and IT services. As with product innovations, service innovations can also be broadened to specifically reflect the organization's value chain and business model.
- *Process innovations:* The third type of innovation is process innovations. What are process innovations? When educating workforces about process innovations, the starting point is to understand what organizational processes are and how they are structured. This is important because it helps workforces to understand the context of their organization's processes, thereby making it easy for them to generate focused ideas for process innovations in the context of the organization's value chain. That said, it's important to understand the following:
  - First, organizations have numerous process elements that are structurally embedded across its core and support functional units, and process innovations can be described or characterized according to the organization's value chain and business model.
  - Second, process activities vary from company to company depending on the type and nature of an organization. For instance, the core and support process activities of a telecom company like AT&T will differ from those of a company in the auto industry like GM. Similarly, the core and support process activities of a financial-sector company like Bank of America will differ from those of a technology company like Apple.
  - Third, process activities are usually out of view of customers, and in most cases, they influence the delivery of services or products in varying ways depending on the value chain and business model of the organization.

The bottom line is that ideas for process innovations generated in core and support functional activities vary from company to company depending on the type and nature of an organization. For instance, in telecom services, innovative systems may be installed to process telephone services in a way not seen on the market before. And in a manufacturing facility, process innovations could include an innovative procedure or technology to enhance competitive advantage in terms of production processes—that is, in relation to product quality, time of production, ability to customize the production process within a short time, ability to produce at low cost, ability to produce in large numbers without compromising on quality, packaging methods, or assembly methods. Other business models where process innovation could be implemented or created include supply chains in supermarkets or department stores, reservation systems and baggage-tracking methods in the airline industry, and parcel-tracking systems by couriers such as FedEx and DHL.

Application of Innovation Engagement Approaches | 73

An example of a cost-saving process innovation is one implemented at PepsiCo's Walkers potato chip plant in Leicester, United Kingdom. The Walkers plant developed a process that involves collecting the rising steam from cookers using a new device that transforms the potato vapors back into water, which is then used for cleaning equipment, washing potatoes, and irrigating lawns and shrubs. This process innovation has saved the company about $1 million annually since its inception.

Here are some simple steps in figure 8-4 that can be helpful when identifying the types of processes on which to focus innovation activities:

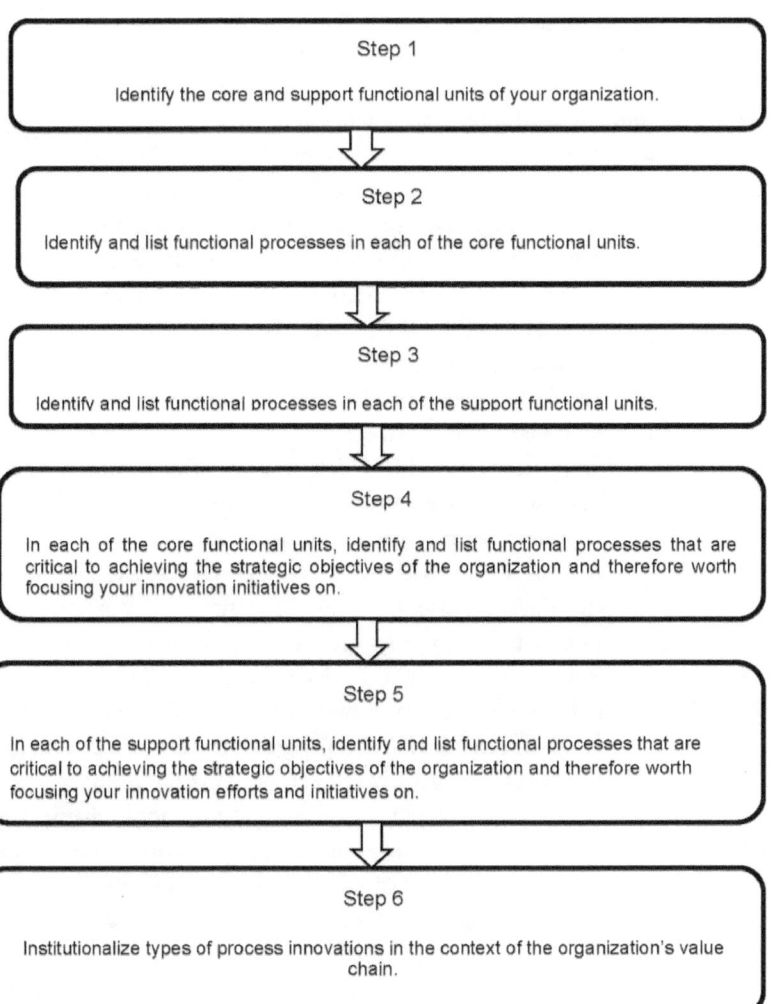

- *Marketing innovations:* The fourth example of types of innovation is marketing innovations. Marketing innovations are usually centered on a number of marketing-related functional elements of the marketing unit of an organization, and the context of marketing innovation ideas usually depends on the type of functional activities that comprise a marketing functional unit—for instance, product promotion, product packaging, product pricing, market or place, and product delivery/distribution. That being said, *marketing innovation* is defined as a process that involves the generation and development of innovative marketing ideas in various marketing-strategy strands, such as the abovementioned marketing functional activities.
- *Customer service innovations:* Before describing customer service innovation, it's important to outline a few aspects of customer service that are helpful in contextualizing its innovations:
  - First, generally, *customer service* is defined as a provision of a series of activities designed to enhance the level of customer satisfaction in a unique way, and it usually involves activities that support the delivery of a product or service, before, during, and after purchase.
  - Second, customer service is said to be either provided by a person or an automated means referred to as self-service (e.g., by internet or by other technological means).
  - Third, in most organizations, customer service is a stand-alone functional unit, just like procurement, finance, marketing, production, and IT. In most cases, the common function of a customer service unit is to manage certain functional activities of interactions with customers, such as returns, complaints, and inquiries. Also related to customer service is the concept of customer experience. The difference between customer service and customer experience, according to many publications, is that in terms of customer service strategies, companies usually develop customer service initiatives that are designed to be implemented in specific areas of the organization, whereas customer experience initiatives are usually aimed at creating an excellent customer experience across all organizational functions, channels, and other touchpoints, such as company products and services and physical contact with customers. Other touchpoints include infrastructural facilities, telephone contact, company website interactions, email interactions, and so forth.
  - Fourth, customer service varies from company to company and is largely determined by the type and nature of an organization. For example, the customer service activities of supermarkets like Walmart and Safeway in the United States or Tesco in the United Kingdom will differ from those of organizations in the hospitality industry, such as Marriott or Hilton Hotels. Similarly, the customer

service activities of telecom companies like AT&T, Verizon, T-Mobile, BT, and Vodafone will differ from the customer service components of airline companies like Delta, Virgin, American Airways, and British Airways.

Given what customer service entails, customer service innovations can be contextualized as follows:

- First, customer service innovations result from innovative ideas that are developed and implemented in customer service–related activities designed to support the delivery of product offerings or service offerings, before, during, and after purchase. In other words, customer service innovations can be described in three categories: before-purchase customer service innovations, during-purchase customer service innovations, and after-purchase customer service innovations.
- Second, customer service innovations are aimed at constantly delivering service or product support in a unique way compared with other competitors on the market, and consequently, they contribute to attracting and retaining customers, thereby adding commercial value to the company.
- Third, the context of customer service innovation differs from company to company depending on the value chain and business model. For instance, customer service innovations for a manufacturing company like 3M would be different from those of a service company like GEICO.
- Fourth, depending on the organization's policy on innovation systems, some customer service innovations can be categorized as follows: (1) *customer service innovations*, which are customer service-related innovations implemented in specific customer service areas, and (2) *customer experience innovations*, which are implemented across all organizational functional units, channels, and other touchpoints and are designed to continually enhance the quality of all interactions between the company and its customers.

• *Innovations aimed at support functional units:* When describing the term *types of innovation*, it has been noted that in addition to the innovations that are generated in the organization's core functional units, there are also types of innovations aimed at back-office activities or support functional units. Because these types of innovation are usually aimed at cost savings and enhancing efficiency, they are often referred to as cost-saving innovations or back-office process innovations. It's also important to know that cost-saving innovations have little effect on the bottom line of an organization compared with innovations in the core areas of the organization's value chain, on which an organization relies for revenue, growth, and competitiveness.

*Educating Workforces about Types of Innovation*

The main takeaway from the foregoing discussion is that, generally, there are different types or forms of innovation, and these are translated in the context of the organization's value chain and business model. That said, how do you educate workforces about the organization's types of innovation?

Two aspects are important. First, the leadership must ensure that all the critical functional activities of the organization's value chain are translated and institutionalized in the types of innovation embraced by the organization. Second, workforces across all functional units must be educated about the organization's types of innovation in simple language using effective communication techniques. There are a number of reasons why translating an organization's types of innovation is an absolute necessity.

First, study after study has revealed that people in organizations have misconception about innovation. In many cases, people think that innovation is just about products, and such a misconception limits the contribution of workforces to innovation. Thus, translating the types of innovation in the context of the organization's value chain helps the workforces to understand that innovation occurs in different forms, and therefore, they can contribute innovative ideas in different forms. Second, it makes it easy for both the leadership and workforces to understand or identify the context of innovation ideas that should be generated, and workforces will thus be able to contribute to the generation of ideas because they understand the different forms of innovation in the context of the organization's business segments and functional units. Third, it helps to create a diverse innovation pipeline for the organization, thereby building a sustainable culture of innovation and creating sources of revenue for the organization. Fourth, it is helpful in determining innovation performance across the organization because innovation performance will be measured according to the types of innovation developed over a period.

*Example*

The earlier discussion on the topic of aligning the meaning of *innovation* with the various functional units of an organization used the example of DM Personal Care Products, a fictitious company that manufactures a variety of personal care products. Let's return to this example and assume we now need to translate and institutionalize types of innovation in the context of the value chain at DM Personal Care Products. The first step is to identify all functional units (core and back-office) of the company. The second step is to translate and institutionalize types of innovations in line with the nature of the core and support functional units and business segments of DM Personal Care Products. Worksheets 8-6 through 8-10 demonstrate how to translate or contextualize the functional units and business segments of DM Personal Care Products into types or forms of innovation. The core functional units are the product-development department, manufacturing department, marketing department, and customer service department, and the five support functional units are the procurement department, HR department, finance and accounting department, IT department, and corporate affairs department. The third step is to identify appropriate and effective techniques, channels, or methods for communicating with and educating workforces about the organization's context of types of innovation. A good example of communication techniques is brochures that use creative illustrations.

Worksheet 8-6. Example of categories of types of product innovations

| Product category | Types of product innovations |
|---|---|
| Body lotions | Body-lotion product innovations |
| Skin cleansing | Skin-cleansing product innovations |
| Hair care | Hair-care product innovations |
| Hand washing | Hand-washing product innovations |

Worksheet 8-7. Example of categories of types of manufacturing-processes innovations

| Manufacturing-processes category | Types of manufacturing-processes innovations |
|---|---|
| Body-lotion manufacturing processes | Body-lotion manufacturing-processes innovations |
| Skin-cleansing manufacturing processes | Skin-cleansing manufacturing-processes innovations |
| Hair-care manufacturing processes | Hair-care manufacturing-processes innovations |
| Hand-washing manufacturing processes | Hand-washing manufacturing-processes innovations |

Worksheet 8-8. Example of categories of types of marketing innovations

| Marketing unit | Types of innovations |
|---|---|
| Product pricing | Pricing innovations |
| Product promotion | Product-promotion innovations |
| Product delivery (*usually a stand-alone unit in large corporations*) | Product-delivery and product- distribution innovations |
| New markets | Innovations for new markets |
| Packaging | Packaging innovations |

Worksheet 8-9. Example of categories of types of customer service innovations

| |
|---|
| Before-purchase customer service innovations |
| During-purchase customer service innovations |
| After-purchase customer service innovations |

Worksheet 8-10. Example of categories of types of innovations in support functional units

| Support functional unit | Types of innovations |
|---|---|

| Procurement department | Innovations in procurement processes |
| HR department | Innovations in HR processes |
| Finance and accounting department | Innovations in accounting processes |
| IT department | Innovations in IT processes |
| Corporate affairs department | Innovations in corporate affairs processes |

o **Innovation Degree**

The preceding section looked at the aspect of *where* innovation occurs or the context in which innovation occurs (i.e., types of innovation). This section looks at *how* innovation occurs in any form or type of innovation. How innovation occurs is referred to as *innovation degree*, and as stated earlier, innovation degree is one of the two conjoint concepts of the dimensionality of innovation.

**Definition**

It is important to understand that innovative ideas create or add value in varying degrees or extents. Thus, *innovation degree* can be defined as the perception of the extent of the newness or novelty of an innovative idea.

This definition entails two vital points:
- First, innovations could be improvements to existing organizational functional activities, such as improvements in products, services, marketing strategy, customer service, procurement, HR, accounting, IT, and so forth.
- Second, some innovations are totally or completely new to the world.
- The point is that whether innovations are improvements or are completely new, the common factor is that an innovation or innovative idea must always be novel; it is the extent of the novelty that differs.

*Categories of Innovation Degree*

The common categories of the extent of the newness of innovations or innovative ideas are *radical* and *incremental*. These are described as follows:

*Radical innovation:* This is the highest extent or range of the perceived newness or novelty of an innovative idea in any type of innovation. In most cases, radical innovations tend to have the following characteristics once launched on the market or implemented in the organization:
- First, radical innovations are usually aimed at completely or totally replacing an existing product, service, process, marketing strategy, or customer service element and result in a whole new way of providing a solution to a problem.
- Second, in a number of cases, radical innovations are a game changer; that is, they transform or disrupt traditional establishments on the market or in the organization, existing products or services, or other aspects of a business model (e.g., processes, marketing, and customer service) in a big way. For instance, think of how Apple's iPod transformed the way we listened to music when it was launched in 2001 and how it disrupted the existence of Sony's Walkman. Also, think of how Amazon's online bookselling services have transformed the industry for brick-and-mortar

bookstores. Think of how AI innovations like Amazon's Echo are transforming how we live and work. Think of how automated teller machines (ATMs) transformed the banking experience—they allow customers to withdraw cash and deposit cash or checks at any time. In other words, radical innovations are usually a complete departure from the current state because everything (100 percent of it) is totally new.
- Third, when implemented, radical innovations often become the talk of the market. In some cases, radical innovations can create a market frenzy; for instance, the iPhone created such a frenzy when it was launched in 2007.

*Incremental innovation:* Generally, this is defined as the extent of the newness or novelty of an innovative idea in which innovative changes or improvements are created or implemented in the existing functional activities of an organization, such as products, services, processes, marketing strategy, and customer service, as well as cost-saving innovations in back-office functional activities. The following are some of the characteristics of incremental innovations:
- First, incremental innovations are aimed at continually satisfying customer needs or solving problems that constantly pop up as a result of loss of effectiveness, efficiency, or competitiveness in the organization's existing functional activities. Consider the following example of incremental innovation:

*Example*
Nike launched its Flyknit running shoes in 2012 as an incremental improvement of its Air Pegasus+ 28 model. The Flyknit is manufactured using a computerized weaving technology that knits the entire upper part of the shoe in a single piece that is then attached to the sole. In contrast, the Air Pegasus+ 28 model needed to have about thirty-five pieces assembled before it was attached to the sole.

The Flyknit is aimed at generating a number of benefits for this category of Nike's product segment, such as the following:
- The new model has thirty-five fewer pieces to assemble than the Air Pegasus+ 28.
- The production of the Flyknit will be much quicker than that of the Air Pegasus+ 28.
- The Flyknit will be produced with less labor than the Air Pegasus+ 28, thereby generating larger profit margins.
- Second, the newness in incremental innovations varies in range or extent, from minor innovative improvements and changes to very big novel changes to an existing product, service, process, marketing strategy, or customer service element. In other words, incremental innovations range from small innovative changes, to moderate innovative changes, to big innovative changes. This book uses the following three categories of incremental innovations:
  - Small incremental innovations
  - Medium incremental innovations
  - Big incremental innovations

# 80 | LEADERSHIP FOR INNOVATION

Figure 8-5 provides a simple diagrammatic depiction of the three ranges of incremental innovations.

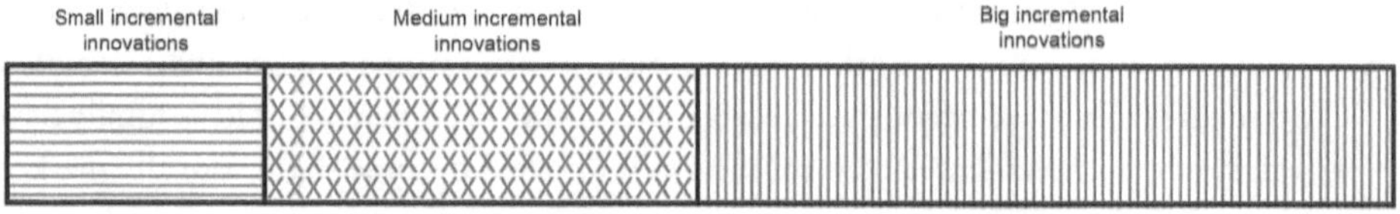

*Figure 8-5. Range of incremental innovations*

- Third, incremental innovations result in small monetary contributions to the organization's bottom line, but in certain cases, incremental innovations can generate breakthrough performance in terms of meeting market needs and providing large monetary contributions to the organization. A good example of a large game-changing incremental innovation is the iPhone, which has proved to be a disruptive and major breakthrough, selling more than one billion units, and has contributed hugely to making Apple the most valuable company in the world, worth more than $700 billion at the time of writing this book. Think of how Uber has transformed ride-sharing services. Uber's ride-sharing model is another example of a big incremental innovation.

Figure 8-6 shows the ascendancy pattern of the categories of innovation degree.

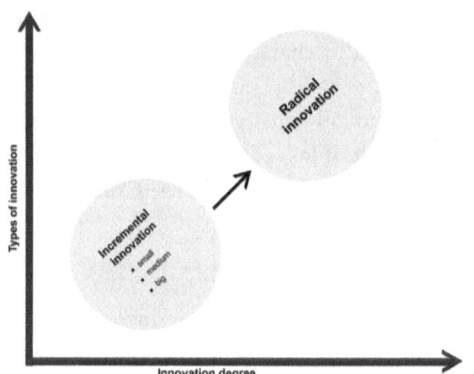

*Figure 8-6. Pattern of innovation degrees*

## Importance of Understanding Innovation Degree

It is important for workforces to understand the concept of innovation degree for the following reasons:

o First, because every innovative idea is perceived to have a particular extent of novelty, that is, incremental or radical, it is difficult for workforces to generate meaningful innovative ideas if they do not understand the aspect of innovation degree because the extent of newness of the innovative idea is a vital aspect that affects the decision-making process for any type of innovation.

o Second, the broad range of choices for the extent of newness of innovative ideas helps workforces to understand that an innovative idea does not always have to be transformational or have a huge impact and that any extent of innovative idea is fine as long as it can fix the problem and has the potential to generate benefits for the organization. Such knowledge encourages workforces to try to generate innovative ideas in the functional activities of the organization in which they feel confident.

o Third, it helps in formulating innovation goals across functional units in that when setting innovation goals, it is necessary to state the extent of novelty—that is, whether the innovation that one desires to generate is radical or incremental. For instance, in the planning goal "to generate four radical innovative ideas related to procurement between February and March of 2018," the word *radical* denotes the degree of the innovative idea.

o Fourth, understanding innovation degree is vital in determining innovation performance across the organization at the corporate, functional-unit, and individual levels. For instance, whether you are determining the number of innovation ideas generated, the number of innovation ideas undergoing development, the number of innovations launched, or the amount of revenue generated or cost savings gained (as described in part III, chapters 9 to 15), it's important to state the innovation degree of the particular innovation launched, generated, or undergoing development. For example, in determining the number of ideas for innovative products generated at Farmers Insurance over a particular period, you would say, "The number of radical innovative home-insurance ideas generated between January and March of 2018."

*Educating Workforces about Innovation Degree*
Given the importance of the concept of innovation degree to innovation ideation and innovation management as a whole, it is important for the organizational leadership to educate workforces about what innovation degree entails and how the categories of innovation degree are aligned with the organization's value chain and business model. The publicity and education should be done using simple language, catchphrases, and visual illustrations that are communicated across the organization using effective techniques.

*Bottom line*
There are three takeaways from this chapter. First, unless workforces are engaged in innovation, the organization's efforts to scale innovation throughout the whole company will remain a rhetorical exercise. Second, instilling innovation in the hearts and minds of workforces is not a natural occurrence; it requires consistent implementation of programs, activities, and approaches aimed at building workforce engagement in advancing innovation across functional units. Third, for leaders to instill innovation in the hearts and minds of workforces it is essential for them (the leaders) to understand and possess innovation engagement skills. That is, by grasping *what* these skills entail and *how* to apply them to help workforces build passion and emotional interest for innovation.

# PART III
# INNOVATION MANAGEMENT SKILLS

**Overview**

In the introduction of the book, we stated that the purpose of the book is threefold:
 i. To explain what leadership for innovation entails in the context of leading employee-driven innovation
 ii. To describe the three essential innovation skill sets required for leading employee-driven innovation
 iii. To explain how to apply the three essential innovation skill sets to build a climate for innovation and make innovation systematic and ongoing across functional units

We have so far looked at two of the three categories of innovation skill sets for leading workforce innovation—that is, we've covered the innovative thinking skill set and how leaders can translate their innovative thinking skills to lead innovation across the organization, and we've covered the innovation engagement skill set, which involves approaches and techniques for engaging workforces in owning the process of creating a culture of innovation.

Part III looks at the third category of innovation skill sets essential for creating a culture of innovation across the organization: innovation management skills. This part looks at *what* these skill sets entail and *how* to apply them.

First and foremost, what are innovation management skills? Generally, organizations operate through a structure of systems designed specifically to deliver the mission of an organization and, ultimately, realize the company's vision. In terms of creating a culture of innovation, remember that you cannot create a culture of innovation across the organization using traditional, non-innovation-oriented management tools. This means that if innovation is to be made a permanent and ongoing habitual process across functional units, it is vital to implement organization-wide innovation-support systems. In the introduction of this book, we stated that the model of leadership for innovation in large part involves the application of various innovation-related tools to make innovation systematic. Systematizing innovation means aligning innovation with the systems of all the functional units of an organization. For example, if company X has the functional units of R&D, production, HR, finance, IT, procurement, marketing, and customer service, systemizing innovation means developing and implementing innovation-oriented strategies, policies, and procedures in the context of each of the eight functional units of company X. However, innovation-oriented systems can be implemented only if the organizational leaders have the skills and abilities to do so. This is where innovation management skills come in. As we shall see, innovation management skills involve the ability to formulate and implement innovation-support systems. What are innovation-support systems? These are the innovation-support strategies, policies and procedures, structures, and technologies aimed at contributing to advancing the culture of innovation across the organization. In this section of the book, we look at examples of innovation management skills and tools and how to apply them to implement innovation-support systems across the organization.

### Aspects of Innovation Management Skills

To explain the context of innovation management skills, part III first covers the following pertinent aspects; (1) context of innovation management skills (2) definition of innovation management skills (3) importance of innovation management skills and (4) expression of innovation management skills. Details of these are as follows:

1. **Context of Innovation Management Skills**

    The term *innovation management skills* is based on the generic meanings of the terms *leadership* and *management*. In an organizational context, it is said that leadership is considered an art focused on winning the hearts and minds of followers, whereas management, in a generic sense, is thought of as a science in which a series of logical steps is followed to implement decisions and functional activities across the organization. Part II of the book described the importance of innovation engagement skills in leading workforce innovation and explained how to engage the hearts and minds of workforces to advance innovation across functional units, and the introduction of the book noted how the three innovation skill sets (i.e., innovative thinking skills, innovation engagement skills, and innovation management skills) for leading innovation can be likened to three pieces of a puzzle, in which each piece plays a vital role in holding the puzzle together. Like the other two skill sets, the innovation management skill set plays a vital role because to cultivate innovation throughout the organization, it is an indispensable necessity to implement innovation-oriented strategies, policies, and procedures across all functional units; otherwise, the leadership's mission of creating an innovation-driven organization risks not being realized.

2. **Definition of *Innovation Management Skills***

    What are innovation management skills? These are the abilities that enable organizational leaders to formulate and implement innovation-support strategies, policies, and procedures in each functional unit of an organization with the purpose of making innovation systemic and helping to create a culture of innovation. In short, innovation management skills are innovation-system-building abilities and competencies applied in the different functional contexts of the organization to make innovation permanent and habitual.

3. **Importance of Innovation Management Skills**
Two reasons why innovation management skills are important in leading workforce innovation are as follows:

   i. *Leaders will be ill-equipped if they do not have the ability to create innovation-support systems.* In order to understand the significance of innovation management skills, it is necessary to recap the two innovation skill sets discussed earlier. The discussion of innovation engagement skills in part II emphasized the importance of instilling innovation engagement in the hearts and minds of workforces if those workforces are to contribute toward advancing innovation across functional units. Part I emphasized the vital role that innovative thinking skills play in role modeling and influencing the innovation performance of workforces. Make no mistake: each of these two categories of innovation skill sets (i.e., innovative thinking skills and innovation engagement skills) is essential to building and sustaining a culture of innovation across functional units. However, these two skill sets can do only so much, and in the absence of innovation management skills, organizational leaders will fall short of the full abilities needed to build a culture of innovation across the organization. Said differently, an organization could have workforces with innovative thinking potential and the most inspirational innovation leadership, but if the organization lacks appropriate and adequate innovation-oriented organizational systems, the organization risks having a meaningless, or unactionable, degree of innovation potential. This can be interpreted as a situation where an organization has a high level of innovation potential but lacks the ability to optimally actualize the potential into an innovation pipeline to drive organizational growth and competitiveness.

   Thus, the importance of each of the three categories of innovation skill sets is context specific in that each fulfills a specific role of innovation-leadership capacity in organizational leaders. That said, in order to make innovation permanent and habitual across functional units, the leadership needs to cultivate capabilities in all three categories of innovation skills.

   ii. *Traditional management models are not effective.* Many analysts and studies have observed that most conventional management models are not designed to drive innovation across the functional units of an organization. For instance, at a conference on innovation held at Harvard Business School in December 2007, panelists felt that traditional management practices have little to contribute to cultivating innovation throughout the organization. Many panelists at this conference felt that the current traditional management models are stacked against innovation performance. Similar observations have been made by other communities and experts in the field of innovation management. For instance, a 2010 report by the Association to Advance Collegiate Schools of Business (compiled by its Task Force on Business Schools and Innovation) observed that business schools across the globe must equip their students with innovation management–oriented tools if the students are to contribute toward advancing innovation in the world of work. In the corporate world, experts have argued that if innovation is to be fostered in organizations, the roles and practices of management should be applied in the context that fosters innovation.

There is no doubt that these observations about the ineffectiveness of traditional management models to advance innovation are accurate. Consider traditional HR models, for instance; most of them, if not all, cannot be used to advance innovation. For example, you cannot identify innovation talent, evaluate the innovation performance of workforces, undertake innovation-talent-succession planning, or design an HR innovation-support strategy using traditional HR models. Similarly, accounting professionals cannot audit or report on the innovation performance of an enterprise using traditional accounting models, just like you cannot use traditional marketing models to design a marketing-related innovation strategy or traditional procurement models to design a procurement-related innovation strategy.

The introduction of this book provided an illustration of the role of every functional unit in implementing innovation-support initiatives to contribute to the organization's mission of building an innovation-driven organization. What this means is that organizational leaders have to develop innovation management abilities to implement initiatives in the context of their functional duties and activities. For instance, a director in charge of a marketing unit should have the ability to create marketing-related innovation goals, marketing-related innovation-challenge questions, assessment and development processes for marketing-related innovation ideas, marketing-related innovation strategies, and a system for measuring marketing-related innovation performance across all components or subunits of the marketing department, such as product pricing, product packaging, product promotion, and product delivery. Similarly, a chief HR officer is expected to build abilities to develop and implement various HR-related innovation-support strategies, such as strategies and policies for recruitment of innovation talent, a framework for workforce innovation-performance evaluation, a framework for innovation-talent-succession planning, an innovation-goal-setting framework for the whole organization, and a framework for translating the dimensions of innovation into an organizational value chain and business model and implementing an organization-wide innovation-performance framework. The same is expected of other heads of functional units and divisions depending on the organization's value chain and business model.

4. **Expression of Innovation Management Skills**
Like any innovation skill, innovation management skills should be applied and expressed in the context of the functional-unit activities of an organization. How

is this done? The following example offers a simple illustration of how innovation management skills can be expressed in each of the functional units of DM Personal Care Products, the fictitious company introduced earlier that manufactures a variety of personal care products.

*Example*

The first step is to outline the core and support (back-office) functional units of DM Personal Care Products. As in the earlier examples, let's assume the company has the following functional units:

*Core functional units*
- Product-development unit, with the following segments:
  o Body-lotions segment
  o Skin-cleansing segment
  o Hair-care segment
  o Hand-washing segment
- Manufacturing-processes department
- Marketing department, with the following units:
  o Pricing unit
  o Product-promotion unit
  o Product-delivery unit
  o New-markets unit
  o Packaging unit
- Customer service department

*Support functional units*
- Procurement department
- HR department
- Finance and accounting department
- IT department
- Corporate affairs department

The second step is translation of the innovation management skills and innovation management functional duties or activities to fit the context of each functional unit.

Worksheets III 1–9 show how innovation management skills and innovation management activities can be expressed in the context of each of the core and support functional units of DM Personal Care Products. Worksheets 1–4 provide some examples of innovation management activities and descriptions of innovation management skills for the core functional units. Worksheets 5–9, introduced in the following subsection, provide some examples of innovation management activities and descriptions of innovation management skills for the support functional units.

## 88 | LEADERSHIP FOR INNOVATION

Worksheet III–1. Examples of innovation management activities and innovation management skills in the product-development functional unit

| Segments | Innovation management activities | Innovation management skills |
|---|---|---|
| • Body lotions<br>• Skin cleansing<br>• Hair care<br>• Hand washing | • Creating innovation-performance job duties and responsibilities in each of the four product segments<br>• Developing and implementing strategies for product innovation in each of the four product segments<br>• Creating goals for product innovation in each of the four product segments<br>• Generating innovation-challenge questions in each of the four product segments<br>• Designing, implementing, and sustaining an effective system for management of innovation ideas for each of the four product segments (i.e., frameworks that include assessment and analysis processes, design processes, innovation-development processes, etc.)<br>• Structuring and reporting innovation performance in each of the four product segments<br>• Developing and implementing any other innovation-support systems and practices in each of the four product segments | • Ability to create innovation-performance job duties and responsibilities in each of the four product segments<br>• Ability to develop and implement strategies for product innovation in each of the four product segments<br>• Ability to create goals for product innovation in each of the four product segments<br>• Ability to generate innovation-challenge questions in each of the four product segments<br>• Ability to design, implement, and sustain an effective system for management of innovation ideas for each of the four product segments (i.e., frameworks that include assessment and analysis processes, design processes, innovation-development processes, etc.)<br>• Ability to structure and report innovation performance in each of the four product segments<br>• Ability to determine, develop, and enact, on an ongoing basis, any other innovation-support systems and practices deemed necessary in each of the four product segments |

Worksheet III–2. Examples of innovation management activities and innovation management skills in the manufacturing-processes functional unit

| Segments | Innovation management activities | Innovation management skills |
|---|---|---|
| • Body lotions<br>• Skin cleansing<br>• Hair care<br>• Hand washing | • Creating innovation-performance job duties and responsibilities for manufacturing processes in each of the four product segments<br>• Developing and implementing strategies for manufacturing-processes innovation in each of the four product segments<br>• Creating goals for manufacturing-processes innovation in each of the four product segments<br>• Generating and creating manufacturing-processes innovation-challenge questions in each of the four product segments<br>• Designing, implementing, and sustaining an effective system for the management of manufacturing-processes innovation ideas for each of the four product segments (i.e., frameworks that include assessment and analysis processes, design processes, innovation-development processes, etc.)<br>• Structuring and reporting manufacturing-processes innovation performance in each of the four product segments<br>• Developing and implementing any other manufacturing-processes innovation-support systems and practices in each of the four product segments | • Ability to create innovation-performance job duties and responsibilities for manufacturing processes in each of the four product segments<br>• Ability to develop and implement strategies for manufacturing-processes innovation in each of the four product segments<br>• Ability to create goals for manufacturing-processes innovation in each of the four product segments<br>• Ability to generate manufacturing-processes innovation-challenge questions in each of the four product segments<br>• Ability to design, implement, and sustain an effective system for the management of manufacturing-processes innovation ideas for each of the four product segments (i.e., frameworks that include assessment and analysis processes, design processes, innovation-development processes, etc.)<br>• Ability to structure and report manufacturing-processes innovation performance in each of the four product segments<br>• Ability to determine, develop, and enact, on an ongoing basis, any other manufacturing-processes innovation-support systems and practices deemed necessary in each of the four product segments |

Worksheet III–3. Examples of innovation management activities and innovation management skills in the marketing functional unit

| Marketing functional component | Innovation management activities | Innovation management skills |
|---|---|---|
| Product promotion | • Creating innovation-centered product-promotion duties and responsibilities for each of the product segments<br>• Developing and implementing innovative promotional strategies for various product platforms<br>• Creating innovative promotional goals for each of the product segments<br>• Generating innovative product-promotion innovation-challenge questions in each of the product segments<br>• Designing, implementing, and sustaining an effective framework for assessing, analyzing, and enacting innovative promotional ideas<br>• Structuring and reporting innovative promotional initiatives and activities undertaken for various product segments | • Ability to create innovation-centered product-promotion duties and responsibilities for each of the product segments<br>• Ability to develop and implement innovative promotional strategies for various product platforms<br>• Ability to create innovative promotional goals for each of the product segments<br>• Ability to generate innovative product-promotion innovation-challenge questions in each of the product segments<br>• Ability to design, implement, and sustain an effective framework for assessing, analyzing, and enacting innovative promotional ideas<br>• Ability to structure and report innovative promotional initiatives and activities undertaken for various product segments |

| | | |
|---|---|---|
| Product pricing | • Creating innovation-centered product-pricing duties and responsibilities for each of the product segments<br>• Developing and implementing product-pricing innovation strategies for various product platforms<br>• Creating product-pricing innovation goals for each of the product segments<br>• Generating product-pricing innovation-challenge questions in each of the product segments<br>• Designing, implementing, and sustaining an effective framework for assessing, analyzing, and enacting product-pricing innovation ideas<br>• Structuring and reporting product-pricing innovation initiatives and activities undertaken for various product segments | • Ability to create innovation-centered product-pricing duties and responsibilities for each of the product segments<br>• Ability to develop and implement product-pricing innovation strategies for various product platforms<br>• Ability to create product-pricing innovation goals for each of the product segments<br>• Ability to generate product-pricing innovation-challenge questions in each of the product segments<br>• Ability to design, implement, and sustain an effective framework for assessing, analyzing, and enacting product-pricing innovation ideas<br>• Ability to structure and report product-pricing innovation initiatives and activities undertaken for various product segments |
| Packaging | • Creating innovation-centered product-packaging duties and responsibilities for each of the product segments<br>• Developing and implementing product-packaging innovation strategies for various product platforms<br>• Creating product-packaging innovation goals for each of the product segments<br>• Generating product-packaging innovation-challenge questions in each of the product segments<br>• Designing, implementing, and sustaining an effective framework for assessing, analyzing, and enacting product-packaging innovation ideas<br>• Structuring and reporting product-packaging innovation initiatives and activities undertaken for various product segments | • Ability to create innovation-centered product-packaging duties and responsibilities for each of the product segments<br>• Ability to develop and implement product-packaging innovation strategies for various product platforms<br>• Ability to create product-packaging innovation goals for each of the product segments<br>• Ability to generate product-packaging innovation-challenge questions in each of the product segments<br>• Ability to design, implement, and sustain an effective framework for assessing, analyzing, and enacting product-packaging innovation ideas<br>• Ability to structure and report product-packaging innovation initiatives and activities undertaken for various product segments |

| | | |
|---|---|---|
| New markets | • Creating duties and responsibilities centered on new-market development for the company's product platforms<br>• Developing and implementing strategies for new-market development for various product platforms<br>• Creating goals for new-market development for each of the product segments<br>• Generating innovation-challenge questions for new-market development for each of the product segments<br>• Designing, implementing, and sustaining an effective framework for assessing, analyzing, and enacting ideas for new-market development<br>• Structuring and reporting initiatives and activities for new-market development undertaken for various product segments | • Ability to create duties and responsibilities centered on new-market development for the company's product platforms<br>• Ability to develop and implement strategies for new-market development for various product platforms<br>• Ability to create goals for new-market development for each of the product segments<br>• Ability to generate innovation-challenge questions for new-market development for each of the product segments<br>• Ability to design, implement, and sustain an effective framework for assessing, analyzing, and enacting ideas for new-market development<br>• Ability to structure and report initiatives and activities for new-market development undertaken for various product segments |
| Product delivery | • Creating innovation-centered product-delivery duties and responsibilities for each of the product segments<br>• Developing and implementing product-delivery innovation strategies for various product platforms<br>• Creating goals for product-delivery innovation for each of the product segments<br>• Generating product-delivery innovation-challenge questions in each of the product segments<br>• Designing, implementing, and sustaining an effective framework for assessing, analyzing, and enacting ideas for product-delivery innovation<br>• Structuring and reporting initiatives and activities for product-delivery innovation undertaken for various product segments | • Ability to create innovation-centered product-delivery duties and responsibilities for each of the product segments<br>• Ability to develop and implement product-delivery innovation strategies for various product platforms<br>• Ability to create goals for product-delivery innovation for each of the product segments<br>• Ability to generate product-delivery innovation-challenge questions in each of the product segments<br>• Ability to design, implement, and sustain an effective framework for assessing, analyzing, and enacting ideas for product-delivery innovation<br>• Ability to structure and report initiatives and activities for product-delivery innovation undertaken for various product segments |

Worksheet III–4. Examples of innovation management activities and innovation management skills in the customer service functional unit

| Functional unit | Innovation management activities | Innovation management skills |
|---|---|---|
| Customer service | • Creating customer service innovation-performance duties and responsibilities centered on the company's business model<br>• Developing and implementing strategies for customer service innovation centered on the company's business model<br>• Creating goals for customer service innovation in the context of the company's business model<br>• Generating customer service innovation-challenge questions in the context of the company's business model<br>• Designing, implementing, and sustaining an effective framework for assessing, analyzing, and enacting ideas for customer service innovation<br>• Structuring and reporting initiatives and activities for customer service innovation undertaken in the context of the company's business model | • Ability to create customer service innovation-performance duties and responsibilities centered on the company's business model<br>• Ability to develop and implement strategies for customer service innovation centered on the company's business model<br>• Ability to create goals for customer service innovation in the context of the company's business model<br>• Ability to generate customer service innovation-challenge questions in the context of the company's business model<br>• Ability to design, implement, and sustain an effective framework for assessing, analyzing, and enacting ideas for customer service innovation<br>• Ability to structure and report initiatives and activities for customer service innovation undertaken in the context of the company's business model |

## Expression of Innovation Management Skills in the Context of Support Functional Units

As indicated earlier, the support functional units of DM Personal Care Products are as follows:

- ❖ Procurement department
- ❖ HR department
- ❖ Finance and accounting department
- ❖ IT department
- ❖ Corporate affairs department

This section illustrates how innovation management functional activities and skills can be expressed. The context of innovation management skills in support functional units involves two aspects:

- o First is the ability to develop and implement innovation-support initiatives aimed at creating a climate for innovation across functional units, especially in the core units of the organization on which growth and the survival of the organization depend.
- o Second is the ability to develop and implement innovation management initiatives focused on encouraging the generation of cost-saving innovation ideas in support functional units.

Given the role of support functional units in advancing workforce innovation, organizational leaders should ensure that they understand the application of innovation management skills in the context of the activities of their organization's support functional units. For illustration purposes, worksheets III–5 to III–9 outline how innovation management skills can be expressed in the context of the support functional units of DM Personal Care Products.

Worksheet III–5. Expressing innovation management activities and innovation management skills in the context of the procurement support functional unit

| Support unit | Innovation management activities | Innovation management skills |
|---|---|---|
| Procurement | • Creating procurement innovation-performance duties and responsibilities<br>• Developing and implementing strategies for procurement innovation, including cost-saving initiatives<br>• Creating goals for procurement innovation<br>• Generating procurement innovation-challenge questions<br>• Structuring and reporting initiatives and activities for procurement innovation<br>• Designing, implementing, and sustaining an effective framework for assessing, analyzing, and enacting ideas for procurement innovation<br>**Innovative procurement cost-saving management activities**<br>• Creating innovative procurement cost-saving duties and responsibilities<br>• Creating innovative procurement cost-saving goals<br>• Designing, implementing, and sustaining an effective framework for assessing, analyzing, and enacting innovative procurement cost-saving ideas | • Ability to create procurement innovation-performance duties and responsibilities<br>• Ability to develop and implement strategies for procurement innovation, including cost-saving initiatives<br>• Ability to create goals for procurement innovation<br>• Ability to generate procurement innovation-challenge questions<br>• Ability to structure and report initiatives and activities for procurement innovation<br>• Ability to design, implement, and sustain an effective framework for assessing, analyzing, and enacting ideas for procurement innovation<br>**Innovative procurement cost-saving management skills**<br>• Ability to create innovative procurement cost-saving duties and responsibilities<br>• Ability to create innovative procurement cost-saving goals<br>• Ability to design, implement, and sustain an effective framework for assessing, analyzing, and enacting innovative procurement cost-saving ideas |

# 96 | LEADERSHIP FOR INNOVATION

Worksheet III–6. Expressing innovation management activities and innovation management skills in the context of the HR support functional unit

| Support unit | Innovation management activities | Innovation management skills |
|---|---|---|
| Human resources (HR) | • Creating duties and responsibilities for HR innovation-performance support<br>• Developing and implementing strategies for HR innovation-performance support, such as the following:<br>  o Strategy for recruitment of innovation talent<br>  o Strategy for workforce innovation-performance appraisal and reward<br>  o Framework for innovation-talent-succession planning<br>  o Strategy for innovation-talent development<br>  o Strategy for workforce diversity<br>• Creating goals for HR innovation-performance support<br>• Generating innovation-challenge questions related to HR innovation-performance support<br>• Structuring and reporting initiatives and activities for HR innovation-performance support<br>**Innovative HR cost-saving management activities**<br>• Creating innovative HR cost-saving duties and responsibilities<br>• Creating innovative HR cost-saving goals<br>• Designing, implementing, and sustaining an effective framework for assessing, analyzing, and enacting innovative HR cost-saving ideas | • Ability to create duties and responsibilities for HR innovation-performance support<br>• Ability to develop and implement strategies for HR innovation-performance support, such as the following:<br>• Strategy for recruitment of innovation talent<br>• Strategy for workforce innovation-performance appraisal and reward<br>• Framework for innovation-talent-succession planning<br>• Strategy for innovation-talent development<br>• Strategy for workforce diversity<br>• Ability to create goals for HR innovation-performance support<br>• Ability to generate innovation-challenge questions related to HR innovation-performance support<br>• Ability to structure and report initiatives and activities for HR innovation-performance support<br>• Innovative HR cost-saving management skills<br>• Ability to create innovative HR cost-saving duties and responsibilities<br>• Ability to create innovative HR cost-saving goals<br>• Ability to design, implement, and sustain an effective framework for assessing, analyzing, and enacting innovative HR cost-saving ideas |

Worksheet III–7. Expressing innovation management activities and innovation management skills in the context of the finance and accounting support functional unit

| Support unit | Innovation management activities | Innovation management skills |
|---|---|---|
| Finance and accounting | • Creating duties and responsibilities for finance and accounting innovation-performance support<br>• Developing and implementing strategies for finance and accounting innovation-performance support<br>• Creating goals for finance and accounting innovation-performance support<br>• Creating innovation-challenge questions for finance and accounting innovation-performance support<br>• Structuring and reporting initiatives and activities for finance and accounting innovation-performance support<br>• Finance and accounting innovative cost-saving activities<br>• Creating duties and responsibilities centered on innovative cost savings in finance and accounting<br>• Creating goals for finance and accounting innovative cost savings<br>• Designing, implementing, and sustaining an effective framework for assessing, analyzing, and enacting innovative ideas for finance and accounting cost savings | • Ability to create duties and responsibilities for finance and accounting innovation-performance support<br>• Ability to develop and implement strategies for finance and accounting innovation-performance support<br>• Ability to create goals for finance and accounting innovation-performance support<br>• Ability to create innovation-challenge questions for finance and accounting innovation-performance support<br>• Ability to structure and report initiatives and activities for finance and accounting innovation-performance support<br>• Finance and accounting innovative cost-saving skills<br>• Ability to create duties and responsibilities centered on innovative cost savings in finance and accounting<br>• Ability to create goals for finance and accounting innovative cost savings<br>• Ability to design, implement, and sustain an effective framework for assessing, analyzing, and enacting innovative ideas for finance and accounting cost savings |

Worksheet III–8. Expressing innovation management activities and innovation management skills in the context of the IT support functional unit

| Support unit | Innovation management activities | Innovation management skills |
|---|---|---|
| Information technology (IT) | • Creating duties and responsibilities for IT innovation-performance support<br>• Developing and implementing strategies for IT innovation-performance support, including collaborative efforts with other functional units to advance innovation through IT initiatives<br>• Creating goals for IT innovation-performance support<br>• Generating innovation-challenge questions for IT innovation-performance support<br>• Structuring and reporting initiatives and activities for IT innovation-performance support<br>**IT innovative cost-saving activities**<br>• Creating duties and responsibilities centered on innovative cost savings in IT-related job positions<br>• Creating goals for IT innovative cost savings<br>• Designing, implementing, and sustaining an effective framework for assessing, analyzing, and enacting ideas for IT innovative cost savings | • Ability to create duties and responsibilities for IT innovation-performance support<br>• Ability to develop and implement strategies for IT innovation-performance support, including collaborative efforts with other functional units to advance innovation through IT initiatives<br>• Ability to create goals for IT innovation-performance support<br>• Ability to generate innovation-challenge questions for IT innovation-performance support<br>• Ability to structure and report initiatives and activities for IT innovation-performance support<br>**IT innovative cost-saving skills**<br>• Ability to create duties and responsibilities centered on innovative cost savings in IT-related job positions<br>• Ability to create goals for IT innovative cost savings<br>• Ability to design, implement, and sustain an effective framework for assessing, analyzing, and enacting ideas for IT innovative cost savings |

Worksheet III–9. Expressing innovation management activities and innovation management skills in the context of the corporate affairs functional unit

| Functional unit | Innovation management activities | Innovation management skills |
|---|---|---|
| Corporate affairs department | • Creating duties and responsibilities for corporate affairs innovation-performance support<br>• Developing and implementing strategies for corporate affairs innovation-performance support, including collaborative efforts with other functional units to advance innovation<br>• Creating goals for corporate affairs innovation-performance support<br>• Generating innovation-challenge questions for corporate affairs innovation-performance support<br>• Structuring and reporting initiatives and activities for corporate affairs innovation-performance support<br>**Corporate affairs innovative cost-saving activities**<br>• Creating duties and responsibilities centered on innovative cost savings in corporate affairs<br>• Creating goals for innovative cost savings in corporate affairs<br>• Designing, implementing, and sustaining an effective framework for assessing, analyzing, and enacting ideas for innovative cost savings in corporate affairs | • Ability to create duties and responsibilities for corporate affairs innovation-performance support<br>• Ability to develop and implement strategies for corporate affairs innovation-performance support, including collaborative efforts with other functional units to advance innovation<br>• Ability to create goals for corporate affairs innovation-performance support<br>• Ability to generate innovation-challenge questions for corporate affairs innovation-performance support<br>• Ability to structure and report initiatives and activities for corporate affairs innovation-performance support<br>**Corporate affairs innovative cost-saving skills**<br>• Ability to create duties and responsibilities centered on innovative cost savings in corporate affairs<br>• Ability to create goals for innovative cost savings in corporate affairs<br>• Ability to design, implement, and sustain an effective framework for assessing, analyzing, and enacting ideas for innovative cost savings in corporate affairs |

## Examples of Innovation Management Skills

Chapters 9–15 provide examples of innovation management skills and abilities and describe how these abilities can be expressed. However, remember that the expression and application of innovation management abilities are context specific in terms of the functional units or business segments of the organization. Also, the innovation management abilities cited are not meant to be exhaustive but to provide some examples.

*Structure*

Part III is divided into seven examples of innovation management abilities that are presented along with examples of how some of these abilities can be applied and translated to the specific functional units and business segments of an organization. The seven examples are presented in form of chapters as follows:

- Chapter 9: Ability to Engage in Innovation-Oriented Planning Activities
- Chapter 10: Ability to Identify Areas for Innovation Focus
- Chapter 11: Ability to Create and Implement Innovation-Performance Job Descriptions and Job Specifications
- Chapter 12: Ability to Create Innovation-Challenge Questions
- Chapter 13: Ability to Formulate Innovation Goals
- Chapter 14: Ability to Design and Implement an Effective Management System for Innovation Ideas
- Chapter 15: Ability to Measure and Report Innovation Performance

## CHAPTER 9
# ABILITY TO ENGAGE IN INNOVATION-ORIENTED PLANNING ACTIVITIES

The first example of innovation management skills is *innovation-oriented planning ability*. What does innovation-oriented planning ability entail? In all management skills, one of the basic and vital abilities required of any organizational leader is planning. In fact, many management publications often describe planning as the first and most important function of management needed at every leadership level of the organization. In leading workforce innovation, innovation-oriented planning ability is not only critical but obligatory because most of the innovation-related activities involve a great deal of planning—hence the importance of organizational leaders' abilities to undertake various innovation-oriented planning activities. To help clarify the expression and application of innovation-oriented planning abilities, this section covers the following aspects: (1) definition of *innovation-oriented planning*, (2) expression of innovation-oriented planning abilities, and (3) illustration of innovation-oriented planning.

### 1. Definition of *Innovation-Oriented Planning*
Innovation-oriented planning is a process that involves creating formats for organizing and implementing the innovation-related functional activities required to achieve desired functional innovation goals that ultimately contribute to overall corporate innovation goals.

## 2. Expression of Innovation-Oriented Planning Abilities

Where are innovation-oriented planning abilities expressed? As stated a number of times, innovation is not reserved for specific functional units or professionals; it's a diverse process of activities that can be undertaken in the different functional contexts of an organization. This means that innovation-oriented planning abilities should be expressed across all the functional units of an organization. Consider the functional units of DM Personal Care Products:

- Product-development functional unit
- Manufacturing-processes functional unit
- Marketing functional unit
- Customer service functional unit
- Procurement functional unit
- HR functional unit
- IT functional unit
- Finance and accounting functional unit
- Corporate affairs functional unit

The leadership would build innovation planning–related skill capabilities and levels in line with the planning demands of the innovation activities and processes of each of the functional units of DM Personal Care Products. In certain cases, some functional units and activities will require complex and high-level innovation-oriented planning abilities.

## 3. Illustration of Innovation-Oriented Planning

Worksheet 9-1 provides a simple format for creating an innovation-oriented action plan for developing and enacting activities to educate workforces about the meaning of *innovation* in the context of the organization's value chain and business model.

Worksheet 9-1. Example of action plan to educate teams about the meaning of innovation

**Objective:** *To develop and implement programs for educating workforces about the meaning of innovation in the context of the organization's value chain and business model*

| Outline of activities and approaches | | **Who:** Individuals responsible for undertaking a particular activity | **When:** Time line for developing and implementing the activity | **Resources:** What will be needed to develop and implement the activity | **Outcome:** Expected outcome from each activity |
|---|---|---|---|---|---|
| Formulate five catchphrases and visual illustrations for educating workforces about the meaning of *innovation* in the context of the organization's value chain and business model | List five approaches or techniques on how to communicate the meaning to workforces | | | | |

| Identify the dates for conducting evaluations to determine how the implementation plan is progressing | | | | | |
|---|---|---|---|---|---|
| **Date:** | **Date:** | **Date:** | **Date:** | **Date:** | **Date:** |
| Outline the aspects that will be evaluated on this date | Outline the aspects that will be evaluated on this date | Outline the aspects that will be evaluated on this date | Outline the aspects that will be evaluated on this date | Outline the aspects that will be evaluated on this date | Outline the aspects that will be evaluated on this date |

## CHAPTER 10
# ABILITY TO IDENTIFY AREAS FOR INNOVATION FOCUS

The second example of innovation management skills is the ability to *identify*, *prioritize*, and *structure* functional-unit areas where innovation should be focused. Recall that one of the premises on which this book is based is that many organizations now view innovation as every employee's job. To make it easy for workforces to understand where they should focus their innovation-ideation efforts, it is helpful for the leadership to outline priority areas for innovation. Worksheet 10-1 provides an example of a simple table that can be used for outlining priority areas on which to focus the generation of innovation ideas.

Ability to Identify Areas for Innovation Focus | 105

Worksheet 10-1. Outlining priority areas for innovation

| Priority areas for generating innovative ideas | Value of the functional activity/business segment or product component |
|---|---|
| Name of functional activity/business segment or product component | |
| Name of functional activity/business segment or product component | |
| Name of functional/business segment or product component | |
| Name of functional/business segment or product component | |
| Date when the outline was done: | |
| Name and position title of the head of the functional unit: | |

*Value*

Note that in worksheet 10-1, the table includes a column on the value that each functional activity or business segment brings to the table in terms of contributing to the growth and competitiveness of the organization and the overall delivery of the organization's mission. This is important because by understanding the value of each business segment or functional unit/activity, workforces will be able to focus their ideation efforts on areas perceived to be of high or considerable value to the organization's growth, competitiveness, and mission. In other words, they will generate innovation ideas with the potential to enhance the value of only the outlined areas for innovation.

The following examples assume we want to outline the areas on which innovation should be focused at DM Personal Care Products, the fictitious company introduced earlier that manufactures a variety of personal care products.

*Steps*

The first step is to outline the core and support functional units of DM Personal Care Products, as follows:

*Core functional units*
- Product-development unit, with the following segments:
  o Body-lotions segment
  o Skin-cleansing segment
  o Hair-care segment
  o Hand-washing segment
- Manufacturing-processes department (as mentioned earlier, the manufacturing-processes department comprises the same segments as the product-development unit)
- Marketing department, with the following units:
  o Pricing unit
  o Product-promotion unit

- o   New-markets unit
- o   Product-delivery unit
- o   Packaging unit
❖ Customer service department

*Support functional units*
- ❖ Procurement department
- ❖ HR department
- ❖ Finance and accounting department
- ❖ IT department
- ❖ Corporate affairs department

The second step is creating tables for listing areas where innovation will be focused in both core and support functional units, as shown in the following example worksheets.

For illustration purposes, worksheet 10-2 is created for the product-development unit.

Worksheet 10-2. Example of how to outline priority areas in product-development unit

| **Body-lotions segment:** List of product categories for the body-lotions segment | Description of the value that each product category aims to deliver |
|---|---|
| Product category A | |
| Product category B | |
| Product category C | |
| Product category D | |
| Date when the outline was done: ||
| Name and position title of the head of the product segment: ||

Similar worksheets would be created for the other three product segments: the skin-cleansing, hair-care, and hand-washing segments.

- ❖ The manufacturing-processes unit has the following categories:
- ❖ Body-lotions manufacturing-processes category
- ❖ Skin-cleansing manufacturing-processes category
- ❖ Hair-care manufacturing-processes category
- ❖ Hand-washing manufacturing-processes category

For illustration purposes, worksheet 10-3 is created for the manufacturing-processes unit.

Worksheet 10-3. Example of how to outline priority areas in manufacturing-processes unit

| **Body-lotions manufacturing-processes category:** List of product segments for the body-lotions manufacturing-processes category | Description of the value that each manufacturing-processes segment aims to deliver |
|---|---|

# Ability to Identify Areas for Innovation Focus | 107

| | |
|---|---|
| Body-lotions manufacturing-processes segment A | |
| Body-lotions manufacturing-processes segment B | |
| Body-lotions manufacturing-processes segment C | |
| Body-lotions manufacturing-processes segment D | |
| Date when the outline was done: | |
| Name and position title of the head of the product category: | |

Similar worksheets would be created for the other three manufacturing-processes categories.

The marketing department has the following functional units:
- Pricing unit
- Product-promotion unit
- Product-delivery unit
- New-markets unit
- Packaging unit

These functional units are presented in five worksheets, as shown in worksheets 10-4 through 10-8.

Worksheet 10-4. Example of how to outline priority areas in pricing subunits

| **Pricing unit:** List of pricing subunits of the marketing functional unit | Description of the value that each of the pricing subunits of the marketing unit aims to deliver |
|---|---|
| Pricing subunit A | |
| Pricing subunit B | |
| Pricing subunit C | |
| Pricing subunit D | |
| Date when the outline was done: | |
| Name and position title of the head of the pricing unit: | |

Worksheet 10-5. Example of how to outline priority areas in product-promotion subunits

| **Product-promotion unit:** List of the product-promotion subunits of the marketing functional unit | Description of the value that each of the product-promotion subunits of the marketing unit aims to deliver |
|---|---|

| | |
|---|---|
| Product-promotion subunit A | |
| Product-promotion subunit B | |
| Product-promotion subunit C | |
| Product-promotion subunit D | |
| Date when the outline was done: | |
| Name and position title of the head of the product-promotion unit: | |

Worksheet 10-6. Example of how to outline priority areas in product-delivery subunits

| **Product-delivery unit:** List of the product-delivery subunits of the marketing functional unit | Description of the value that each of the product-delivery subunits of the marketing unit aims to deliver |
|---|---|
| Product-delivery subunit A | |
| Product-delivery subunit B | |
| Product-delivery subunit C | |
| Product-delivery subunit D | |
| Date when the outline was done: | |
| Name and position title of the head of the product-delivery unit: | |

Worksheet 10-7. Example of how to outline priority areas in new-markets subunits

| **New-markets unit:** List of the new-markets subunits of the marketing functional unit | Description of the value that each of the new-markets subunits of the marketing unit aims to deliver |
|---|---|
| New-markets subunit A | |
| New-markets subunit B | |
| New-markets subunit C | |
| New-markets subunit D | |
| Date when the outline was done: | |
| Name and position title of the head of the new-markets unit: | |

Worksheet 10-8. Example of how to outline priority areas in packaging subunits

| **Packaging unit:** List of the packaging subunits of the marketing functional unit | Description of the value that each of the packaging subunits of the marketing unit aims to deliver |
|---|---|
| Packaging subunit A | |
| Packaging subunit B | |
| Packaging subunit C | |
| Packaging subunit D | |
| Date when the outline was done: ||
| Name and position title of the head of the packaging unit: ||

The customer service unit is the last functional unit of the core units or departments of DM Personal Care Products. Normally, customer service subunits are structured according to the size and business model of an organization. The leadership should ensure that customer service priority areas for innovation are outlined in simple terms.

Worksheet 10-9 provides an example of how the customer service priority subunits can be outlined simply to make it easy for workforces to generate innovative ideas.

Worksheet 10-9. Example of how to outline priority areas in customer service subunits

| **Customer service functional unit:** List of the customer service subunits | Description of the value that each of the customer service subunits aims to deliver |
|---|---|
| Customer service subunit A | |
| Customer service subunit B | |
| Customer service subunit C | |
| Customer service subunit D | |
| Date when the outline was done: ||
| Name and position title of the head of the customer service unit: ||

*Support Units: How Do You Identify and Prioritize Areas in Support Functional Units to Focus Innovation?*

As stated before, innovation ideas in support functional units are normally generated for cost-saving purposes. Thus, the goal here is to illustrate how to outline priority areas for cost-saving innovation ideas in the support functional units of DM Personal Care Products, which are as follows:

❖ Procurement department
❖ HR department
❖ Finance and accounting department
❖ IT department
❖ Corporate affairs department

For illustration purposes, a sample worksheet for the procurement unit is shown in worksheet 10-10.

Worksheet 10-10. Example of how to outline priority areas in procurement subunits

| **Procurement functional unit:** Identify and list the procurement subunits to focus generation of cost-saving innovation ideas | Describe the value that each procurement subunit aims to deliver |
|---|---|
| Procurement subunit A | |
| Procurement subunit B | |
| Procurement subunit C | |
| Procurement subunit D | |
| Date when the outline was done: ||
| Name and position title of the head of the procurement unit: ||

Similar worksheets could be used for the other four support functional units listed previously.

## CHAPTER 11
# ABILITY TO CREATE AND IMPLEMENT INNOVATION-PERFORMANCE JOB DESCRIPTIONS AND JOB SPECIFICATIONS

The third example of innovation management skills is the ability to create and implement innovation-performance job descriptions and job specifications. Remember that many organizations are now making innovation every employee's job. However, it's important to bear in mind that innovation performance in organizations does not take place in a vacuum; it's enacted by workforces in the form of performance by undertaking specific innovation-related tasks. This means that if employees are to effectively execute innovation-related tasks and duties, it is a must that organizational leaders integrate innovation-related duties and responsibilities in the job descriptions of the employees. If innovation-performance duties are not stated or specified in employees' job descriptions, the innovation performance of workforces is left to chance, with the hope that they'll execute innovation-related activities based on the encouragement and instructions of the leadership. Such an expectation is dead on arrival! This approach will give zero results in terms of workforces contributing to the innovation performance of the organization. There's so much innovation-talent potential that is being hindered from being actualized because of, in large part, lack of innovation-performance guidelines in the form of job descriptions. However, creating these innovation-performance duties requires abilities to do so by the leadership, and this is where this section comes into play.

# 112 | LEADERSHIP FOR INNOVATION

The question is, *How do you formulate innovation-performance job descriptions and job specifications?* This chapter answers that question and covers the following topics:
1. Generic definitions of *job description* and *job specification*
2. Definition of *innovation-performance job descriptions* and *job specifications*
3. How to formulate innovation-performance job descriptions and job specifications

## 1. Generic Definitions of *Job Description* and *Job Specification*

o *Job description:*, A job description is generally a list of duties performed for a particular job.
o *Job specification:* A job specification is the knowledge, skills, and abilities, along with the associated education, training, and experience, required to successfully perform the duties outlined in a job description.

## 2. Definition of *Innovation-Performance Job Descriptions* and *Job Specifications*

Innovation-performance job descriptions and job specifications are defined as follows:
i. **Innovation-Performance Job Descriptions**

An innovation-performance job description is an outline of innovation-related duties and responsibilities. There are three categories of innovation-performance duties and responsibilities: *innovative thinking–related duties and responsibilities, innovation engagement–related duties and responsibilities,* and *innovation management– related duties and responsibilities.* These are outlined as follows:

o *Innovative thinking–related duties and responsibilities:* These are duties and responsibilities that are centered on the identification of problems/needs and opportunities and the generation of innovative ideas/solutions to deal with the identified challenges and add commercial value to the organization.

Note that specific duties and responsibilities vary by organization and by functional unit. In terms of functional units, innovative ideas can be generated in either core or support functional units. Some of the core functional units could include the product-development unit, manufacturing-processes unit, market-strategy-development unit, and customer service unit. Support functional units could include HR, IT, procurement, finance and accounting, corporate affairs, and so forth. Also bear in mind that innovative ideas generated in support functional units are mainly centered on cost-saving ideas.

o *Innovation engagement–related duties and responsibilities:* These are innovation-performance duties and responsibilities that involve the application of various organizational resources to design and implement initiatives on a regular basis that are aimed at educating workforces about innovation through informative and inspirational messages using different communication approaches and techniques.

o *Innovation management–related duties and responsibilities:* These are innovation-performance duties and responsibilities that are focused on the continual design and implementation of various frameworks, strategies, policies, procedures, and action plans that contribute to managing, systemizing, and advancing innovation performance across the functional units of the organization.

ii. **Innovation-Performance Job Specifications**
Innovation-performance job specifications are the characteristics, abilities, knowledge, and experience needed to perform innovation performance–related duties and responsibilities.

*Categories*

There are three categories of innovation-performance job specifications: *innovative thinking, innovation engagement,* and *innovation management*. Brief details of each are as follows:

o *Innovative thinking job specifications:* These are the characteristics, knowledge, abilities, and experience required to perform innovative thinking–related duties and responsibilities.

o *Innovation engagement job specifications:* These are the characteristics, knowledge, abilities, and experience required to perform innovation engagement–related duties and responsibilities.

o *Innovation management job specifications*: These are the characteristics, knowledge, abilities, and experience required to perform innovation management–related duties and responsibilities.

iii. **How to Formulate Innovation-Performance Job Descriptions and Job Specifications**
Worksheets 11-1 and 11-2 can be used to create innovation-performance job descriptions and job specifications.

Worksheet 11-1. Innovation-performance job description

| Name of department: Position title: | | |
|---|---|---|
| Categories of innovation-performance duties and responsibilities | | |
| Innovative thinking–related duties and responsibilities | Innovation engagement–related duties and responsibilities | Innovation management–related duties and responsibilities |

Worksheet 11-2. Innovation-performance job specification

| Name of department: Position title: | | |
|---|---|---|
| Categories of innovation-performance job specifications | | |
| Innovative thinking abilities | Innovation engagement abilities | Innovation management abilities |

## CHAPTER 12
# ABILITY TO CREATE INNOVATION-CHALLENGE QUESTIONS

Recall that part I of this book defined *innovation* as a process that involves four aspects: (i) identifying a need or problem, (ii) generating an innovative idea to fix the identified problem, (iii) transforming the innovative idea into a solution not seen on the market before, and (iv) converting the solution to monetary value. The relevant part for this section is the first aspect of identifying needs or problems. If the goal is to implement organization-wide innovation, it is important that workforces have the tools for identifying different contexts of problems and needs. However, developing such tools requires specific skills. Thus, the fourth example of the innovation management skill set is the ability to create and implement innovation-challenge questions across the organization. This chapter covers the following aspects: (1) the definition of *innovation-challenge questions*, (2) the importance of innovation-challenge questions, and (3) how to manage innovation-challenge questions across functional units.

### 1. The Definition of *Innovation-Challenge Questions*
Innovation-challenge questions are pinpointing exploratory questions formulated to reveal specific organizational or community problems/needs or business opportunities requiring innovative solutions.

In other words, innovation-challenge questions are innovation-related questions or challenges that are strategically formulated, on a continual basis, to reveal a specific need, problem, or opportunity in the context of the organization's value chain or business model to encourage and invoke workforces to generate innovative ideas that specifically target the characteristics of the identified need, problem, or business opportunity.

*Framework for Innovation-Challenge Questions*
In order to leverage innovation-challenge questions in terms of ensuring that the practice contributes to making innovation everyone's job in the organization, it is important for the leadership to create a simple framework for managing the practice of innovation-challenge questions across functional units. Practice in this sense means the continual formulation of innovation-challenge questions across the functional units or business segments of an organization.

## 2. The Importance of Innovation-Challenge Questions
Why are innovation-challenge questions important in making innovation every employee's job? The following are three reasons:
  i. It helps to guide and stimulate workforces to generate focused and pinpointed innovative ideas. Because innovation-challenge questions reveal specific organizational or community problems/needs or business opportunities that require innovative solutions, they encourage workforces to generate innovative ideas with a high degree of accuracy to meet the characteristics of the identified need, problem, or business opportunity in the context of the business segments or functional units of the organization.
  ii. Innovation-challenge questions encourage workforces to realize innovative thinking potential. Getting workforces to participate in the ideation processes of the organization is not an easy undertaking because innovation is not an expected practice for most organizations, and organizational attitudes toward innovation have, over the years, led many people to misconstrue innovation as the responsibility of certain functional units and professionals because organizations have consigned or designated innovation to these specific units. Thus, if organizational leaders desire to successfully scale innovation organization-wide, it is important to adopt a range of tools and practices aimed at helping workforces to progressively build their innovative thinking abilities. One such practice is creating a framework for formulating innovation-challenge questions on a continual basis. This is because innovation-challenge questions will potentially encourage and help workforces across functional units to build, over time, the attitude of participating in generating innovation ideas and, eventually, make innovative thinking habitual.
  iii. It promotes the continual flow of different types and degrees of innovative ideas. The fact that innovation-challenge questions are aimed at ensuring the continual identification of problems/needs and generation of innovative ideas means that they contribute to building a pipeline for the continual flow of different types and degrees of innovative ideas across the organization's value chain and business segments, which ultimately contributes to advancing innovation-led growth and competitiveness.

## 3. How to Manage Innovation-Challenge Questions across Functional Units

In order to leverage innovation-challenge questions so that the practice contributes to making innovation a responsibility of everybody across functional units, the leadership should build the capability to ensure that there's continual formulation of innovation-challenge questions in every functional unit of an organization. This involves creating a framework aimed at making the practice of innovation-challenge questions sustainable.

The question is, *How do you ensure that there is a continual flow of innovation-challenge questions across all core and support functional units of the organization?* One of the approaches is the formation of a committee, such as an *innovation-challenge-questions committee* (ICQC), whose role is to coordinate and oversee the creation of innovation-challenge questions across all the core and support functional units of an organization. The ICQC should also be empowered to create various subcommittees. The role of the subcommittees is to formulate innovation-challenge questions in the context of functional units or business segments on a regular basis, as and when needs, problems, and other opportunities related to particular functional units or business segments emerge.

Note that the composition and operational aspects of the committees should be sanctioned and fully supported by the CEO and the top leadership of the organization.

### Roles of ICQC and Subcommittees

Once the main committee and subcommittees are established, their role is to ensure that they regularly brainstorm approaches for sustaining the continual formulation and phrasing of effective innovation-challenge questions in all the functional units or business/product segments of the organization. Formulation of effective innovation-challenge questions means generating innovation questions that have the potential to contribute toward advancing innovation in the organization through their ability to stimulate the generation of innovative solutions from workforces.

There are a number of approaches and measures committees can take to enable continual generation and formulation of effective innovation-challenge questions. The following are some of them:

i. Formulating frameworks for aligning innovation-challenge questions across all functional units and business/product segments
ii. Formulating innovation-challenge questions that contribute to broadening the organization's business-model identity
iii. Ensuring that good innovation-challenge questions are formulated
iv. Creating databases of innovation drivers
v. Conducting periodic review of the innovation-challenge questions
vi. Collaborating and conferring with various heads of functional units
vii. Creating good innovation-challenge-questions worksheets

Each of these aspects is outlined as follows:

i. *Formulating frameworks for aligning innovation-challenge questions across all functional units and business/product segments*: One of the approaches that can be engaged by the ICQC is to ensure that respective subcommittees regularly generate and formulate innovation-challenge questions that correlate with the activities of the particular functional units or business/product segments that the committees are responsible for. The ICQC should also ensure that the formulation of innovation-challenge questions is cascaded down to every component of the functional unit or business/product segment that has been identified as critical. The question is, *How do you cascade innovation-challenge questions?* All organizations are structured in functional units or departments. And these functional units are further broken down into various small components. Thus, cascading innovation-challenge questions means formulating *thoughtful* innovation-centered questions for all the critical functional activities, business segments, or product components of an organization. The term *thoughtful innovation-centered questions* implies formulating innovation-challenge questions that reveal the inner need, problem, or business opportunity of a particular component or context. In order to realize this goal, the leadership should ensure that the organization's ICQC facilitates (through subcommittees) the formulation of frameworks for cascading innovation-challenge questions across all functional units and business segments.

*Illustration*

Let's assume we wish to create a framework for cascading innovation-challenge questions across the functional units of DM Personal Care Products. The first step is to identify the core and support functional units of DM Personal Care Products, as follows:

*Core functional units*
- Product-development unit, with the following segments:
  o Body-lotions segment
  o Skin-cleansing segment
  o Hair-care segment
  o Hand-washing segment
- Manufacturing-processes department
- Marketing department, with the following units:
  o Pricing unit
  o Product-promotion unit
  o Product-delivery unit
  o New-markets unit
  o Packaging unit
- Customer service department

*Support functional units*
- Procurement department
- HR department
- Finance and accounting department
- IT department
- Corporate affairs department

118 | LEADERSHIP FOR INNOVATION

The second step is to align various core and support functional unit activities to the innovation-challenge-questions framework.

As an example, the following steps show how to create a simple framework for aligning innovation-challenge questions in the body-lotions segment of the product-development unit of DM Personal Care Products:

*Steps*
1. Identify a product type within the body-lotions segment; for instance, let's assume lotion X is a type of lotion manufactured by DM Personal Care Products
2. Identify all the critical components of lotion X (i.e., from the value aspects of the lotion to packaging) on which the innovation-challenge questions will be focused
3. Identify the number of innovation-challenge questions to be formulated within a particular period

Figure 12-1 charts these steps.

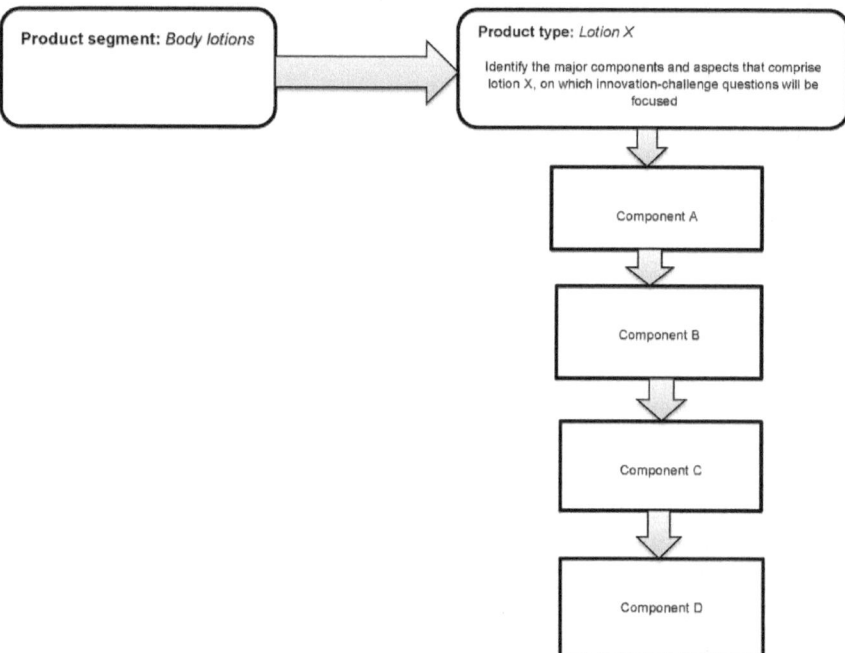

**Note:** The innovation-challenge questions should be formulated periodically in the context of each of the product components of lotion X.

The same process would be replicated for the other core functional units of DM Personal Care Products (i.e., manufacturing processes, marketing, and customer service).

*Support Functional Units*

In terms of support functional units, innovation occurs in the context of cost savings. Thus, the innovation-challenge questions should be formulated in the form of cost-saving innovation-challenge questions in the context of the activities of each support functional unit. The support units for DM Personal Care Products are as follows:

- o  Procurement
- o  HR
- o  Finance and accounting
- o  IT
- o  Corporate affairs

ii. *Formulating innovation-challenge questions that contribute to broadening the organization's business-model identity*: Effective innovation-challenge questions should not only enhance the innovation performance of the organization's existing business model but also contribute to corporate growth. Thus, the top leadership should ensure that ICQCs not only focus on incremental innovation-challenge questions that encourage the generation of small incremental innovative ideas but also on the formulation of innovation-challenge questions that contribute toward broadening the business identity of the organization. This could be done by formulating innovation-challenge questions that seek to explore business spaces for new business models. Many companies have achieved tremendous growth as a result of venturing into nontraditional business opportunities. A good example is Apple, Inc. Over the years, Apple has been leveraging its innovation capabilities to broaden its identity in nontraditional areas such as music, smartphones, and smartwatches. 3M is another company that leverages its innovation capabilities to constantly explore business opportunities outside its traditional spaces. At an annual shareholders' meeting on May 30, 2011, George Buckley, 3M's chairman, president, and CEO, told shareholders that the new innovation heyday for 3M was now, citing simultaneous growth in multiple businesses across the company, and noted that 3M had always relied on exploring new innovative business opportunities outside its traditional spaces. In highlighting growth in multiple markets, Buckley described new opportunities in fast-growing segments like software and electronics, as well as advances in core and traditional areas such as abrasives, adhesives, industrial tape, and office products. And the third example is Nokia, which began its operations as a paper mill company in 1865. In 1912, Nokia added manufacturing of electrical cable to its business model; in 1967, it expanded to paper, rubber, and cable; in 1982, it installed the digital telephone switch, the DX200; in 1987, it launched the Mobira Cityman, the company's first nonbulky mobile phone; and finally, in 1991, the first-ever Global System for Mobile communication (GSM) call was made using Nokia equipment.

Conversely, however, some companies are struggling to survive because they have defined themselves too narrowly, instead of thinking of how they can broaden their business identity with their resources.

iii. *Ensuring that good innovation-challenge questions are formulated*: Understanding the meaning of innovation-challenge questions and knowing areas where the innovation-challenge questions should be formulated is one thing; however, generating or creating innovation-challenge questions that can effectively elicit innovative solutions from workforces is another. So one of the approaches is for the organizational leadership to ensure that every innovation-challenge question that is formulated and publicized to workforces is of good quality in terms of the ability to elicit effective innovative solutions. That said, the question would be, *What are the characteristics of good innovation-challenge questions?* Here are some suggestions:

- Questions should be focused and pinpointed in terms of bringing out the need, problem, or opportunity that requires innovative ideas
- Questions should use simple and plain language
- Ensure that there is only one innovation-challenge question per need, problem, or opportunity
- Questions should be preceded by a brief outline of the factors influencing the need for innovative ideas in a particular functional unit or business/product segment. Some of the drivers of innovation could include the following:
  - Part of company strategy to realize the company vision through innovation performance
  - Customer need or problem
  - Complaints from customers
  - Product recalls
  - Intense competition
  - Disruptive industry trends/practices
  - Transforming or broadening the organization's business model
  - Market trends and consumer demands
  - Cost-saving measures
  - Global trends
  - Government vision, policy, or regulation
  - Disasters
  - Epidemics

iv. *Creating databases of innovation drivers:* As stated in the preceding point, there are many diverse factors (both internal and external) that influence innovation in organizations. For instance, one of the factors influencing innovation in organizations is disruptive industry trends or changes in industry practices. In relation to this is Nokia's case. On February 11, 2011, Nokia announced that it would migrate from its mobile operating system Symbian (Symbian OS). In his speech to Nokia staff in March 2011, former Nokia CEO Stephen Elop explained his decision to dump Symbian OS as being based on the fact that Apple and Google had changed the industry from handset focused to software focused and that Nokia's Symbian OS had fallen too far behind to have any hope of catching up. Thus, a change in industry practices, as in the Nokia case, is one of the major influencing factors of innovation in many companies because a company will have to innovate to replace the disrupted offering with one that can compete against the market trends. Also, note that factors that influence innovation differ from organization to organization and from sector to sector. For instance, innovation at Dow, an energy company, is influenced by a host of factors that are different from those influencing a company in the financial sector like Bank of America, a technology company like Dell, a telecom company like AT&T, a hospitality company like Marriott, an airline company like Southwest

Airlines, and so forth. That said, innovation drivers are a key resource to influencing innovation in organizations, and therefore, it's critical for any organization that has made innovation a key part of its growth and competitiveness to constantly keep tabs on the various innovation drivers that can be leveraged to advance innovation. There are many approaches that organizations can use to keep track of the various forces in the business environment. In relation to innovation-challenge questions, this book suggests creating some form of database for storing various aspects and contexts of factors influencing innovation across the organization. The ICQC should ensure that innovation-challenge-questions subcommittees across functional units create databases of various innovation drivers within the context of the areas the subcommittees are responsible for. The databases should be updated regularly to reflect the trends, needs, and problems of each particular functional unit or business/product segment. The trends and needs, as stated earlier, are used as the basis for formulating innovation-challenge questions, which in turn stimulate the generation of innovative ideas by workforces.

v. *Conducting periodic reviews of the innovation-challenge questions*: The fifth measure is for the ICQC to not only coordinate the formulation of innovation-challenge questions but also to ensure that, over time, existing innovation-challenge questions are regularly reviewed and updated to reflect current factors that are influencing innovation in the organization and, in some cases, include future scenarios likely to affect the components of the functional units, a particular product, or the organization.

vi. *Collaborating and conferring with various heads of functional units:* As mentioned, the role of ICQCs is to ensure that they regularly come up with innovation-challenge questions that have the potential to stimulate workforces across functional units to generate innovative ideas on a regular basis. One of the approaches in ensuring that this objective is realized is for committees to regularly collaborate and confer with various heads of functional units on a number of aspects related to innovation-challenge questions, including brainstorming and discussing ideas about the various needs, problems, and opportunities of the organization's functional units that could be used to formulate innovation-challenge questions. Committees could also use the collaborative interactions with heads of functional units to obtain information on the innovation goals of functional units and then use this information when formulating innovation-challenge questions for the respective functional units and components.

vii. *Creating good innovation-challenge-questions worksheets:* In order to ensure that the intended purposes of innovation-challenge questions are realized, the organizational leadership should ensure that the ICQC and all the subcommittees understand the importance of creating good innovation-challenge-questions worksheets. Good innovation-challenge-questions worksheets are those with sufficient questioning characteristics that will help elicit effective innovative ideas correlating to particular needs or problems highlighted in the innovation-challenge questions.

The questions would then be, *How do you create worksheets for formulating innovation-challenge questions on a regular basis? What aspects should be included in the innovation-challenge-questions worksheet so that the right innovation-challenge questions are formulated to effectively elicit innovative ideas or solutions from workforces?* The following are some of the aspects to take into account when creating innovation-challenge-questions worksheets:

- Include a provision for the type of innovation-challenge questions of the functional unit for which the innovation-challenge-questions worksheet is meant. Part II of this book described innovation dimensions as the main ways in which innovation occurs or is implemented and noted that there are two aspects that make up innovation dimensions: types of innovation and innovation degree. It was also stated that in order to understand types of innovation, the first step is to understand that innovation is implemented across the business categories and functional units of an organization by being translated into types of innovation. Thus, in order to guide workforces on the types of innovation-challenge questions, it is important that the innovation-challenge-questions worksheet has a provision for the type of innovation-challenge questions that the worksheet is meant for.
- Include a provision indicating the specific functional-unit component or business/product segment for which the innovation-challenge questions are meant. For instance, indicate a particular product or service segment if the innovation-challenge-questions worksheet is meant for a particular product or service segment, and if the innovation-challenge-questions worksheet is meant for a particular marketing component, state the name of the component. And similarly, if the innovation-challenge-questions worksheet is meant for a manufacturing processes–related component or customer service–related component, indicate this on the worksheet.
- Include a provision specifying the innovation degree—that is, whether the worksheet is meant for incremental or radical innovation-challenge questions.
- Include a provision describing the factors influencing the need for innovative solutions in the functional unit or business/product segment.
- You could also include a provision for the time frame within which innovative ideas that are targeted at solving particular problems, meeting particular needs, or exploring business opportunities shall be collected. For instance, a provision could note, "Submission of innovative ideas for [functional unit or product category here] innovation-challenge questions is between January and April of 2018."

## Example 1

In this example, a fictitious scenario is used to create an innovation-challenge-questions worksheet. Environmental Solutions, a fictitious company that specializes in developing innovative environmental solutions, is approached by a government agency responsible for regulating forestry activities to help the agency come up with an innovative solution for taking forest inventories.

*Current System*
Currently, the foresters from the government agency take inventories of trees by hiking through representative plots and recording each tree. They extrapolate from those samples to get the general sense of the land. The bigger and more diverse the forest, the more plots that must be sampled.

*The Problem*
This method has frustrated staff in the government agency because the system is inefficient and not very effective. For instance, workers are unable to gather information from ground sampling alone, and in addition, the system is very time consuming and uses a lot of workforce power.

*Application of Innovation-Challenge Questions*
Let's assume that Environmental Solutions has a director responsible for operations. As a starting point, the operations director creates an ICQC and tasks the committee with two goals: (1) to create a forest inventory innovation-challenge-questions worksheet and (2) to formulate (using the worksheet) innovation-challenge questions in the context of a forest inventory, which in turn will stimulate the generation of innovative ideas for creating the forest inventory system.

Worksheet 12-1 provides an example of a forest inventory innovation-challenge-questions worksheet that could be used in this scenario.

Worksheet 12-1. Innovation-challenge-questions for Forest Inventory Unit

| Type of innovation-challenge questions: Forest inventory innovation-challenge questions ||
|---|---|
| Product or service segment: Forest Inventory Unit ||
| Name of innovation-challenge-question committee: Forest Inventory Committee ||
| Date when the innovation-challenge questions were publicized to workforces: March 15, 2018 ||
| The worksheet is divided into two parts: part I is for radical innovation-challenge questions, and part II is for incremental innovation-challenge questions. ||
| Part I<br>Innovation degree: Radical innovation-challenge questions ||
| Describe factors influencing the need for the generation of radical innovative ideas for the Forest Inventory Unit | Context of the radical innovation-challenge questions: Forest Inventory Unit |

| | |
|---|---|
| o The current system is inefficient and not very effective.<br>o The Forest Inventory Unit is unable to get information from ground sampling alone.<br>o The current system also involves a lot of work. | ***Radical innovation-challenge question:***<br>*What radical forest inventory solution/method would help the Forest Inventory Unit to undertake the inventory tasks in the following list?* |

| | |
|---|---|
| 1. | Tally the *sizes* of the trees in a more efficient and effective manner |
| 2. | Tally the *number* of trees in a more efficient and effective manner |
| 3. | Tally the *species* of the trees in a more efficient and effective manner |
| 4. | Locate the ideal mushroom habitat |
| 5. | Complete items 1–4 with less manpower |
| 6. | Establish a system that will also result in the creation of detailed inventories to help maximize timber yields |

**Part II**
**Innovation degree:** Incremental innovation-challenge questions

| **Describe factors influencing the need for the generation of incremental innovative ideas for the Forest Inventory Unit** | **Incremental innovation-challenge questions** |
|---|---|
| No consideration for this category | No consideration for this category |
| | |
| | |
| | |
| | |
| | |
| | |
| | |

**Time frame for submission of forest inventory innovative ideas from Environmental Solutions after publication of the forest inventory innovation-challenge questions:** One month (*March 15–April 15, 2018*)

**Innovation-challenge-questions status report:** At the end of the submission time frame, the committee should submit a status report noting the following:
- Number of forest inventory innovation-challenge questions formulated within the prescribed time period
- Number of forest inventory innovative ideas generated as a result of the forest inventory innovation-challenge questions publicized to Environmental Solutions staff

**Names and positions of subcommittee members:**

## Example 2

This second example illustrates how to apply the innovation-challenge-questions worksheet to the core and support functional units of DM Personal Care Products, which are outlined as follows:

*Core functional units*
- Product-development unit, with the following segments:
    o Body-lotions segment
    o Skin-cleansing segment
    o Hair-care segment
    o Hand-washing segment
- Manufacturing-processes department
- Marketing department, with the following units:
    o Pricing unit
    o Product-promotion unit
    o Product-delivery unit
    o New-markets unit
    o Packaging unit
- Customer service department

*Support functional units*
- Procurement department
- HR department
- Finance and accounting department
- IT department
- Corporate affairs department

Worksheets 12-2 through 12-7 show how the innovation-challenge-questions worksheets can be formulated for the context of each of the core and support functional units.

Worksheet 12-2. Type of innovation-challenge questions in product-development unit

| |
|---|
| **Product segment:** Body-lotions segment |
| **Name of innovation-challenge-question subcommittee:** Body-Lotions ICQC Subcommittee |
| **Date when the innovation-challenge questions will be publicized to workforces:** February 1, 2018 |
| **Indicate challenge questions according to innovation degree:** part I is for radical product innovation-challenge questions, and part II is for incremental product innovation-challenge questions |

| Part I: Radical product innovation-challenge questions ||
|---|---|
| Describe factors influencing the need for the generation of radical product innovation ideas in the body-lotions segment | Formulate radical product innovation-challenge questions in the context of the components of the body-lotions segment |
|  |  |

| Part II: Incremental product innovation-challenge questions ||
|---|---|
| Describe factors influencing the need for the generation of incremental product innovation ideas in the body-lotions segment | Formulate incremental product innovation-challenge questions in the context of the components of the body-lotions segment |
|  |  |

**Time frame for submission of innovative ideas:** The period within which innovation ideas aimed at solving problems, meeting needs, or exploring business opportunities revealed in the particular innovation-challenge questions shall be collected. For instance, "Submission of innovative ideas for the innovation-challenge questions for the product-development functional unit is between January and April of 2018."

**Innovation-challenge-questions status report:** At the end of every quarter of the year, each subcommittee should submit a status report stating the following:
- Number of innovation-challenge questions formulated over a particular period
- Number of innovation-challenge questions that stimulated generation of innovation ideas from workforces

This information can be obtained from the respective committees responsible for collecting innovation ideas from workforces.

**Note:** Subcommittees should create frameworks for storing the innovation-challenge questions for which they are responsible.

**Names and positions of subcommittee members:**

Worksheet 12-2 could also be applied to the other three product segments:
- Skin-cleansing segment
- Hair-care segment
- Hand-washing segment

Worksheet 12-3. Type of innovation-challenge questions in manufacturing-processes department

| **Manufacturing-processes segments:** Align the innovation-challenge-questions worksheet to each of the manufacturing-processes segments, that is: <br>• Body-lotions manufacturing-processes segment <br>• Skin-cleansing manufacturing-processes segment <br>• Hair-care manufacturing-processes segment <br>• Hand-washing manufacturing-processes segment ||
|---|---|
| **Name of innovation-challenge-question subcommittee:** Manufacturing-Processes ICQC Subcommittee ||
| **Date when the innovation-challenge questions will be publicized to workforces:** February 1, 2018 ||
| **Indicate challenge questions according to innovation degree:** part I is for radical manufacturing-processes innovation-challenge questions, and part II is for incremental manufacturing-processes innovation-challenge questions ||
| **Part I: Radical manufacturing-processes innovation-challenge questions** ||
| Describe factors influencing the need for the generation of radical manufacturing-processes innovative ideas | Formulate radical manufacturing-processes innovation-challenge questions in the context of each of the four manufacturing-processes segments outlined in this worksheet |
|  |  |
|  |  |
|  |  |
| **Part II: Incremental manufacturing-processes innovation-challenge questions** ||
| Describe factors influencing the need for the generation of incremental manufacturing-processes innovative ideas | Formulate incremental manufacturing-processes innovation-challenge questions in the context of each of the four manufacturing-processes segments outlined in this worksheet |

|   |   |
|---|---|
|   |   |
|   |   |
|   |   |
|   |   |

**Time frame for submission of innovative ideas:** The period within which innovation ideas aimed at solving problems, meeting needs, or exploring business opportunities revealed in the particular innovation-challenge questions shall be collected. For instance, "Submission of innovative ideas for the innovation-challenge questions for the manufacturing-processes functional unit is between January and April of 2018."

**Innovation-challenge-questions status report:** At the end of every quarter of the year, each subcommittee should submit a status report stating the following:
- Number of innovation-challenge questions formulated over a particular period
- Number of innovation-challenge questions that stimulated generation of innovation ideas from workforces

This information can be obtained from the respective committees responsible for collecting innovation ideas from workforces.

**Note:** Subcommittees should create frameworks for storing the innovation-challenge questions for which they are responsible.

**Names and positions of subcommittee members:**

Worksheet 12-4. Type of innovation-challenge questions in Marketing department—pricing unit

| |
|---|
| **Marketing unit:** Pricing unit |
| **Name of innovation-challenge-question subcommittee:** Pricing ICQC Subcommittee |
| **Date when the innovation-challenge questions will be publicized to workforces:** February 1, 2018 |
| **Indicate challenge questions according to innovation degree:** part I is for radical pricing innovation-challenge questions, and part II is for incremental pricing innovation-challenge questions |

| Part I: Radical pricing innovation-challenge questions ||
|---|---|
| Describe factors influencing the need for the generation of radical pricing innovation ideas in the body-lotions segment | Formulate radical pricing innovation-challenge questions in the context of the body-lotions segment |
|  |  |

| Part II: Incremental pricing innovation-challenge questions ||
|---|---|
| Describe factors influencing the need for the generation of incremental pricing innovation ideas for existing products | Formulate incremental innovation-challenge questions in the context of pricing for existing products |
|  |  |

| **Time frame for submission of innovative ideas:** The period within which innovation ideas aimed at solving problems, meeting needs, or exploring business opportunities revealed in the particular innovation-challenge questions shall be collected. For instance, "Submission of innovative ideas for the innovation-challenge questions for the pricing unit is between January and April of 2018." |
|---|
| **Innovation-challenge-questions status report:** At the end of every quarter of the year, each subcommittee should submit a status report stating the following:<br>• Number of innovation-challenge questions formulated over a particular period<br>• Number of innovation-challenge questions that stimulated generation of innovation ideas from workforces<br>This information can be obtained from the respective committees responsible for collecting innovation ideas from workforces.<br>**Note:** Subcommittees should create frameworks for storing the innovation-challenge questions for which they are responsible. |
| Names and positions of subcommittee members: |

This worksheet format could also be applied to three of the four remaining marketing units:
- Product-promotion unit
- Product-delivery unit
- Packaging unit

You will notice that the new-markets unit is not included in this list. The reason is that the worksheet for this unit is formulated differently. Whereas worksheet 12-4 uses the terms *radical* and *incremental innovation-challenge questions* to express the degree of newness of a marketing innovative idea, worksheet 12-5 characterizes the extent of new markets as *new unserved markets* and *new-market segments*. These two terms are defined as follows:
- *New unserved market* denotes a completely new geographical area not served by the organization or its competitors; this is covered in part I of worksheet 12-5
- *New-market segment* means a segment within an existing wider market already served by the company and its competitors; this is covered in part II of worksheet 12-5

The other aspect to bear in mind is that new-market ideas are usually generated for the organization's existing products.

Worksheet 12-5. Type of innovation-challenge questions in new-markets unit

| |
|---|
| **Marketing unit:** New-markets unit |
| **Name of innovation-challenge-question subcommittee:** New-Markets ICQC Subcommittee |
| **Date when the innovation-challenge questions will be publicized to workforces:** February 1, 2018 |
| **Innovation degree takes two forms when formulating innovation-challenge questions for new markets:** part I is for new-unserved-market innovation-challenge questions, and part II is for new-market-segment innovation-challenge questions |

| Part I: New-unserved-market innovation-challenge questions ||
|---|---|
| **Describe factors influencing the need for the generation of new-unserved-market innovative ideas for particular existing products** | **Formulate new-unserved-market innovation-challenge questions in the context of a particular existing product** |
| | |
| | |
| | |
| | |

| Part II: New-market-segment innovation-challenge questions ||
|---|---|
| **Describe factors influencing the need for the generation of new-market-segment innovative ideas for particular existing products** | **Formulate new-market-segment innovation-challenge questions in the context of a particular existing product** |
| | |
| | |
| | |
| | |

**Time frame for submission of innovative ideas:** The period within which innovation ideas aimed at exploring new-market opportunities for existing products revealed in innovation-challenge questions shall be collected. For instance, "Submission of innovative ideas for the innovation-challenge questions for new-market ideas for [name of product] is between January and April of 2018."

# Ability to Create Innovation-Challenge Questions | 131

| |
|---|
| **Innovation-challenge-questions status report:** At the end of every quarter of the year, each subcommittee should submit a status report stating the following:<br>• Number of innovation-challenge questions formulated over a particular period<br>• Number of innovation-challenge questions that stimulated generation of innovation ideas from workforces<br>This information can be obtained from the respective committees responsible for collecting innovation ideas from workforces.<br>**Note:** Subcommittees should create frameworks for storing the innovation-challenge questions for which they are responsible. |
| **Names and positions of subcommittee members:** |

As noted earlier, customer service innovations can be categorized in three contexts:
- Before-purchase customer service innovations
- During-purchase customer service innovations
- After-purchase customer service innovations

This means that the innovation-challenge-questions worksheets ought to be formulated in the context of the above categories; worksheet 12-6 provides an example.

Worksheet 12-6. Type of innovation-challenge questions in customer service unit

| | |
|---|---|
| **Functional unit:** Customer service | |
| **Name of innovation-challenge-question subcommittee:** Before-Purchase Customer Service ICQC Subcommittee | |
| **Date when the innovation-challenge questions will be publicized to workforces:** February 1, 2018 | |
| **Indicate challenge questions according to innovation degree:** part I is for radical before-purchase customer service innovation-challenge questions, and part II is for incremental before-purchase customer service innovation-challenge questions | |
| **Part I: Radical before-purchase customer service innovation-challenge questions** | |
| **Describe factors influencing the need for the generation of radical before-purchase customer service innovative ideas** | **Formulate radical before-purchase customer service innovation-challenge questions** |
| | |
| | |
| | |
| | |
| **Part II: Incremental before-purchase customer service innovation-challenge questions** | |
| **Describe factors influencing the need for the generation of incremental before-purchase customer service innovation ideas** | **Formulate incremental before-purchase customer service innovation-challenge questions** |

# 132 | LEADERSHIP FOR INNOVATION

| | |
|---|---|
| | |
| | |
| | |
| | |

| |
|---|
| **Time frame for submission of innovative ideas:** The period within which innovation ideas aimed at solving problems, meeting needs, or exploring business opportunities revealed in the particular innovation-challenge questions shall be collected. For instance, "Submission of innovative ideas for the innovation-challenge questions for the customer service unit is between January and April of 2018." |
| **Innovation-challenge-questions status report:** At the end of every quarter of the year, each subcommittee should submit a status report stating the following:<br>• Number of innovation-challenge questions formulated over a particular period<br>• Number of innovation-challenge questions that stimulated generation of innovation ideas from workforces<br>This information can be obtained from the respective committees responsible for collecting innovation ideas from workforces.<br>**Note:** Subcommittees should create frameworks for storing the innovation-challenge questions for which they are responsible. |
| **Names and positions of subcommittee members:** |

Worksheet 12-6 could also be applied to the other two categories of customer service innovations:

- During-purchase customer service innovations
- After-purchase customer service innovations

## *Support Functional Units*

This section illustrates how to *create* innovation-challenge questions in support units. Recall that innovation in support (back-office) functional units is normally implemented for cost-saving purposes. Thus, the innovation-challenge questions for support functional units should be focused on cost savings and phrased in the context of the activities of the support functional unit.

Worksheet 12-7 provides an example of the innovation-challenge-questions worksheet applied to the procurement support functional unit of DM Personal Care Products; worksheets for the other support functional units would follow a similar format.

Worksheet 12-7. Type of innovation-challenge questions in procurement department

| |
|---|
| **Name of innovation-challenge-question subcommittee:** Procurement ICQC Subcommittee |
| **Date when the innovation-challenge questions will be publicized to workforces:** February 1, 2018 |

| List of critical procurement functional components | Factors influencing the need for the generation of particular procurement innovative ideas | Procurement innovation-challenge questions |
|---|---|---|
| | | |
| | | |
| | | |
| | | |
| | | |

**Time frame for submission of innovative ideas:** The period within which innovation ideas aimed at providing solutions for procurement cost-saving innovation-challenge questions shall be collected. For instance, "Submission of innovative ideas for the innovation-challenge questions for the procurement functional unit is between January and April of 2018."

**Innovation-challenge-questions status report:** At the end of every quarter of the year, each subcommittee should submit a status report stating the following:
- Number of innovation-challenge questions formulated over a particular period
- Number of innovation-challenge questions that stimulated generation of innovation ideas from workforces

This information can be obtained from the respective committees responsible for collecting innovation ideas from workforces.

**Note:** Subcommittees should create frameworks for storing the innovation-challenge questions for which they are responsible.

Names and positions of subcommittee members:

Worksheet 12-7 could also be replicated for the other four support functional units
- ❖ HR department
- ❖ Finance and accounting department
- ❖ IT department
- ❖ Corporate affairs department

## CHAPTER 13
# ABILITY TO FORMULATE INNOVATION GOALS

G oal setting is one of the most common and vital organizational practices. It is equally as vital when it comes to scaling innovation performance across functional units. That said, the fifth example of innovation management skills is the ability to create various contexts of innovation goals across functional units.

The question is, *How do you create various categories of innovation goals across core and support functional units?* To answer this question, chapter 13 looks at the following aspects: (1) the definition of *innovation goals*, (2) the importance of organizational leaders' possession of innovation goal-setting abilities, (3) guidelines for creating innovation goals in core and support functional units, and (4) how to create functional-unit innovation goals.

### 1. The Definition of *Innovation Goals*
Innovation goals are statements expressing the desired future state of innovation performance to be attained within a specified period in the context of the specified level of the organization (i.e., individual level, departmental level, corporate level).

### 2. The Importance of Organizational Leaders' Possession of Innovation Goal-Setting Abilities
Why is it important for organizational leaders to possess innovation goal-setting abilities? The following are four reasons:
   i. *Innovation goal setting motivates workforces to generate innovative ideas.* In whatever context of performance activities, performance goal setting plays a vital role in driving performance. In fact, numerous behavioral philosophies have linked goal setting to

motivation to perform and the realization of the purpose of a particular performance activity. One often-quoted theory is Aristotle's philosophy of final causality- That is, *action caused by a purpose*. In other words, *goal setting can incite action*. And in an article by Dr. Edwin Locke, an organizational-behavior philosopher, that was published in a 1968 issue of the *Journal of Organizational Behavior and Human Performance*, Locke argues that employees are motivated when they have clear performance goals and are provided feedback about their performance. The question then is, *How does this description apply to innovation goals?* Although the context of this description is generic, the concepts can also be linked to innovation goal setting. This is so because innovation performance is driven by certain factors—such as revenue or profit goals, market-share goals, customer satisfaction goals, functional-unit-performance goals, and so forth—that incite employees to set individual innovation goals and consequently stimulate them to generate innovative ideas to meet their particular innovation-performance goals and ultimately contribute to the functional-unit goals for innovation and overall goals for corporate innovation. Thus, setting goals for functional-unit innovation contributes to inciting and motivating workforces to generate innovative ideas, and in turn, these ideas fuel the advancement of innovation across the organization.

ii. *Employees and teams will understand what is expected of them in terms of contributing to innovation*. Related to the first point, goal-setting theory suggests that one of the effective tools for making progress on goals is ensuring that participants in a group with a common goal are clearly aware of what is expected from them as a whole. In terms of innovation, innovation goal setting contributes to ensuring that teams across functional units are clearly aware of the role of their functional units in advancing innovation. This means that teams will not only understand but will also internalize what is expected of them as individuals and also as part of the larger team in advancing the innovation performance of the functional unit.

iii. *Determining or measuring innovation performance involves, in large part, setting and reviewing innovation goals*. Part II of this book defined *dimensions of innovation* as ways in which innovation occurs (where and how) across the value chain and noted that understanding this is vital to determining the occurrence of innovation in a particular organization's functional context. What this means is that determining or measuring innovation performance involves setting and reviewing innovation goals. Hence, organizational leaders must understand what innovation goals are and know how to formulate or set innovation goals for various contexts.

iv. *Harnessing the power of innovation goals requires knowledge of all categories of innovation goals*. The ultimate aim of all categories of innovation goals is to contribute toward realizing the organizational vision of creating an innovation-driven enterprise; however, whether this is achieved depends on how the leadership uses the innovation goal-setting process. For instance, one of the categories of innovation goals is *workforce innovation ideation goals*. These are innovation goals set by teams or individual employees. This category of innovation goals is critical to achieving goals for functional-unit innovation, and likewise, goals for functional-unit innovation are critical to achieving corporate-level innovation goals. It's therefore important

## 136 | LEADERSHIP FOR INNOVATION

that leaders understand what each category of innovation goals entails and how to set such goals; otherwise, it will be difficult to use the innovation goal-setting process to advance innovation across the organization. Hence the need for organizational leaders to possess abilities to formulate innovation goals in different contexts.

*Illustration*

Figure 13-1 provides an example of a simple corporate innovation goal-setting flowchart.

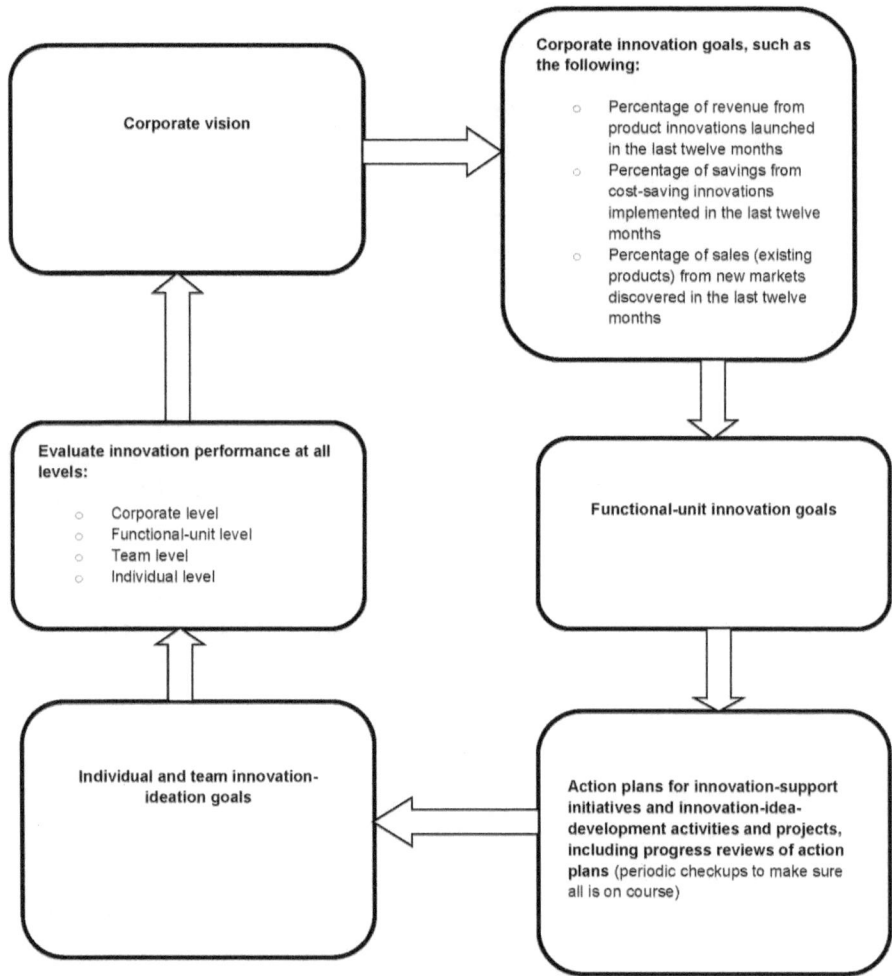

*Figure 13-1. Goal-setting flowchart*

## 3. Guidelines for Creating Innovation Goals in Core and Support Functional Units

In any goal-setting process, certain aspects need to be taken into consideration. This section suggests some guidelines that can be applied when creating functional-unit innovation goals in both core and support functional units, as follows:

i. Review the following aspects:
   o Organizational vision
   o Corporate innovation goals
ii. Review and describe factors driving innovation performance in the particular functional unit.
iii. Ensure that the leadership creates the right types of worksheets for different categories and contexts of innovation goals.

## 4. How to Create Functional-Unit Innovation Goals

Let's return to the example of DM Personal Care Products and assume we wish to create a worksheet for formulating radical and incremental innovation goals for core and support units based on the value chain and business model of the company. The specific steps in the process are described next.

*Steps*

The first step is to outline the core and support functional units:

*Core functional units*
- Product-development unit, with the following segments:
   o Body-lotions segment
   o Skin-cleansing segment
   o Hair-care segment
   o Hand-washing segment
- Manufacturing-processes department
- Marketing department, with the following units:
   o Pricing unit
   o Product-promotion unit
   o Product-delivery unit
   o New-markets unit
   o Packaging unit
- Customer service department

*Support functional units*
- Procurement department
- HR department
- Finance and accounting department
- IT department
- Corporate affairs department

The second step is outlining, in summary form, the organization's corporate goals. See table 13-1 for five example categories of corporate innovation goals.

Table 13-1. Categories of corporate innovation goals

| Category of innovation goals | Description of goals | |
|---|---|---|
| **Corporate innovation-support goal** | To implement three to four different innovation-support initiatives (in all categories: innovative thinking, innovation engagement, and innovation management) across all functional units and business segments between January and March of 2018 | |
| **Innovation-ideation goal** | To generate 10 percent more innovative ideas across the organization between January and March of 2018 than during the same period in 2017 | |
| **Innovation-idea-development goal** | To have 6 percent more innovation ideas undergoing development between January and March of 2018 than during the same period in 2017 | |
| **Innovation-launch goal** | To launch or implement 4 percent more innovations between January and March of 2018 than during the same period in 2017 | |
| **Monetary innovation goals** | | |
| Percentage of revenues | Percentage of savings | Percentage of sales from new markets |
| 1.5 percent of the overall revenue should come from product innovations launched in the last six months | 2 percent of the overall savings should come from cost-saving innovations implemented in the last six months | 2.5 percent of overall sales (from existing products) should come from new markets discovered in the last six months |

The third step is creating worksheets for outlining the innovation goals in each functional unit. Worksheets 13-1 through 13-5 are for the core functional units, and worksheets 13-6 through 13-10 are for the support functional units. The worksheets have two parts: part I is for radical innovation goals, and part II is for incremental innovation goals. Each notes important aspects that should be included in the worksheet.

Worksheet 13-1. Innovation goals for the product-development department

| Radical and Incremental Product-Innovation-Goals Worksheet |
|---|
| **Name of functional unit:** Product-development department<br>**Name of segment:** Body-lotions segment<br>**Date:**<br>**Head of segment:** |
| Part I<br>**Radical Product Innovation Goals** |
| **Centered on three aspects:**<br>• Number of radical product innovation ideas to be generated<br>• Number of radical product innovation ideas to be undergoing development<br>• Number of radical product innovations to be launched |

| Number of radical product innovation ideas for body-lotions segment to be generated over a particular period | Number of radical product innovation ideas for body-lotions segment to be undergoing development over a particular period | Number of radical body-lotions innovations to be launched over a particular period |
|---|---|---|
| For instance:<br>• To generate five radical (completely new to the world) product innovation ideas in the body-lotions segment between January and March of 2018 | • To ensure that the unit has three radical product innovation ideas in the body-lotions segment undergoing development between January and March of 2018 | • To launch two radical product innovations in the body-lotions segment between January and March of 2018 |

**Number of radical product innovation goals set:**

**Review date:**

## Part II
### Incremental Product Innovation Goals

**Centered on three aspects:**
- Number of incremental product innovation ideas to be generated
- Number of incremental product innovation ideas to be undergoing development
- Number of incremental product innovations to be launched

| Number of incremental product innovation ideas for body-lotions segment to be generated over a particular period | Number of incremental product innovation ideas for body-lotions segment to be undergoing development over a particular period | Number of incremental body-lotions innovations to be launched over a particular period |
|---|---|---|
| For instance:<br>• To generate six incremental product innovation ideas for improving the existing body-lotion products between January and March of 2018 | • To ensure that the unit has four incremental product innovation ideas for improving the existing body-lotion products undergoing development between January and March of 2018 | • To launch three incremental product innovations in the body-lotions segment between January and March of 2018 |

**Number of incremental product innovation goals set:**

**Review date:**

Similar worksheets would be created for the other three product segments:
- ❖ Skin-cleansing segment
- ❖ Hair-care segment
- ❖ Hand-washing segment

Worksheet 13-2. Innovation goals for the manufacturing-processes department

| Radical and Incremental Manufacturing-Processes Innovation Goals |||
|---|---|---|
| **Name of functional unit:** Manufacturing-processes department<br>**Name of segment:** Body-lotions manufacturing-processes segment<br>**Date:**<br>**Head of segment:** |||
| **Part I**<br>**Radical Manufacturing-Processes Innovation Goals** |||
| **Centered on three aspects:**<br>• Number of radical manufacturing-processes innovation ideas to be generated<br>• Number of radical manufacturing-processes innovation ideas to be undergoing development<br>• Number of radical manufacturing-processes innovations to be implemented |||
| Number of radical manufacturing-processes innovation ideas to be generated in the body-lotions segment over a particular period | Number of radical manufacturing-processes innovation ideas for the body-lotions segment to be undergoing development over a particular period | Number of radical manufacturing-processes innovations to be implemented over a particular period |
| For instance:<br>• To generate five radical (completely new to the world) product innovation ideas in the body-lotions segment between January and March of 2018 | • To ensure that the unit has three radical product innovation ideas in the body-lotions segment undergoing development between January and March of 2018 | • To launch two radical product innovations in the body-lotions segment within a development budget of $2.5 million per radical innovation idea between January and March of 2018 |
| **Number of radical manufacturing-processes innovation goals set:** |||
| **Review date:** |||
| **Part II**<br>**Incremental Manufacturing-Processes Innovation Goals** |||
| **Centered on three aspects:**<br>• Number of incremental manufacturing-processes innovation ideas to be generated<br>• Number of incremental manufacturing-processes innovation ideas to be undergoing development<br>• Number of incremental manufacturing-processes innovations to be implemented |||
| Number of incremental manufacturing-processes innovation ideas to be generated in the body-lotions segment over a particular period | Number of incremental manufacturing-processes innovation ideas for the body-lotions segment to be undergoing development over a particular period | Number of incremental manufacturing-processes innovations to be implemented over a particular period |

| | | |
|---|---|---|
| For instance:<br>• To generate six incremental product innovation ideas for improving the existing body-lotion products between January and March of 2018 | • To ensure that the unit has four incremental product innovation ideas for improving the existing body-lotion products undergoing development between January and March of 2018 | • To launch three incremental product innovations in the body-lotions segment between January and March of 2018 |
| **Number of incremental manufacturing-processes innovation goals set:** | | |
| **Review date:** | | |

Similar worksheets would be created for the other manufacturing processes in the other three segments:

❖ Skin-cleansing manufacturing processes
❖ Hair-care manufacturing processes
❖ Hand-washing manufacturing processes

Worksheet 13-3. Innovation goals for the marketing department

| | | |
|---|---|---|
| **Radical and Incremental Marketing Innovation Goals** | | |
| **Name of functional unit:** Marketing department<br>**Name of unit:** Pricing unit<br>**Date:**<br>**Head of unit:** | | |
| **Part I**<br>**Radical Pricing Innovation Goals** | | |
| **Centered on three aspects:**<br>• Number of radical pricing innovation ideas to be generated<br>• Number of radical pricing innovation ideas to be undergoing development<br>• Number of radical pricing innovations to be implemented | | |
| Number of radical pricing innovation ideas to be generated for existing products over a particular period | Number of radical pricing innovation ideas to be undergoing development for existing products over a particular period | Number of radical pricing innovations to be implemented for existing products over a particular period |
| For instance:<br>• To generate five radical pricing innovation ideas between January and March of 2018 | • To have three radical pricing innovation ideas undergoing development between January and March of 2018 | • To launch two radical pricing innovations between January and March of 2018 |
| **Number of radical pricing innovation goals set:** | | |
| **Review date:** | | |

# 142 | LEADERSHIP FOR INNOVATION

| Part II<br>Incremental Pricing Innovation Goals |||
|---|---|---|
| **Centered on three aspects:**<br>• Number of incremental pricing innovation ideas to be generated<br>• Number of incremental pricing innovation ideas to be undergoing development<br>• Number of incremental pricing innovations to be implemented |||
| **Number of incremental pricing innovation ideas to be generated for existing products over a particular period** | **Number of incremental pricing innovation ideas to be undergoing development for existing products over a particular period** | **Number of incremental pricing innovations to be implemented for existing products over a particular period** |
| For instance:<br>• To generate five incremental pricing innovation ideas between January and March of 2018 | • To have three incremental pricing innovation ideas undergoing development between January and March of 2018 | • To launch two incremental pricing innovations between January and March of 2018 |
| **Number of incremental pricing innovation goals set:** |||
| **Review date:** |||

Similar worksheets could also be created for three of the four remaining marketing units:
- Product-promotion unit
- Product-delivery unit
- Packaging unit

Once again, as in chapter 12 on creating an innovation-challenge-questions framework, you'll notice that the new-markets unit is not included in the list. This is because different terminology is used when it comes to setting new-market goals, and thus, a different worksheet format is needed. When creating goals for new-market ideation, the extent of newness for new-market innovative ideas is expressed as new unserved markets and new-market segments (rather than radical vs. incremental innovations). This is illustrated in worksheet 13-4. Also, see chapter 12 for the interpretation of the two terms *new unserved market* and *new-market segment*.

Worksheet 13-4. New-market ideation goals

*Name of functional unit:* Marketing department
**Name of unit:** New-markets unit
**Date:**
**Head of unit:**
**Category of products:** Existing products

## Ability to Formulate Innovation Goals | 143

| Part I<br>New-Unserved-Market Ideation Goals ||| 
|---|---|---|
| **Centered on three aspects:**<br>• Number of new-unserved-market ideas to be generated<br>• Number of new-unserved-market ideas to be undergoing development<br>• Number of new-unserved-market ideas to be launched |||
| **Number of new-unserved-market ideas to be generated** | **Number of new-unserved-market ideas to be undergoing development** | **Number of new-unserved-market ideas to be launched** |
| For instance:<br>• To generate five new-unserved-market ideas for the company's existing products between January and March of 2018 | • To have three new-unserved-market ideas undergoing development between January and March of 2018 | • To launch two new-unserved-market ideas between January and March of 2018 |
| **Number of new-unserved-market ideation goals set:** |||
| **Review date:** |||
| Part II<br>New-Market-Segment Ideation Goals |||
| **Centered on three aspects:**<br>• Number of new-market-segment ideas to be generated in an already-existing larger market<br>• Number of new-market-segment ideas to be undergoing development<br>• Number of new-market-segment ideas to be launched |||
| **Number of new-market-segment ideas to be generated** | **Number of new-market-segment ideas to be undergoing development** | **Number of new-market-segment ideas to be launched** |
| For instance:<br>• To generate five new-market-segment ideas for the company's existing products between January and March of 2018 | • To have three new-market-segment ideas undergoing development between January and March of 2018 | • To launch two new-market-segment ideas between January and March of 2018 |
| **Number of new-market-segment ideation goals set:** |||
| **Review date:** |||

As when creating innovation-challenge-questions worksheets, the format used for creating customer service innovation goals is in the context of the following three categories:
- Before-purchase customer service innovations
- During-purchase customer service innovations
- After-purchase customer service innovations

Worksheet 13-5 provides an example of how to formulate innovation goals for the customer service department.

Worksheet 13-5. Innovation goals for the customer service department

| Radical and Incremental Customer Service Innovation Goals |||
| --- | --- | --- |
| **Name of functional unit:** Customer service department<br>**Category of customer service:** Before-purchase customer service<br>**Date:**<br>**Head of unit:** |||
| **Part I**<br>**Before-Purchase Radical Customer Service Innovation Goals** |||
| **Centered on three aspects:**<br>• Number of before-purchase radical customer service innovation ideas to be generated<br>• Number of before-purchase radical customer service innovation ideas to be undergoing development<br>• Number of before-purchase radical customer service innovations to be launched |||
| Number of before-purchase radical customer service innovation ideas to be generated over a particular period | Number of before-purchase radical customer service innovation ideas to be undergoing development over a particular period | Number of before-purchase radical customer service innovations to be launched over a particular period |
| For instance:<br>• To generate five before-purchase radical customer service innovation ideas between January and March of 2018 | • To have three before-purchase radical customer service innovation ideas undergoing development between January and March of 2018 | • To launch two before-purchase radical customer service innovations between January and March of 2018 |
| **Number of before-purchase radical customer service innovation goals set:** |||
| **Review date:** |||
| **Part II**<br>**Before-Purchase Incremental Customer Service Innovation Goals** |||
| **Centered on three aspects:**<br>• Number of before-purchase incremental customer service innovation ideas to be generated<br>• Number of before-purchase incremental customer service innovation ideas to be undergoing development<br>• Number of before-purchase incremental customer service innovations to be launched |||
| Number of before-purchase incremental customer service innovation ideas to be generated over a particular period | Number of before-purchase incremental customer service innovation ideas to be undergoing development over a particular period | Number of before-purchase incremental customer service innovations to be launched over a particular period |

| For instance: <br> • To generate five before-purchase incremental customer service innovation ideas between January and March of 2018 | • To have three before-purchase incremental customer service innovation ideas undergoing development between January and March of 2018 | • To launch two before-purchase incremental customer service innovations between January and March of 2018 |
|---|---|---|
| **Number of before-purchase incremental customer service innovation goals set:** ||| 
| **Review date:** |||

### Support Units: Creating Innovation Goals for Support Functional Units

Part I of the book discussed in detail the role of support functional units in advancing the culture of innovation across the organization by developing and implementing different forms of innovation-support initiatives within the context of the activities of the support functional units. In addition, recall that the innovation-support initiatives are mainly aimed at advancing innovation in the core functional units on which the organization's growth and competitiveness depend. With that in mind, the innovation goal-setting approach for support functional units is categorized into two contexts: (1) innovation-support goals and (2) cost-saving innovation goals.

The two types of innovation goals for support functional units are defined as follows:

i. *Innovation-support goals*: These are types of innovation goals that are intended for developing and implementing various innovation-support initiatives aimed at creating a climate of innovation in all the functional units of the organization.

ii. *Cost-saving innovation goals:* These are types of innovation goals intended for generating and developing radical and incremental cost-saving innovation ideas in support functional units over a particular period.

To continue our example, we next need to formulate innovation-support goals and cost-saving innovation goals in the context of the support functional units of DM Personal Care Products, as follows:

- ❖ Procurement department
- ❖ HR department
- ❖ Finance and accounting department
- ❖ IT department
- ❖ Corporate affairs department

Worksheets 13-6 through 13-10 show how to formulate innovation goals for these support units. Each worksheet is divided into two parts: part I is for innovation-support goals, and part II is for cost-saving innovation goals.

146 | LEADERSHIP FOR INNOVATION

Worksheet 13-6. Innovation goals for the procurement department

**Procurement Innovation-Support Goals** (Part I) and
**Procurement Cost-Saving Innovation Goals** (Part II)

**Department:** Procurement department
**Date:**
**Head of department:**

### Part I
### Procurement Innovation-Support Goals

| Procurement functional components *(examples)* | Procurement innovation-support goals to be implemented in each procurement component over a particular period *(examples)* |
|---|---|
| Develop and implement purchasing and contract-management instructions, policies, and procedures | • To integrate innovation performance into the company's procurement contracts between January and March of 2018 |
| Locate vendors of supplies; interview them in order to determine product availability and terms of sale | • To locate vendors of supplies that are able to meet the company's respective innovation needs and aspirations between April and June of 2018 |
| Prepare reports regarding market conditions and merchandise costs | • To prepare and produce reports on the vendors with the ability to meet the company's innovation needs between July and August of 2018 |

**Number of procurement innovation-support goals set:**

**Review date:**

### Part II
### Radical and Incremental Procurement Cost-Saving Innovation Goals

| Radical Procurement Cost-Saving Innovation Goals | Incremental Procurement Cost-Saving Innovation Goals |
|---|---|
| | |

Ability to Formulate Innovation Goals | 147

| Number of radical procurement cost-saving innovation ideas to be generated within a particular period | Number of radical procurement cost-saving innovation ideas to be undergoing development within a particular period | Number of radical procurement cost-saving innovation ideas to be implemented within a particular period | Number of incremental procurement cost-saving innovation ideas to be generated within a particular period | Number of incremental procurement cost-saving innovation ideas to be undergoing development within a particular period | Number of incremental procurement cost-saving innovation ideas to be implemented within a particular period |
|---|---|---|---|---|---|
| For instance:<br>• To generate six radical procurement innovative ideas aimed at improving efficiency and reducing procurement-related costs by [X percent] between January and March of 2018 | • To have five radical procurement innovative ideas aimed at improving efficiency and reducing procurement-related costs by [X percent] undergoing development between January and March of 2018 | • To implement four radical procurement innovation ideas aimed at improving efficiency and reducing procurement-related costs by [X percent] between January and March of 2018 | • To generate ten incremental procurement innovative ideas aimed at improving efficiency and reducing procurement-related costs by [X percent] between January and March of 2018 | • To have seven incremental procurement innovative ideas aimed at improving efficiency and reducing procurement-related costs by [X percent] undergoing development between January and March of 2018 | • To implement four incremental procurement innovation ideas aimed at improving efficiency and reducing procurement-related costs by [X percent] between January and March of 2018 |

Number of radical and incremental procurement cost-saving innovation goals set:

Review date:

Worksheet 13-7. Innovation goals for the HR department

**HR Innovation-Support Goals (Part I) and**
**HR Cost-Saving Innovation Goals (Part II)**

Department: HR department
Date:
Head of department:

## Part I
### HR Innovation-Support Goals

| HR functional components *(examples)* | HR innovation-support goals to be implemented in each HR component over a particular period *(examples)* |
|---|---|
| Change management | • To implement at least three innovation engagement programs across the organization between January and February of 2018 |
| Recruitment and selection | • To implement a strategy for aligning innovation to the organization's recruitment and selection practices between April and May of 2018 |
| Workforce performance assessments | • To design and implement workforce innovation-performance evaluation across the organization between June and July of 2018 |
| Succession planning | • To design and implement innovation talent-succession planning across the organization between August and September of 2018 |

Number of HR innovation-support goals set per particular period:

Review date:

## Part II
### Radical and Incremental HR Cost-Saving Innovation Goals

| Radical HR cost-saving innovation goals | Incremental HR cost-saving innovation goals |
|---|---|
| | |

## Ability to Formulate Innovation Goals | 149

| Number of radical HR cost-saving innovation ideas be to generated within a particular period | Number of radical HR cost-saving innovation ideas to be undergoing development within a particular period | Number of radical HR cost-saving innovation ideas to be implemented within a particular period | Number of incremental HR cost-saving innovation ideas to be generated within a particular period | Number of incremental HR cost-saving innovation ideas to be undergoing development within a particular period | Number of incremental HR cost-saving innovation ideas to be implemented within a particular period |
|---|---|---|---|---|---|
| For instance: To generate six radical HR innovative ideas aimed at improving efficiency and reducing HR-related costs by [X percent] between January and March of 2018 | To have five radical HR innovative ideas aimed at improving efficiency and reducing HR-related costs by [X percent] undergoing development between January and March of 2018 | To implement four radical HR innovation ideas aimed at improving efficiency and reducing HR-related costs by [X percent] between January and March of 2018 | To generate ten incremental HR innovative ideas aimed at improving efficiency and reducing HR-related costs by [X percent] between January and March of 2018 | To have seven incremental HR innovative ideas aimed at improving efficiency and reducing HR-related costs by [X percent] undergoing development between January and March of 2018 | To implement four incremental HR innovation ideas aimed at improving efficiency and reducing HR-related costs by [X percent] between January and March of 2018 |
| Number of radical and incremental HR cost-saving innovation goals set: | | | | | |
| Review date: | | | | | |

Worksheet 13-8. Innovation goals for the finance and accounting department

**Accounting Innovation-Support Goals** (Part I) and
**Accounting Cost-Saving Innovation Goals** (Part II)

**Department:** Finance and accounting department
**Date:**
**Head of department:**

### Part I
### Accounting Innovation-Support Goals

| Accounting functional components *(examples)* | Accounting innovation-support goals to be implemented in each accounting component over a particular period *(examples)* |
|---|---|
| Reporting financial performance of the organization over a particular period | • To develop a framework for measuring and reporting the innovation performance of the organization between January and February of 2018<br>• To help four functional units design frameworks for measuring and reporting their innovation performance between March and May of 2018 |
| Advising on investment potential of projects | • To contribute toward designing a framework for assessing the investment and innovative potential of the innovation ideas between June and July of 2018 |
| Contributing toward designing reward frameworks | • To contribute toward designing a model for rewarding and recognizing the innovation performance of workforces between August and September of 2018 |
| Advising on the budgeting for innovation ideas | • To design a funding framework for funding innovation ideas between October and November of 2018 |

**Number of finance and accounting innovation-support goals set:**

**Review date:**

### Part II
### Radical and Incremental Accounting Cost-Saving Innovation Goals

| Radical Accounting Cost-Saving Innovation Goals | Incremental Accounting Cost-Saving Innovation Goals |
|---|---|
|  |  |

| Number of radical accounting cost-saving innovation ideas to be generated within a particular period | Number of radical accounting cost-saving innovation ideas to be undergoing development within a particular period | Number of radical accounting cost-saving innovation ideas to be implemented within a particular period | Number of incremental accounting cost-saving innovation ideas to be generated within a particular period | Number of incremental accounting cost-saving innovation ideas to be undergoing development within a particular period | Number of incremental accounting cost-saving innovation ideas to be implemented within a particular period |
|---|---|---|---|---|---|
| For instance: To generate six radical accounting innovative ideas aimed at improving efficiency and reducing accounting-related costs by [**X percent**] between January and March of 2018 | To have five radical accounting innovative ideas aimed at improving efficiency and reducing accounting-related costs by [**X percent**] undergoing development between January and March of 2018 | To implement four radical accounting innovation ideas aimed at improving efficiency and reducing accounting-related costs by [**X percent**] between January and March of 2018 | To generate ten incremental accounting innovative ideas aimed at improving efficiency and reducing accounting-related costs by [**X percent**] between January and March of 2018 | To have seven incremental accounting innovative ideas aimed at improving efficiency and reducing accounting-related costs by [**X percent**] undergoing development between January and March of 2018 | To implement four incremental accounting innovation ideas aimed at improving efficiency and reducing accounting-related costs by [**X percent**] between January and March of 2018 |

**Number of radical and incremental accounting cost-saving innovation goals set:**

**Review date:**

Worksheet 13-9. Innovation goals for the IT department

IT Innovation-Support Goals (Part I) and
IT Cost-Saving Innovation Goals (Part II)

Department: IT department
Date:
Head of department:

### Part I
### IT Innovation-Support Goals

| IT functional components *(examples)* | IT innovation-support goals to be implemented in each IT component over a particular period *(examples)* |
|---|---|
| Evaluation of system specifications for business requirements | • To review all innovation tools and resource capabilities of the organization between January and March of 2018 for the purpose of determining the kind of innovation-information package the IT unit can come up with as a contribution toward building an organization-wide innovation-support capability |
| Work closely with other functional units to prioritize business information needs | • To collaborate with other functional units between May and June of 2018 for the purpose of identifying their information needs and determining possibilities of setting up various intraorganizational information-resource systems to support advancement of innovation across the organization |
| Develop and implement efficient and cost-effective solutions | • To collaborate with other functional units and contribute, between July and August of 2018, at least five IT-related cost-effective and efficient ways of implementing and sustaining innovation-support programs |
| Implementation, support, and inventory control of applications used in the organization | • To create frameworks, between September and October of 2018, for storing various categories of innovation ideas:<br>  ○ Innovation ideas generated in various business clusters and functional units<br>  ○ Innovation ideas undergoing development<br>  ○ Innovations launched or implemented |

**Number of IT innovation-support goals set:**

**Review date:**

Ability to Formulate Innovation Goals | 153

## Part II
### Radical and Incremental IT Cost-Saving Innovation Goals

| Radical IT Cost-Saving Innovation Goals | | | Incremental IT Cost-Saving Innovation Goals | | |
|---|---|---|---|---|---|
| Number of radical IT cost-saving innovation ideas to be generated within a particular period | Number of radical IT cost-saving innovation ideas to be undergoing development within a particular period | Number of radical IT cost-saving innovation ideas to be implemented within a particular period | Number of incremental IT cost-saving innovation ideas to be generated within a particular period | Number of incremental IT cost-saving innovation ideas to be undergoing development within a particular period | Number of incremental IT cost-saving innovation ideas to be implemented within a particular period |
| For instance: To generate eight radical IT innovative ideas aimed at improving efficiency and reducing costs in various functional units of the organization by [X percent] between January and March of 2018 | To have six radical IT innovative ideas aimed at improving efficiency and reducing costs in various functional units of the organization by [X percent] undergoing development between January and March of 2018 | To implement eight radical IT innovation ideas aimed at improving efficiency and reducing costs in various functional units of the organization by [X percent] between January and March of 2018 | To generate ten incremental IT innovative ideas aimed at improving efficiency and reducing costs in various functional units of the organization by [X percent] between January and March of 2018 | To have seven incremental IT innovative ideas aimed at improving efficiency and reducing costs in various functional units of the organization by [X percent] undergoing development between January and March of 2018 | To implement five incremental IT innovation ideas aimed at improving efficiency and reducing costs in various functional units of the organization by [X percent] between January and March of 2018 |

**Number of radical and incremental IT cost-saving innovation goals set:**

**Review date:**

Worksheet 13-10. Innovation goals for the corporate affairs department

**Corporate Affairs Innovation-Support Goals** (Part I) and
**Corporate Affairs Cost-Saving Innovation Goals** (Part II)

**Department:** Corporate affairs department
**Date:**
**Head of department:**

## Part I
### Corporate Affairs Innovation-Support Goals

| Corporate affairs functional components<br>*(examples)* | Corporate affairs innovation-support goals to be implemented in each component over a particular period<br>*(examples)* |
|---|---|
| Represent the company's brand and reputation in public, through both oral and written communications | • To create five innovation slogans and catchphrases between January and February of 2018 aimed at publicizing the company's innovation culture to the outside world |
| Work with other functional-unit teams to develop effective internal communication strategies | • To develop, in collaboration with other functional units, two innovation engagement initiatives between March and June of 2018, as follows:<br>  o To come up with a documentary on the vision of the company and how the company has made innovation performance a key component in realizing its vision<br>  o To record and produce video statements of the company's top leadership on various aspects of how they are supporting and steering innovation performance across the organization |
| Develop and implement strategic initiatives that promote the company and the industry's position on important public policy issues | • To come up with one media program between May and July of 2018 aimed at complementing government efforts to promote innovative thinking in colleges and universities |
| Champion the company's values and the highest ethical standards in the conduct of its business to the outside world | • To create five innovation-focused illustrations between March and April of 2018 aimed at publicizing the innovation culture of the company to the outside world |

Ability to Formulate Innovation Goals | 155

| Number of corporate affairs innovation-support goals set: |
|---|

**Review date:**

### Part II
### Radical and Incremental Corporate Affairs Cost-Saving Innovation Goals

| Radical Corporate Affairs Cost-Saving Innovation Goals | | Incremental Corporate Affairs Cost-Saving Innovation Goals | |
|---|---|---|---|
| Number of radical corporate affairs cost-saving innovation ideas to be generated within a particular period | Number of radical corporate affairs cost-saving innovation ideas to be implemented within a particular period | Number of incremental corporate affairs cost-saving innovation ideas to be generated within a particular period | Number of incremental corporate affairs cost-saving innovation ideas to be implemented within a particular period |
| For instance: To generate six corporate affairs radical innovative ideas aimed at improving efficiency and reducing corporate affairs–related costs by [**X percent**] between January and March of 2018 | To have five radical corporate affairs innovative ideas aimed at improving efficiency and reducing corporate affairs–related costs by [**X percent**] undergoing development between January and March of 2018 | Number of incremental corporate affairs cost-saving innovation ideas to be undergoing development within a particular period | Number of incremental corporate affairs cost-saving innovation ideas to be implemented within a particular period |
| | To implement four radical corporate affairs innovation ideas aimed at improving efficiency and reducing corporate affairs–related costs by [**X percent**] between January and March of 2018 | To generate ten incremental corporate affairs innovative ideas aimed at improving efficiency and reducing corporate affairs–related costs by [**X percent**] between January and March of 2018 | To have seven incremental corporate affairs innovative ideas aimed at improving efficiency and reducing corporate affairs–related costs by [**X percent**] undergoing development between January and March of 2018 | To implement four incremental corporate affairs innovation ideas aimed at improving efficiency and reducing corporate affairs–related costs by [**X percent**] between January and March of 2018 |

**Number of radical and incremental corporate affairs cost-saving innovation goals set:**

**Review date:**

## CHAPTER 14
# ABILITY TO DESIGN AND IMPLEMENT AN EFFECTIVE MANAGEMENT SYSTEM FOR INNOVATION IDEAS

As I was writing this book, I was also working on a small invention idea called the CT Holder, as mentioned earlier. I contracted a renowned US invention consulting firm to conduct a detailed analysis and provide me with specific advice regarding the investment potential of the CT Holder. My conversations with the consulting firm grew beyond the CT Holder project. I would chat with the team that was assigned to assess the CT Holder project, generally, about product development and the importance of an effective idea-assessment process and why most invention ideas or innovation ideas do not make it on the market: once launched on the market, they fail to meet customer expectations and become a flop. Further, study after study has observed the importance of an effective innovation-idea management system for not only the success of innovation ideas but also, overall, for building a sustainable climate for innovation. For instance, a report titled *"Literature Review of Idea Management"* (by Anna Rose Vagn Jensen) published in proceeding of NordDesign Conference, in 2012 by Aalborg University, Denmark, outlines various studies and reports on idea management. Therefore, this area is a must-have ability for organizational leaders who want to play a role in not only making innovation a key part of the organization's business strategy but also every employee's job. So the sixth example of innovation management skill is the ability of organizational leaders to design, implement, and sustain an effective innovation-idea management system across functional units

# An Effective Management System for Innovation Ideas | 157

Usually, innovation-idea management systems have lots of moving parts. This book tries to simplify the framework as much as possible by dividing the topic into the following aspects: (1) the definition of *innovation-idea management system*, (2) the importance of innovation-idea management systems, (3) innovation-idea management committees, and (4) aspects of the innovation-idea management framework.

## 1. The Definition of *Innovation-Idea Management System*

An innovation-idea management system is defined as an organizational process that involves creating tools, techniques, and procedures for assessing and developing, on a continual basis, innovative ideas into solutions that contribute monetary value to the organization.

## 2. The Importance of Innovation-Idea Management Systems

Why is the innovation-idea management system important? The following are three reasons:

i. Unless they are assessed and developed, innovation ideas are worthless. It's often said that human progress depends on ideas. Although the accuracy of this statement is indisputable—clearly, human progress has always been driven by ideas—it's important to bear in mind that unless they are developed, ideas cannot bring about human progress. In short, raw ideas cannot bring about human advancement. To harness ideas to bring about human development, ideas have to be developed, and at the core of an idea-development exercise is an effective assessment process to ensure that only ideas with a high potential for generating the intended results are developed. In relation to the context of an organization, one could say that although the growth of any organization depends on ideas, unless they are developed into something that adds value to the organization's cause, innovation ideas by themselves cannot grow or advance an organization. As the old saying goes, "Clever business ideas that cannot be commercialized are nothing more than dead trees." This concept underpins the importance of building effective innovation-idea-development systems for developing ideas into solutions to fix problems/needs and contribute monetary value, growth, and competitiveness to an organization.

From the foregoing discussion, we can see how important it is for leaders to possess the ability to design and manage an innovation-idea management system because innovation performance and the culture of innovation depend on the ability to translate the innovative ideas into the intended results. What this means is that without the ability and institutional capability to translate the ideas, the whole mission of advancing innovation will be rendered unattainable because innovative ideas represent the core lifeline for innovation performance.

ii. It is difficult to determine the investment potential of innovation ideas. Without an effective innovation-idea management system, an organization would end up developing ideas that have little or no potential to make it on the market. For instance, as mentioned earlier, there is a cliché around Silicon Valley, California, that only one out of one hundred patented invention products makes it on the market, indicative of the fact that many ideas fail to make it. Numerous other factors contribute to the success or failure of an innovation on the market, but if we were to rate the significance of the innovation-idea management system to innovation success on, say, a scale of 1 to 5, with 5 being the highest in significance, we would put it at 5 to denote its importance. That's how vital an innovation-idea management system is. In an interview with the *Wall Street Journal* in November 2015 on the role of CFOs in fostering innovation, Deloitte chief innovation officer John Levis emphasized the importance of an effective innovation-idea management process in sustaining an innovation culture in an organization. "Coming into this role," Levis said, "I expected the biggest challenge to be generating new ideas because being an innovative company requires generating a lot of new ideas on a sustainable basis. I was completely wrong about that; we had no problem with ideation. Instead," he said, "the real challenge was figuring out a process to evaluate the many ideas being proposed so that the truly top-shelf ideas could be advanced." This and many other reasons underscore the importance of organizational leaders having the necessary abilities and competencies to design and implement an innovation-idea management system.

iii. The system could be harnessed as a motivating factor for workforces to generate innovation ideas. A number of studies and analysts have pointed out that one of the reasons for workforces' lack of ability to innovate is because many organizations do not have effective innovation-idea management systems. The impact of a lack of an effective innovation-idea management system is that it discourages workforces from participating in generating innovation ideas. Multiple reports and analysts have observed that no matter how much you encourage workforces to innovate, they will not be forthcoming if an organization does not have an effective innovation-idea management procedure. The foregoing underpins how vital innovation-idea management skills are to innovation leadership and management.

## 3. Innovation-Idea Management Committees

Developing a system aimed at scaling ideation across all functional units requires approaches that will help to effectively manage the large volumes of diverse ideas from workforces across the organization, especially huge organizations with hundreds of thousands of employees. One approach is for the top leadership to ensure that the organization has a corporate-wide innovation-idea management system that encourages the participation of workforces in the generation of innovative ideas and also ensures that workforces get involved in managing the innovation-idea management system. One of the approaches for ensuring the participation of workforces in managing the innovation-idea pipeline of the organization is the formation of various innovation-idea management committees, whose composition should be as diverse as possible in terms of seniority of employees and functional representation.

*What Are Innovation-Idea Management Committees?*
Innovation-idea management committees are collaborative groups established within an organization to contribute toward establishing and sustaining an efficient and effective organization-wide innovation-idea management system so that the organization can have a fit-for-purpose system for receiving, assessing, developing, and launching/implementing innovative ideas that add meaningful commercial value to the organization.

# An Effective Management System for Innovation Ideas | 159

*Implementation Plan for Creating Committees*
The starting point for establishing innovation-idea management committees is figuring out who will be responsible for establishing the committees. The CEO and other C-suite executives should form a task force to be charged with the responsibility of creating various innovation-idea management committees across functional units and divisions. For instance, the task force could be referred to as the task force for creating innovation-idea committees (TCIIC). For credibility purposes and to show top-leadership support, the chairperson of the task force should be nominated by the CEO and his or her C-suite executives. In terms of functions, the top leadership could be responsible for outlining terms of reference and detailing the functions of the TCIIC. Some of the functions could include the following:

- Creating an action plan for establishing various innovation-idea management committees
- Ensuring that the TCIIC constantly collaborates and confers with the innovation-idea management committees to ensure that each of the groups has put in place their respective structures and functions within the scope of their objectives
- Reporting periodically to the CEO and the top leadership of the organization regarding the following:
  - Status of formation of various innovation-idea management committees
  - How far each of the committees has progressed in drafting its functions
- Creating a consolidated manual containing the following aspects:
  - The structure of all the innovation-idea management committees of the organization
  - The functions of each innovation-idea management committee
  - An outline and visual illustration of various procedures and processes pertaining to the organization's innovation-idea management system

*Illustration: Creating Innovation-Idea Management Committees*
Suppose we wish to come up with a task force for creating various innovation-idea management committees in the core and support functional units of DM Personal Care Products, the fictitious company introduced earlier. The first step is to outline the functional units and the business segments, as follows:

*Core functional units*
- Product-development unit, with the following segments:
  - Body-lotions segment
  - Skin-cleansing segment
  - Hair-care segment
  - Hand-washing segment
- Manufacturing-processes department
- Marketing department, with the following units:
  - Pricing unit
  - Product-promotion unit
  - Product-delivery unit

- o New-markets unit
- o Packaging unit
- ❖ Customer service department

*Support functional units*
- ❖ Procurement department
- ❖ HR department
- ❖ Finance and accounting department
- ❖ IT department
- ❖ Corporate affairs department

The second step is to create an action plan for establishing various innovation-idea management committees across functional units. Worksheet 14-1 is a sample worksheet for creating an action plan to establish innovation-idea management committees. The worksheet is divided into two parts: part I is for the activities to create committees responsible for formulating *innovation-idea submission* and *innovation-idea self-assessment procedures*, and part II is for creating committees for each of the five stages of the innovation-development process, listed as follows:
- o Innovation-idea reception
- o Innovation-idea assessment
- o Innovation development
- o Innovation launch/implementation
- o Post-launch/post-implementation evaluations

Worksheet 14-1. Example of action plan for creating innovation-idea management committees

| Part I |   |   |   |
|---|---|---|---|
| **Objectives:** To create a committee responsible for designing two procedures:<br>• Innovation-idea submission process<br>• Innovation-idea self-assessment process ||||
| **Activities to be undertaken** | **Actionable time frame for commencement and completion of each activity** | **Team responsible for undertaking the task** | **Output:** Expected work to be produced as a result of the activities |
| To create a committee responsible for formulating the innovation-idea submission and innovation-idea self-assessment processes | [**Note appropriate time frame**] | Task force for creating innovation-idea committees | Formation of the innovation-idea submission and self-assessment processes committee |

# An Effective Management System for Innovation Ideas | 161

| Part II | | | |
|---|---|---|---|
| **Objective:** To create committees for each of the five stages of the innovation-development process, as follows:<br>• Innovation-idea reception committees<br>• Innovation-idea assessment committees<br>• Innovation-development committee<br>• Innovation-launch committee<br>• Post-launch/post-implementation-evaluations committee | | | |
| **Activities to be undertaken** | **Actionable time frame for commencement and completion of each activity** | **Team responsible for undertaking the task** | **Output:** Expected work to be produced as a result of the activities |
| To create the innovation-idea reception committee | **[Note appropriate time frame]** | Task force for creating innovation-idea committees | Formation of the innovation-idea reception committee |
| To create the product innovation-idea assessment committees | **[Note appropriate time frame]** | Task force for creating innovation-idea committees | Formation of respective product innovation-idea assessment committees |
| To create manufacturing-processes innovation-idea assessment committees | **[Note appropriate time frame]** | Task force for creating innovation-idea committees | Formation of respective manufacturing-processes innovation-idea assessment committees |
| To create marketing-strategy innovation-idea assessment committees | **[Note appropriate time frame]** | Task force for creating innovation-idea committees | Formation of respective marketing-strategy innovation-idea assessment committees |
| To create customer service innovation-idea assessment committees | **[Note appropriate time frame]** | Task force for creating innovation-idea committees | Formation of respective customer service innovation-idea assessment committees |
| To create innovation-development committees | **[Note appropriate time frame]** | Task force for creating innovation-idea committees | Formation of respective innovation-development committees |
| To create innovation-launch/implementation committees | **[Note appropriate time frame]** | Task force for creating innovation-idea committees | Formation of respective innovation-launch/implementation committees |

| To create post-launch/post-implementation-evaluation committees | [**Note appropriate time frame**] | Task force for creating innovation-idea committees | Formation of post-launch/post-implementation-evaluation committees |

**Innovation-idea management committees for support functional units**

Earlier, we indicated that innovation ideas in support functional units are aimed at cost-saving purposes.

Thus, there should be a committee or committees to exclusively deal with cost-saving innovation ideas for support functional units. The formation of a cost-saving innovation-idea management committee or committees should be included in the action plan as follows:

| **Activity to be undertaken** | **Actionable time frame for commencement and completion of activity** | **Team responsible for undertaking the task** | **Output:** Expected work to be produced as a result of the activity |
|---|---|---|---|
| To create innovation-idea management committees (and subcommittees) for support functional units | [**Note appropriate time frame**] | Task force for creating innovation-idea committees | Formation of innovation-idea management committees (and subcommittees) for support functional units |

Innovation-idea management committees (and subcommittees) could be formed for each of the support functional units (e.g., HR, procurement, IT, etc.).

*Functions of Innovation-Idea Management Committees*

As previously stated, one of the roles of the TCIIC is ensuring that all the various committees have clear functional roles. This necessitates the following:

o All innovation-idea management committees should collaborate with the TCIIC when formulating committee functions.

o All the proposed functions of each committee and other guidelines pertaining to the innovation-idea management process across the organization should be compiled into a manual to guide workforces about the organization's innovation-idea management system. The manual should be written and illustrated in simple and clear language that all workforces can understand. As a sign of involvement and support from the top leadership, the manual should be reviewed and approved for use by the CEO of the organization.

*Disbanding the Task Force for Creating Innovation-Idea Committees*

Once the essential aspects of the organization's innovation-idea management framework are up and running in terms of the respective committees and the creation of the manual (i.e., describing the structure and functions of committees and the processes and procedures of the organization-wide innovation-idea management system), the TCIIC can be disbanded. Once disbanded, a mechanism should be put in place to ensure that

An Effective Management System for Innovation Ideas | 163

the innovation-idea management system is continually effective. One such mechanism of ensuring effective continuity is to have periodic reviews and evaluations of the organization's innovation-idea management system. In addition, performance reviews of all the innovation-idea management committees will need to be undertaken from time to time. An ad hoc committee could be established to undertake such reviews. The frequency of reviews should be stated in the organization's innovation-idea-management-system manual. The periodic review of the innovation-idea management system could take place every three, six, or twelve months depending on what the leadership deems fitting. Also, reasons or factors that would trigger periodic reviews should be outlined in the manual.

### 4. Aspects of the Innovation-Idea Management Framework

In order to build a sustainable and effective innovation-idea management system, the CEO and the C-suite executives should ensure that the organization implements the right framework. The question then would be, *What kind of aspects should one include in the organization's innovation-idea management framework to make it implementable and effective?*

This section suggests a number of tools and techniques that can contribute to developing and sustaining an effective and replicable crosscutting innovation-idea management system. The framework is based on the following: (1) experience from my CT Holder invention idea-assessment process, (2) experience from training and consulting engagements with a number of organizations in various countries, and (3) inquiries and information gathered from some US companies.

Aspects included in the framework are as follows:

i. Innovation-idea preliminary self-assessment
ii. Innovation-idea submission process
iii. Innovation-development process, which includes the following aspects:
    o Stage 1: Innovation-idea reception procedure
    o Stage 2: Innovation-idea assessment process
    o Stage 3: Innovation-development pipeline
    o Stage 4: Innovation launch or implementation
iv. Post-launch/post-implementation evaluation

Figure 14-1 provides a simple summary of the components or stages of the innovation-idea management framework.

## 164 | LEADERSHIP FOR INNOVATION

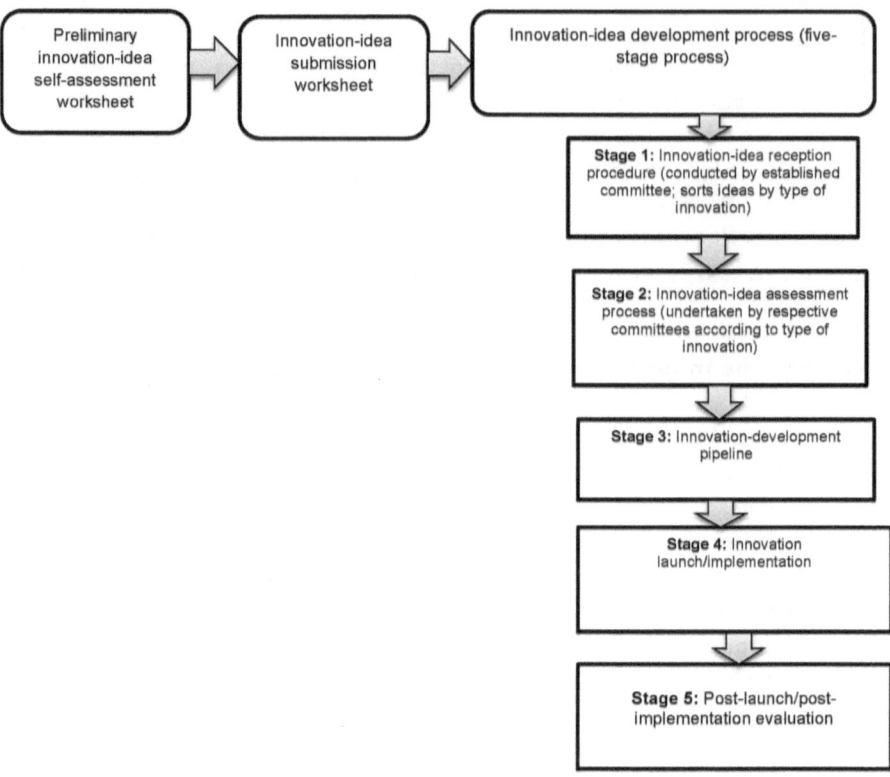

*Figure 14-1. Innovation-idea management framework*

Each of the aspects is described in more detail as follows:

i. **Creating the preliminary innovation-idea self-assessment process:** What is the preliminary innovation-idea self-assessment? It is a tool that employees can apply to conduct an initial assessment of an innovation idea they have generated to determine whether the idea is innovative enough and has investment potential before submitting it for further assessment.

The preliminary innovation-idea self-assessment is one of the vital components or stages of the innovation-idea management for the following five reasons:

- o First, it helps workforces to understand what constitutes an innovative idea—because not every idea is innovative. By subjecting their ideas to the initial self-assessment, they will understand the characteristics of an innovative idea because the self-assessment has embedded checkpoints that are useful for determining whether an idea is indeed innovative.
- o Second, it gives workforces an initial indication of whether an innovation idea has the potential to be developed into an innovation and is therefore worth pursuing—that is, whether the idea is actionable in the sense that it can actually be developed with the organization's resources.

# An Effective Management System for Innovation Ideas | 165

- o Third, it helps in preventing innovation-idea management committees from being inundated with noninnovative ideas or ideas with insignificant investment potential, thereby freeing space and time for potential innovation ideas.
- o Fourth, it contributes to sustaining an efficient idea-assessment process because most ideas that will be received or submitted for assessment will have gone through an initial vetting process, therefore cutting down on delays for releasing the idea-assessment results (in terms of ideas that have progressed to the next stage) determined by various idea-assessment committees.
- o Fifth, as mentioned earlier, it is often said that only one out of one hundred invention ideas makes it on the market, so conducting an initial assessment of innovative ideas encourages workforces to submit ideas that have a chance of being progressed and considered for further development.

*Aspects to Include When Creating Criteria for the Preliminary Innovation-Idea Self-Assessment Process*

To ensure that the preliminary innovation-idea self-assessment process is fit for its purpose, it's important to include relevant aspects that will help workforces have an initial indication of whether an idea is, indeed, innovative and has investment potential. The following are some of the questions that could be included in the preliminary innovation-idea self-assessment:

- o What purpose will the innovation idea uniquely fulfill that is not being fulfilled by the existing products, services, processes, marketing strategies, or customer service functions?
- o What gap does the innovation idea seek to fill that the existing products, services, processes, marketing strategies, and customer service functions are not addressing effectively?
- o What problem does the innovation idea seek to fix that the market has failed to identify or is not fixing effectively?
- o If it's a cost-saving innovation idea to be implemented in any of the organization's support functional units, what costs does the innovation idea seek to save?
- o What improvements does the innovation idea seek to contribute?
- o How will the innovation idea contribute to the monetary goals of the organization?
- o Is the innovation idea environmentally friendly?
- o What safety risks does the innovation idea pose? How will the risks be mitigated?
- o Development time line: Will the innovation idea take a reasonable time to implement or bring to the market, or does it potentially have a longer time line?

Worksheet 14-2 is an example of a preliminary innovation-idea self-assessment worksheet.

Worksheet 14-2. Preliminary innovation-idea self-assessment

| |
|---|
| Functional purpose: *What functional purpose will the innovation idea fulfill?* |
| Need: What need or problem does the innovation idea seek to solve that is not being addressed effectively by the organization? |
| Problem: What problem does the innovation idea seek to fix that the market has failed to identify or is not fixing effectively? |
| Monetary value: How will the innovation idea contribute to the monetary goals of the organization? Is the return worth the investment? Is the cost of investment reasonable? |
| Environment: Is the innovation idea environmentally friendly? |
| Safety issues: What safety risks does the innovation idea pose? How will the risks be mitigated? |
| Development time line: Will the innovation idea take a reasonable time to implement or bring to the market? |

| | |
|---|---|
| Name(s) and department(s) of employee(s) who generated the innovation idea: | |
| Date of the initial idea self-assessment: | |

**Note:** An earlier suggestion was to create committees to exclusively deal with cost-saving innovation ideas for support functional units; similarly, preliminary innovation-idea self-assessment processes for cost-saving innovation ideas generated in support functional units could also be created.

ii. **Innovation-Idea Submission Process**

The second stage is innovation-idea submission, which is defined as a stage designed for workforces to outline an innovation-idea proposal and, once the idea is outlined, submit it to the respective committee for further assessment.

What purpose does the innovation-idea submission serve? According to my experience with organizations, one of the most common innovation-capability weaknesses in many organizations is the lack of an appropriate process that workforces can use to submit their innovation ideas to the relevant system for determination. And analysts in idea management have often cited the lack of a submission process as one of the factors responsible for the lack of meaningful ideation in many companies. Certainly, employees wouldn't have much incentive to generate innovation ideas if an organization had no clear process for submitting such ideas. The following are three reasons why the innovation-idea submission process is important:

- o First, it provides workforces with a convenient and orderly procedure for submitting innovation ideas to the organizational leadership.
- o Second, it encourages workforces to generate innovation ideas because they know there is a system to attend to their ideas.

# An Effective Management System for Innovation Ideas | 167

  o  Third, it encourages workforces to submit ideas that specifically focus on meeting a need or solving a problem innovatively.

Worksheet 14-3 provides a sample innovation-idea submission worksheet.

Worksheet 14-3. Innovation-idea submission

| What is the category of the innovation idea?<br>Choose one of the following:<br>❑ **Product/service**<br>❑ **Process** (manufacturing or service production processes)<br>❑ **Market strategy**<br>❑ **Customer service**<br>*(Check appropriate box.)* ||
|---|---|
| What type of innovation idea is it? | **Examples of classifying innovation ideas**<br>For the service segments of an insurance company, the types of innovation ideas could be categorized as follows:<br>• Home-insurance services (*home-insurance innovation ideas*)<br>• Business-insurance services (*business-insurance innovation ideas*)<br>• Travel-insurance services (*travel-insurance innovation ideas*)<br>• Motor vehicle–insurance services (*motor vehicle–insurance innovation ideas*)<br>*Process innovation:* service-production-process innovation ideas, service-delivery innovation ideas, etc.<br>*Marketing innovation:* promotion innovation ideas, pricing innovation ideas, packaging innovation ideas, etc.<br>*Customer service innovation:* innovation ideas focused on customer service segments |
| Describe your innovation idea. What is it? ||
| What need or problem does your innovation idea seek to fix? ||
| What innovation degree is the idea (radical or incremental)? ||
| How will the innovation idea fix the identified need or problem? ||
| What benefits will your innovation idea contribute to the organization and/or its clients and the community? ||
| What advantage(s) does the innovation idea have over existing ideas? ||
| How will the innovation idea contribute or add commercial value to the organization? ||

| Name(s) and department(s) of employee(s) who have sponsored the innovation idea: | |
|---|---|
| Date of submission: | |
| What are the comments and decision of the relevant idea assessment committee?<br>Options:<br>❖ Proceed for further assessment<br>❖ Reject<br>❖ Put on hold | |

There are two things to bear in mind regarding creating innovation-idea submission worksheets:

- o First, the committee responsible for creating idea-submission worksheets could create different submission worksheets for each functional unit or type of innovation.
- o Second, the committee could also create two types of submission worksheets—that is, one for assessing revenue generation–focused innovation ideas and one for assessing cost-saving innovation ideas for support functional units.

The next question is, *What factors should one take into account when formulating the preliminary innovation-idea self-assessment and innovation-idea submission processes?* Five considerations that should be taken into account are as follows:

- o *Type and nature of the organization's industry:* Some industries, such as pharmaceuticals, food, and cosmetics, have rigorous innovation-idea assessment processes because the nature of the industry demands very high safety standards and effectiveness. Because of this, innovation-idea assessment processes (especially for pharmaceutical products) are rigorous, and it often takes years before a new product is on the market. According to a statement by the US Food and Drug Administration (FDA), when a company develops a drug, it undergoes about three and a half years of laboratory testing before an application is made to the FDA to begin testing the drug in humans, and that's just part of the lengthy FDA review and clearance process. The purpose of the lengthy review process is to prevent companies from launching potentially injurious and dangerous products. For instance, in 2005, the drug maker Biogen and Elan introduced a drug for multiple sclerosis called Tysabri. Within three months of the drug's launch on the market, two deaths were linked to the drug, and the drug was pulled from the market. As a result of the two deaths, Biogen and Elan was plunged into a crisis.

- *Type of innovation idea*: As stated before, there are different types of innovation ideas. Thus, based on the differences among the types of innovation, there are certain factors that need to be considered when formulating preliminary innovation-idea self-assessment and innovation-idea submission processes so that the processes can be effective for the different types of innovation ideas.
- *Degree of perceived risk in return on investment:* The core purpose of pursuing any innovation idea is to realize the expected monetary-value return. However, in order to realize the return, the company needs to invest the level of resources commensurate with the type and degree of the innovation idea. Thus, the risk aspect should be included in the preliminary innovation-idea self-assessment and innovation-idea submission processes and phrased in a manner aimed at effectively eliciting the required risk aspects from the innovation idea under assessment.
- *Level of regulation*: This point is similar to the first one. Naturally, every industry is regulated in one way or another, and industry regulation takes many forms. Also, as stated in the first point, the intensity of regulation depends on the nature of the industry. Because of their nature, some industries have multiple layers of regulation. That is, some industries are subjected to sectoral regulatory regimes promulgated by a government authority, as well as self-regulation approaches by industry associations. The point here is that when formulating preliminary innovation-idea self-assessment and innovation-idea submission processes, the innovation-idea assessment factors that are adopted to be included in the assessment process should take into account the rigorous regulatory nature of the industry.
- *Degree of innovation idea*: The context of this point is that the extent of newness of the innovation idea plays a role when formulating innovation-idea assessment factors. For example, because of the level of investment that is usually required to develop radical innovation ideas, radical ideas tend to be subjected to a rigorous set of assessment factors. Conversely, incremental innovation ideas are not usually subjected to the same assessment factors and level of scrutiny as radical innovation ideas. Thus, the innovation degree must be taken into account when formulating innovation-idea assessment factors.

iii. **Creating the Innovation-Development Process**

The third component of the innovation-idea management system is the innovation-development process. What is an innovation-development process? It is a procedure that involves assessing innovation ideas and making decisions for progressing innovative ideas from conception through development to the full launch or implementation of an innovation.

In other words, an innovation-development process is an integration of assessment and development stages and activities used to develop or translate an innovative idea into an innovation.

The second question would be, *Where does the innovation-development process begin?* As outlined earlier, the process starts with preliminary self-assessment by employees. Once employees take their innovation ideas through a preliminary innovation-idea self-assessment process and are convinced that their ideas could be considered for further strategic development, the next step is submitting the innovation ideas to the relevant committee for a painstaking due-diligence process and onward development of an innovation.

The most common name used to describe the process of developing ideas into innovations is called the *stage-gate* model. The model was created by Dr. Robert Cooper of McMaster University in Canada. Adopted by many companies around the globe, the stage-gate model is a technique in which an idea-development process is divided into *stages* separated by what are referred to as *gates*. And each gate has criteria or factors used by a steering committee to progress the idea to the next stage of development.

This book suggests an innovation-development process that comprises the following components or stages:
1. Innovation-idea reception procedure
2. Innovation-idea assessment process
3. Innovation project teams
4. Guidelines for creating innovation project teams
5. Innovation-development stage
6. Innovation launch/implementation

Each of these components is described in the following subsections.

## 1. Innovation-Idea Reception Procedure

The innovation-idea reception procedure is the first component of the innovation-development process. *What does it involve?* Once an employee describes his or her innovation idea using the *innovation-idea submission worksheet*, the next stage involves submitting the worksheet to an *innovation-idea reception committee* (IIRC) for determination and onward progression.

Because handling "raw ideas" or unpatented innovation ideas is one of the most delicate tasks, with potential legal and rights-ownership implications, the CEO and top leadership of the organization, through relevant committees or offices, should ensure that the IIRC is supported with the formulation of guidelines for managing the innovation-idea reception procedure. Given the intricacies of ownership implications, the organization's legal team should be involved in drafting the ownership and confidentiality guidelines, which should eventually be approved by the organization's C-suite leadership and the board and adopted as part of the innovation-idea management policy. Some of the aspects that could be included in the innovation-idea reception procedure are as follows:

- o *Certificate of idea submission:* This should be written in the form of a guidelines manual and issued to all workforces. The document should outline the various processes involved in the organization's innovation-development process.

# An Effective Management System for Innovation Ideas | 171

- *Confidentiality statement:* This statement should be phrased in a way that informs and guides workforces about the level of confidentiality they are expected to exercise pertaining to any idea under consideration and the expiry of such confidentiality. The confidentiality statement should be signed by both parties (the employee[s] and the receiving party, in this case, the IIRC).
- *Idea-ownership acknowledgment statement:* The purpose of this statement is for workforces to acknowledge that innovation ideas submitted for assessment and eventual development will remain the property of the organization unless under certain circumstances, such as the following:
  - If the idea is withdrawn from the innovation-development process by the employee(s) who generated the idea or by the organization
  - If the idea does not make it through the innovation-idea assessment procedure or does not qualify for *idea storage* (for future consideration)

Figure 14-2 provides an example of a simple innovation-idea reception process, with the following steps: *(See figure 14.2 on next page.)*

- Step 1: Ideas are received and sorted according to the types of innovation ideas
- Step 2: Ideas are stored in the innovation-idea database facilities
- Step 3: Ideas are conveyed to respective innovation-idea assessment committees for further determination

## Innovation-Idea Database

What is an innovation-idea database? It is a kind of idea-storage facility for innovation ideas awaiting transmission to respective innovation-idea assessment procedures. To enable easy management of the database, it should be designed in a simple manner. One of the aspects to bear in mind when designing the database is categorizing it according to *types of innovation ideas* and *degree of innovation ideas.*

The IIRC, whose composition should have a representation of the top leadership, should be responsible for the storage of ideas. The organization's IT functional unit should be responsible for the establishment of the innovation-idea database, under the supervision of a senior executive. This task could also be outsourced.

*Uses of Innovation-Idea Database*

The uses of the innovation-idea database may vary depending on the type of framework that the leadership prefers to adopt. In most cases, the innovation-idea database serves three purposes: (1) storing innovation ideas awaiting assessment, (2) storing rejected ideas, and (3) storing ideas that have been put on hold for future consideration.

Worksheet 14-4 is a sample of an action plan worksheet for creating an innovation-idea database.

172 | **LEADERSHIP FOR INNOVATION**

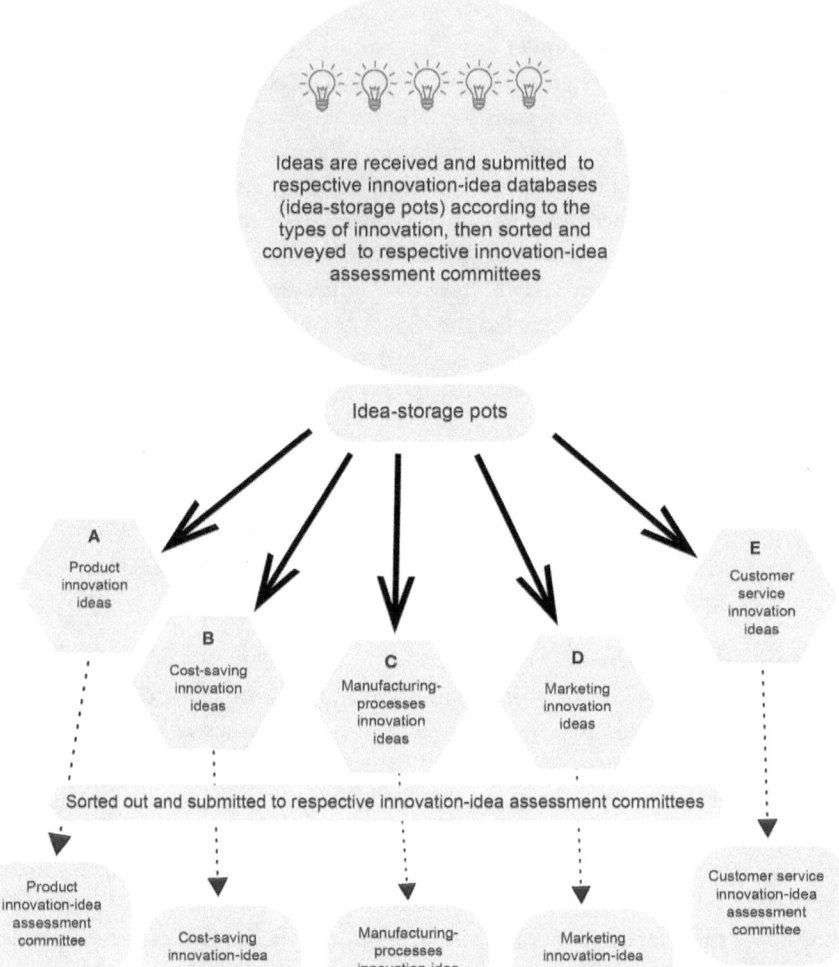

*Figure 14-2. Innovation-dea reception process*

Worksheet 14-4. Action plan for creating innovation-idea database

| **Objective:** To create an innovation-idea database for three purposes: (1) storing innovation ideas awaiting assessment, (2) storing innovation ideas that have been put on hold for future consideration, and (3) storing rejected ideas ||||
|---|---|---|---|
| **Activities:** List of activities leading to creating the innovation-idea database | **Time frame:** The actionable time line when each activity shall be conducted | **Who:** Individuals or subcommittee who will be responsible for undertaking each activity | **Output:** A completed innovation-idea database |

|  |  |  |  |
|--|--|--|--|
|  |  |  |  |
|  |  |  |  |
|  |  |  |  |
|  |  |  |  |
|  |  |  |  |

| Evaluation: Identify the dates for conducting evaluations to determine how this action plan is progressing. ||||
|---|---|---|---|
| Date: | Date: | Date: | Date: |
| State aspects that will be evaluated on this date. | State aspects that will be evaluated on this date. | State aspects that will be evaluated on this date. | State aspects that will be evaluated on this date. |

## 2. Innovation-Idea Assessment Process

The second component of the innovation-development process is the *innovation-idea assessment process,* which is defined as a stage or component of the overall innovation-development process that consists of a series of factors used as criteria for determining the innovative and investment potential of ideas submitted by workforces.

*Who should conduct the innovation-idea assessment process?* The recommended method is that it should be undertaken by innovation-idea assessment committees categorized by type of innovation idea. Numerous aspects are involved in the innovation-idea assessment process:

- o Formation of innovation-idea assessment committees
- o Formation of special ad hoc assessment committees
- o Ensuring that innovation-idea assessment processes are effective
- o Functions of innovation-idea assessment committees
- o Factors to include in the innovation-idea assessment process
- o Aspects to consider when creating idea-progression valves
- o Action plans for creating innovation-idea assessment processes
- o Creating schedules for assessing innovation ideas
- o Reviewing and updating the innovation-idea assessment process
- o Aspects to consider when creating the innovation-idea assessment process
  Each of the above is described in the following subsections.

- o *Formation of innovation-idea assessment committees*
  As indicated earlier, one way of systemizing innovation across the organization is ensuring that the top leadership leads in implementing systems that not only encourage and allow participation of workforces through generation of innovation ideas but also ensure that a large portion of workforces take part in managing the system that contributes to sustaining the organization's innovation pipeline. One of the approaches for accomplishing this is the formation of diverse innovation-idea assessment committees across functional units.

The CEO should ensure that the organization has simple and clear guidelines on how the innovation-idea assessment committees shall be created, and the guidelines should emphasize diversity in composition.

Some of the innovation-idea assessment committees could include the following:

- Product innovation-idea assessment committee (and perhaps also subcommittees to assess different types of product innovation ideas)
- Process innovation-idea assessment committee (perhaps numerous committees for various process innovation ideas depending on the nature of the processes of an organization, e.g., multiple process innovation-idea assessment committees for the various process units of a large manufacturing company)
- Marketing innovation-idea assessment committee (perhaps also various subcommittees for assessing different marketing strategy-related ideas, e.g., new-market innovation ideas, promotion innovation ideas, pricing innovation ideas, and product-delivery innovation ideas)
- Customer service innovation-idea assessment committee (and perhaps subcommittees for various customer service innovation-idea components)
- Cost-saving innovation ideas in support functional units, such as:
    - HR cost-saving innovation ideas
    - Procurement cost-saving innovation ideas
    - IT cost-saving innovation ideas
    - Accounting innovation ideas

o *Formation of special ad hoc assessment committees*

Special ad hoc assessment committees could also be established for innovation ideas that are highly technical and complex and that require particular expertise and competencies to determine their innovative and investment potential.

o *Ensuring that innovation-idea assessment processes are effective*

The innovation-idea assessment process is the fulcrum of any innovation-idea management system and, ultimately, the innovation performance of an organization. Thus, ensuring that the innovation-idea assessment processes are efficient and effective is vital. Why? Let's take a look at a basic perspective. It's common knowledge that all businesses are created by ideas, right? But once established, businesses require continual generation and development of ideas across the value chain to thrive and survive; otherwise, the business will go belly-up. In fact, it's often said, "The difference between success and failure in business is the ability to generate and translate ideas into value that sustains an organization on a long term basis." While acknowledging the importance of ideas, it is also important for the leadership to understand that although businesses rely on ideas, not every idea will grow and prosper in a business. It's only ideas with innovative and investment potential that contribute to the sustainable growth and prosperity of a business. This is the reason why it's important for the leadership to ensure that the innovation-idea assessment processes are efficient and effective so that the innovation ideas that are generated across the organization are continually developed into different types and degrees of innovations that will ultimately contribute to realizing the innovation-led growth and

## An Effective Management System for Innovation Ideas | 175

prosperity of the organization. Recall that only one out of one hundred inventions succeeds on the market. This reinforces the importance of establishing an efficient and effective innovation-idea assessment process to ensure that, as much as possible, only ideas with a high potential for success are selected for further development.

o   *Functions of innovation-idea assessment committees*
The following are examples of the functions of innovation-idea assessment committees:
- *Receiving innovation ideas*: Once ideas are collected from workforces by the IIRC, the next stage is submitting the ideas to respective innovation-idea assessment committees. So the role of idea assessment committees in this context is to receive ideas for assessment.
- *Creating idea-progression valves*: One of the basic functions of each of the innovation-idea assessment committees is to come up with what this book refers to as *idea-progression valves* for their respective areas of focus.

  What are idea-progression valves? Idea-progression valves are a set of factors to which an innovation idea is subjected to determine the extent to which the innovation idea meets a particular threshold factor or attribute in order to progress to the next progression valve along the innovation-idea assessment process and, at the end of all the embedded progression valves, determine whether the idea under consideration has accumulated sufficient *scores* or *points* to warrant further development through the innovation-development process or gets rejected and stored in the innovation-idea database for future consideration.
- *Assessing and recommending innovation ideas*: As indicated previously, one of the vital roles of the innovation-idea assessment committees is to determine whether an innovation idea meets the set criteria and qualifies to move on to the next stage for further assessment and development.
- *Adhering to confidentiality and nondisclosure policy*: One of the measures that should be aligned with the innovation-development process is the organization's confidentiality and nondisclosure policy on innovation ideas received from workforces. The policy should include a number of aspects relating to the confidentiality of the innovation ideas, including a requirement that anybody involved in dealing with the innovation ideas must sign a confidentiality statement for his or her respective responsibility regarding innovation ideas. That includes innovation-idea assessment committee members.

o   *Factors to include in the innovation-idea assessment process*
What factors should make up the criteria for assessing innovation ideas? The innovation-idea assessment process is a vital decision-making process that begins the journey of turning innovation ideas into innovations that could potentially transform an organization and also change the world. As stated earlier, the innovation-idea assessment process comprises a set of assessment factors referred to as idea-progression valves by which innovation ideas are evaluated for progression to the next stage of the idea-development process. In other words, idea-progression

valves are a set of criteria that constitute a basis on which an innovation idea is judged to determine whether the innovation idea should progress or should be put on hold or rejected.

*Illustration: Idea progression valves*

The word *valves* in the term *idea-progression valves* is being used metaphorically, in the sense that similar to how the heart valves of humans allow blood to flow in a certain direction, idea-progression valves constitute a set of factors embedded in the innovation-idea assessment process, and these factors qualify innovation ideas to move toward the next "valve" (comprising another set of assessment factors) for further determination until the innovation idea passes through all the established idea-progression valves and, ultimately, a decision is made as to whether the innovation idea qualifies for further development. Thus, the factors in the idea-progression valves should be thoughtful in probing the innovative potential and simple to understand.

Figure 14-3 provides a simple illustration showing how the idea-progression valves are embedded in the innovation-idea assessment process.

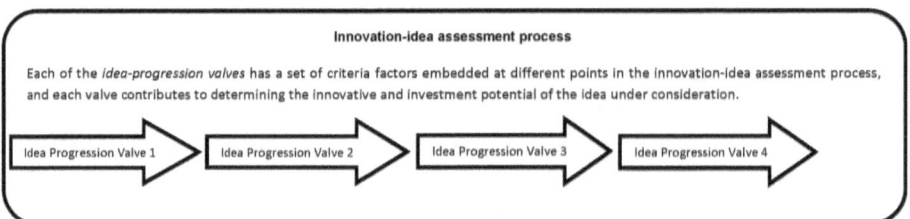

*Figure 14-3. Innovation-idea assessment*

The following are some of the factors that could be embedded in the idea-progression valves:

- *Clear-purpose valve:* Is the purpose of the innovation idea clearly outlined, in terms of how the idea will fix the problem or meet the need?
- *Marketability-analysis valve:* If the innovation idea is a product or service, what is the potential for marketability and demand?
- *Cost-of-investment analysis valve:* Is the cost of the investment reasonable?
- *Return-on-investment analysis valve:* Is the return worth the investment?
- *Development-time-line valve:* Will the innovation idea take a reasonable time to bring to the market, or will it take a long period?
- *Safety analysis valve:* What safety risks does the innovation idea pose? How will the risks be mitigated?
- *Environmental analysis valve:* Is the innovation idea environmentally sustainable?
- *Patentability analysis valve:* Is the innovation idea patentable?
- *Context analysis valve:* Does the innovation idea fall within the organization's business model and availability of resources (financial, human, technological, etc.)?

## An Effective Management System for Innovation Ideas | 177

*Innovation Quotient*

What is an *innovation quotient* in relation to the evaluation of innovation ideas? It is a mechanism used to complement the determination of the value of innovation potential in ideas. The innovation quotient is a kind of scorecard in which the innovation idea must accumulate a minimum score or number of points to qualify for moving to the next innovation-development stage; the points are then used to determine the extent to which the innovation idea under consideration meets the set of factors in the idea-progression valve by which the innovation idea is being assessed.

Each idea-progression valve has an appropriate score or number of points to allocate to an innovation idea as the idea moves along the innovation-idea assessment process. The total score or points accumulated at the end of assessment by the idea under consideration are then used to help determine whether the innovation idea qualifies for further development. The following example clarifies the process.

*Example: Formulating an Innovation Quotient*

The steps in the process of formulating a simple innovation quotient for idea-assessment purposes are as follows:

- *Step 1:* List all the criteria factors that have been adopted for evaluating a particular type of innovation idea. For instance, let's assume that the procurement functional unit for company X has adopted the following three factors as criteria for evaluating procurement innovation ideas:
  - Value proposition
  - Implementation feasibility
  - Cost-effectiveness
- *Step 2:* Create a table of predetermined sets of points or scores, and align them to the criteria factors based on the degree of criticalness of the factor (i.e., the higher the degree of criticalness, the more points that should be allocated to that particular factor under consideration). Table 14-1 provides examples of three criteria factors and the allocation of rating points per factor.

Table 14-1. Example of innovation-idea assessment criteria

| Innovation-idea assessment criteria factors | Allocation of rating points per factor<br>**Note:** *Only one number (from each set of four numbers) should be allocated for each criteria factor, based on the quality of the idea in relation to the criteria factor under consideration* |
|---|---|
| Implementation feasibility | 20-25-30-35 |
| Cost-effectiveness | 40-45-50-55 |
| Value proposition of the innovation idea | 55-60-65-70 |
| **Total points awarded:** | |

- *Step 3:* Create a table indicating the level of innovativeness in one column and a range of ratings in another (see table 14-2). The range of ratings (from step 2) will be applied to show the level of innovativeness of the idea and, ultimately, help in determining the innovation value of the idea under consideration.

Table 14-2. Example of determining range of innovativeness

| Level of innovativeness | Corresponding range of ratings for each level of innovativeness |
|---|---|
| Low or not innovative | 0–55 |
| Averagely innovative | 56–110 |
| Moderately innovative | 111–145 |
| Highly innovative | 146–160 |
| Exceptionally innovative | 161–180 |
| **Name of the innovation idea:**<br>**Level of innovativeness:**<br>**Range of level of innovativeness:**<br>**Decision:** Given the level of innovativeness, *what is the decision?* Options:<br>• Progress to next stage<br>• Reject<br>• Put on hold | |

**Note:** Because of the contextual differences of innovation ideas, innovation-idea assessment committees should come up with idea-progression valves in relation to the *type* and *context* of the innovation ideas they are responsible for. For instance, product platforms should have product idea-progression valves in the context of the particular product platform, as should manufacturing process, marketing, customer service, and so forth. For innovation ideas that may require complex and specific sets of assessment factors, respective innovation-idea assessment committees could create subcommittees or ad hoc committees to specifically develop idea-progression valves to deal with certain innovation ideas. Also, the appropriate committees should periodically review and modify (when necessary) the sets of assessment factors for their respective idea-progression valves.

o *Aspects to consider when creating idea-progression valves*
What aspects do you need to consider when creating idea-progression valves? There are a number to consider when establishing idea-progression valves or criteria of factors for assessing and determining the investment potential of an innovation idea. The following are four aspects:
- *The nature of industry*: As stated earlier, some industry sectors are subjected to strict and rigorous government regulatory regimes. Thus, when establishing innovation-idea assessment frameworks, the first question should be whether the organization operates in an industry that is tightly or strictly regulated, such as pharmaceuticals, food, and cosmetics. For an organization that operates in

an industry with strict and rigorous regulatory processes, committees need to come up with strict, rigorous product innovation-idea assessment factors that, to some extent, mirror those of government regulatory regimes. An example of a strictly regulated industry, as stated earlier, is the pharmaceutical industry. In an interview with *Bloomberg Businessweek*, Erik Gordon, a professor at the University of Michigan's Ross School of Business, said that developing major new drugs in the United States is harder than in the past. "Only 16% of drugs under development," Gordon said, "ever get regulatory approval. This has led to some companies like Abbott Laboratories and Johnson & Johnson to rely more on non-drug businesses, such as medical devices."

- *Size of the organization:* In large organizations, innovation-idea management systems are usually flooded with hundreds of ideas. In order to cope with such a situation, the top leadership needs to ensure that the organization establishes lean but efficient and effective innovation-idea assessment criteria frameworks to cope with the influx of innovation ideas submitted.
- *Type of innovation idea:* Business segments, business processes, product platforms, or business functional units differ in functional characteristics, and naturally, the innovation ideas generated in the various business segments and functional units of the organization will differ from one another in a number of aspects. This is the basis for the suggestion that each business segment, product platform, or functional unit should have its own innovation-idea assessment criteria that take into account the characteristics of the particular unit or segment. The main purpose is to ensure that the idea-progression valves are embedded with criteria factors that take into account the context of the particular type of innovation idea.
- *Degree of innovation ideas:* As stated earlier, the degree of innovation, in most cases, will influence or guide the characteristics of the factors that should be included in the innovation-idea assessment criteria. For instance, a radical product innovation idea may not be subjected to the same level or extent of assessment that an incremental product innovation idea is subjected to. In most cases, radical product innovation ideas are subjected to more rigorous and exhaustive processes and procedures than are incremental innovation ideas; this is because of the development resource demands and risks that accompany radical innovation ideas.

o *Action plans for creating innovation-idea assessment processes*
The CEO should ensure that the task force for creating innovation-idea committees coordinates and collaborates with various innovation-idea assessment committees to guarantee that assessment committees come up with action plans for creating innovation-idea assessment processes.

Worksheet 14-5 is a sample worksheet for creating an action plan for an innovation-idea assessment process.

Worksheet 14-5. Example of an action plan for product innovation-idea assessment

| Objective: *To create an action plan for a product innovation-idea assessment process* ||||||
|---|---|---|---|---|---|
| **Activities:** List of tasks that will be undertaken to create an action plan for a product innovation-idea assessment process | **Time frame:** The actionable time frame within which each listed task shall be completed | **Who:** The individual(s) or subcommittee responsible for undertaking the tasks | **Resources:** The resources needed to undertake each task | **Output:** A complete action plan for a product innovation-idea assessment process ||
| 1. | | | | ||
| 2. | | | | ||
| 3. | | | | ||
| 4. | | | | ||
| 5. | | | | ||
| **Evaluation:** Identify the dates for conducting evaluations to determine how this action plan is progressing. ||||||
| Date: | Date: | Date: | Date: | Date: ||
| State aspects that will be evaluated on this date. | State aspects that will be evaluated on this date. | State aspects that will be evaluated on this date. | State aspects that will be evaluated on this date. | State aspects that will be evaluated on this date. ||

As stated earlier, the number of innovation-idea assessment committees depends on a number of aspects, such as the nature and size of the organization and also what the top leadership considers as the right number of committees. Each innovation-idea assessment committee should come up with an action plan for creating innovation-idea assessment processes. Normally, the innovation-idea assessment action plans should be aligned to the particular functional units and business segments of an organization. For instance, action plans in the context of the core functional units of DM Personal Care Products would be stated as follows:

- Action plan for creating product innovation-idea assessment process
- Action plan for creating manufacturing-processes innovation-idea assessment process
- Action plan for creating marketing innovation-idea assessment process
- Action plan for creating customer service innovation-idea assessment process

Cost-saving innovation-idea assessment committee(s) for support functional units should come up with versions of action plans for creating innovation-idea assessment processes for reviewing cost-saving innovation ideas in those units. For example, action plans in the context of DM Personal Care Products would be aligned to each support functional unit as follows:

- *Action plan for creating HR cost-saving innovation-idea assessment process*
- *Action plan for creating procurement cost-saving innovation-idea assessment process*
- *Action plan for creating IT cost-saving innovation-idea assessment process*
- *Action plan for creating finance and accounting cost-saving innovation-idea assessment process*
- *Action plan for creating corporate affairs cost-saving innovation-idea assessment process*

o *Creating schedules for assessing innovation ideas*
One of the aspects that contributes to making innovation-idea management efficient is ensuring that the leadership creates an orderly procedure for assessing innovation ideas generated by workforces. And one of the aspects that contributes to enhancing the efficiency of the innovation-idea assessment procedure is ensuring that the innovation-idea assessment committees come up with respective schedules for assessing innovation ideas and moving them through to the next stage, which in this framework is referred to as the innovation-development stage. Thus, one of the aspects to be undertaken by innovation-idea assessment committees is to create schedules for considering innovation ideas submitted within a particular period. The creation of an innovation-idea assessment schedule is one of the vital activities of the innovation-idea management system, so the leadership should ensure that each innovation-idea assessment committee comes up with an innovation-idea assessment schedule that is fit for the purpose. Depending on a number of factors, such as the size of the organization, the number of ideas received, and the nature of the ideas received (in terms of types and degrees of innovation ideas), the innovation-idea assessment schedules could be weekly, biweekly, monthly, bimonthly, quarterly, and so forth.

o *Reviewing and updating the innovation-idea assessment process*
Recall that the efficacy of the innovation-idea assessment process is critical because it contributes to sustaining a fit-for-purpose innovation-development process. One of the approaches for continually enhancing the efficiency and capability of innovation-idea assessment processes across the organization is to ensure that idea-assessment committees are encouraged to periodically review and update or modify their respective idea-progression valves, which, as indicated earlier, comprise the assessment-criteria factors. Periodic reviews are important for a number of reasons. For instance, periodic reviews contribute to ensuring that at any given point, every aspect of the assessment-criteria factors is relevant to the reason it has been included in a particular idea-progression valve. Worksheet 14-6 is a sample worksheet for creating an action plan for reviewing and updating idea-progression valves.

Worksheet 14-6. Example of an action plan for reviewing idea-progression valves

| Objective: *To create an action plan for reviewing and updating idea-progression valves* ||||| 
|---|---|---|---|---|
| **Activities:** List of criteria factors that are due for review | **Time frame:** The actionable time frame within which the task of reviewing and updating each of the listed criteria factors shall be conducted | **Who:** The individual(s) or subcommittee responsible for undertaking the task of reviewing and updating the identified assessment factors | **Resources:** The resources needed to undertake each task of reviewing and updating the assessment criteria factors | **Output:** Reviewed and updated assessment criteria factors or idea-progression valves and submission of a summary report to the top leadership |
| 1. | | | | |
| 2. | | | | |
| 3. | | | | |
| 4. | | | | |
| 5. | | | | |
| **Evaluation:** Identify the dates for conducting evaluations to determine how this action plan is progressing. |||||
| **Date:** | **Date:** | **Date:** | **Date:** | **Date:** |
| State aspects that will be evaluated on this date. | State aspects that will be evaluated on this date. | State aspects that will be evaluated on this date. | State aspects that will be evaluated on this date. | State aspects that will be evaluated on this date. |

- *Aspects to consider when creating the innovation-idea assessment process*

  Because the innovation-idea assessment process is one of the critical components of the innovation-development process, the leadership should ensure that the assessment-criteria factors and other procedures that are incorporated in the idea-progression valves for determining innovative and investable potential of the ideas are effective.

  The following are some of the aspects to take into account when creating organization-wide innovation-idea assessment processes:
  - Each innovation-idea assessment process should be embedded with the following:
    - The right number of idea-progression valves
    - Different contexts of assessment-criteria factors at each idea-progression valve to elicit specific data about the innovation idea under consideration
  - Each innovation-idea assessment committee should come up with a set of factors that should be applied as criteria for assessing and determining the innovation potential of the ideas as they progress along the various stages of the innovation-idea assessment process.

## An Effective Management System for Innovation Ideas | 183

- All innovation-idea assessment processes should be approved by the top leadership of the organization.
- The lines of consultation and collaboration between the innovation-idea assessment committees and innovation-idea reception committee should be clear.
- Depending on the size of the organization and the nature and number of ideas generated or submitted, innovation-idea assessment committees could establish subcommittees at various stages of the innovation-idea assessment process to assess specific innovation ideas.
- If subcommittees are created, the functions of such subcommittees should be clearly defined.
- For an innovation idea to progress to the next stage for further assessment and subsequently progress to the innovation-development stage, the idea must meet the set standard criteria factors embedded in each idea-progression valve.
- The specific objectives of the assessment factors at each idea-progression valve along the innovation-idea assessment process should be clearly outlined.
- If the innovation idea does not accumulate a sufficient score or number of points along the innovation-idea assessment process and fails to make it to the next stage for further development, the innovation idea should be put on hold for future consideration.
- There is no one-size-fits-all or general standardized number of innovation-idea assessment stages that should be established in the innovation-idea assessment process. The number of stages included depends on certain factors, such as the following:
  - The number of innovation-idea assessment stages that the organization deems effective to determine the investment potential of the innovation idea before it progresses for further development
  - The nature of the innovation idea: Some ideas may require only a few assessment stages, whereas others might need rigorous assessment processes for number of reasons, such as the following:
    - Risk levels involved
    - Doubts on return on investment
    - Type of innovation
    - Degree of innovation involved
    - Government regulatory procedures (e.g., in the pharmaceutical industry)

## 3. Innovation Project Teams

The third component or stage of the innovation-development process involves creating *innovation project teams*. Once innovation ideas are assessed, passed through the idea-progression valves, and recommended for further development by the respective innovation-idea assessment committees, the next step involves committees submitting the innovation ideas (the business case) to the top leadership of the organization for onward implementation of a series of innovation project activities that will result in the development

## 184 | LEADERSHIP FOR INNOVATION

of an innovation. What are innovation project teams? An innovation project team is a group of staff with complementary skills and competencies charged with the responsibility to undertake specific innovation-development tasks and activities that ultimately result in developing or transforming an innovation idea into an innovation.

Whose responsibility is it to create the teams? Recall that the top leadership should ensure that the organization develops a manual outlining all the critical components of the organization's innovation-idea management system. One of the components that should be included in the manual is a section on guidelines for the creation of innovation project teams. The guidelines should be applied whenever the leadership is creating an innovation project team. For every innovation project, the leadership should ensure that the innovation project team comprises skilled and competent team members who are able to develop an *innovation project charter*, which the team will ultimately use to deliver a successful innovation project.

The simple illustration in figure 14-4 depicts the process of submitting innovative and investment-potential ideas to the top leadership and the formation of innovation project teams by the top leadership.

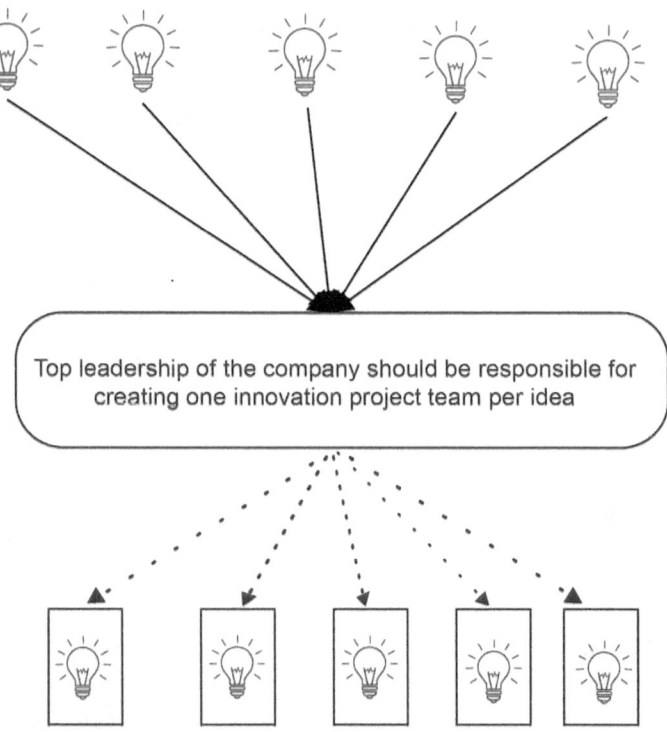

*Figure 14-4. Example of a process for submitting innovative ideas*

## 4. Guidelines for Creating Innovation Project Teams

The fourth component of the innovation-development process involves formulating guidelines for creating the innovation project teams. This process should be considered one of the vital components of the innovation-development process because it is these guidelines that are applied to create innovation project teams, and it is the project teams that will ultimately deliver the end result in the form of an innovation. Thus, when formulating guidelines, every aspect should be aimed at contributing toward having a set of guidelines that are effective in helping to come up with the right project team that will be able to deliver a successful innovation project within the context of the innovation idea. That said, a number of factors influence the aspects that should be included in the guidelines for creating innovation project teams. Some of the factors include the following:

- *Types of innovation ideas:* Innovation ideas are characterized by different dynamics that affect how they are assessed and how they are developed. This means that the dynamics of a particular type of innovation idea will influence how the innovation ideas in that category are developed. For instance, the dynamics of product innovation ideas, process innovation ideas, marketing innovation ideas, customer service innovation ideas, HR cost-saving innovation ideas, finance and accounting cost-saving innovation ideas, and procurement cost-saving innovation ideas will influence the kind of innovation talent that should constitute a particular innovation project team.
- *Innovation degree:* The extent of innovativeness of an idea, in most cases, influences the kind of skills and competencies that the team members should possess.
- The technical complexity of the innovation idea
- The scale of the innovation project
- The size of budget required to develop the innovation idea into an innovation
- The personnel needed to work on the innovation project, for instance, number of core and support staff to undertake the innovation-development project
- The life-cycle steps of the innovation-development project
- *The leader of the innovation project:* The appointment of the person to lead the innovation project (*innovation project manager*) will also be influenced by a number of aspects, for instance, whether it's the automatic practice of the organization that the innovator(s) of the idea should lead the innovation project or whether the decision of who leads the innovation project shall be determined on a case-by-case basis. Even in instances where appointment of an innovation project manager is determined on a case-by-case basis, guidelines should outline factors to consider when appointing the innovation project manager.

*Guidelines on Expectations for Innovation Project Teams*
In addition to the guidelines for *creating* innovation project teams, it's also important to have a set of guidelines on *what is expected of each innovation project team* once formed. The purpose of the guidelines is to ensure that each innovation project team comes up with an innovation project charter in the context of the innovation project and consequently applies it to manage and successfully deliver an innovation project.

## 186 | LEADERSHIP FOR INNOVATION

An innovation project charter (IPC) is an outline of what needs (duties and responsibilities) to be accomplished and how the innovation project will proceed. The following are some of the aspects that could be included in the innovation project charter:

- o Guidelines on creating an innovation project structure
- o Formulation of tasks and activities that individuals or subcommittees will be responsible for
- o Formulation of actionable time lines throughout the innovation-development process
- o Clear outline of financial resources needed to complete an innovation project
- o Guidelines on how to review and evaluate an innovation project
- o Guidelines on creating innovation project plans

### 5. Innovation-Development Stage

The fifth component of the innovation-development process is the innovation-development stage. What does this component involve?

This component consists of a series of innovation-development stages and processes for transforming an innovation idea into an innovation. The number of innovation-development stages varies from organization to organization. This book recommends the three stages illustrated in figure 14-5.

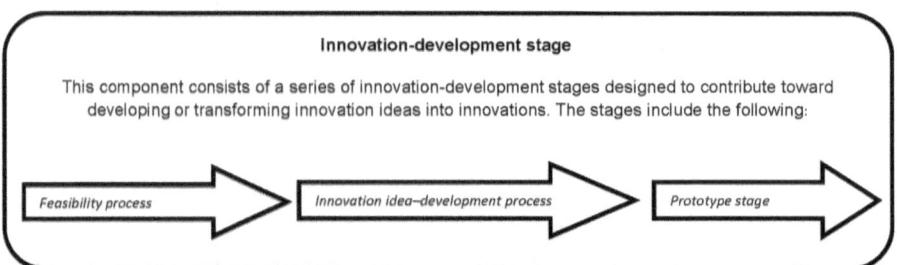

*Figure 14-5. Example of innovation-development stages*

The three stages are interpreted in table 14-3.

# An Effective Management System for Innovation Ideas | 187

Table 14-3. Interpretation of the Innovation-Development Stages

| Feasibility process | Innovation idea–development process | Prototype stage |
|---|---|---|
| This stage involves respective innovation project teams undertaking a feasibility review, which is a detailed analysis to determine whether, based on the information provided by the innovation-idea assessment process, the innovation project should move on to the next stage, which is the development stage. The question then is, What criteria are applied to conduct a feasibility review? The same factors that were applied in the innovation-idea assessment processes can be used (some aspects may require more detailed analysis). | This stage involves the innovation-development project teams establishing an innovation-development project plan (i-DPP). The i-DPP should describe, in detail, the following aspects:<br>• **Leadership structure:** The top leadership of the organization should ensure that the innovation-development project is under good leadership that is able to put in place clearly defined roles so that the team members undertake their specific roles effectively and contribute to the development process of transforming the idea into an innovation.<br>• **Tasks:** A list of tasks or activities that individuals or subcommittees in the innovation-development project team will undertake should be created by the leadership of the innovation project. The tasks should have milestones that are described as SMART: specific, measurable, actionable, realistic, and time-bound.<br>• **Human resources:** The project plan should outline, in detail, the human resources needs in terms of expertise (core and support staff) and the total number of staff required.<br>• **Financial resources:** The project plan should include a clear outline of financial resources needed to complete the innovation project.<br>• **Time frame:** The project plans should include realistic, actionable time frames throughout the innovation-development project. The time frames should be frequently reviewed and updated to help teams stay on task, and the teams should ensure that they are updating the top leadership of the | This stage involves the ultimate delivery of a finished innovation in the form of a sample or prototype. Once completed, the prototype should undergo extensive testing and evaluation. |

|   |   |
|---|---|
|   | organization with periodic reports about the innovation's progress.<br>• ***The project should be on course:*** The innovation-development teams should ensure that the innovation project continues to progress within the company's approved technical and financial goals and is constantly aligned to meeting the need or solving the problem for which the idea was generated. |

## 6. Innovation Launch/Implementation

The sixth and final component of the innovation-development process is the launch of an innovation on the market or implementation of an innovation in the organization's system. In this book, *launching* an innovation means introducing the innovation on the market for direct procurement by customers, whereas the *implementation* of an innovation refers to the application of an innovation for efficiency or customer experience purposes within an organization's system.

The innovation-launch component suggested in this book has two stages: (1) the innovation testing stage and (2) the innovation-launch stage. Figure 14-6 shows a simple illustration of the two stages, and table 14-4 provides an interpretation of the stages.

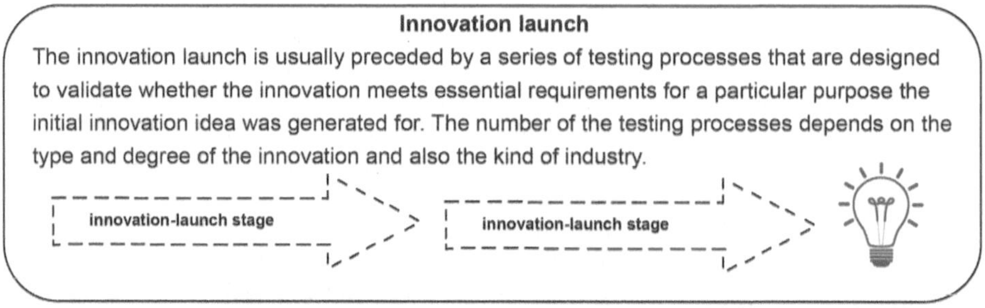

**Innovation launch**
The innovation launch is usually preceded by a series of testing processes that are designed to validate whether the innovation meets essential requirements for a particular purpose the initial innovation idea was generated for. The number of the testing processes depends on the type and degree of the innovation and also the kind of industry.

→ innovation-launch stage → innovation-launch stage

*Figure 14-6. Example of innovation launch stages*

Table 14-4. Interpretation of the innovation-launch stages

| Innovation-testing stage | Innovation-launch stage |
|---|---|
| Whatever the type of innovation (e.g., product innovation, service innovation, process innovation, marketing innovation, customer service innovation, or any type of innovation in the context of the organization's value chain and functional units), the purpose of the testing stage is to provide validation for the innovation. In this book, *innovation validation* is defined as a process by which an innovation is proven | This is the last stage of the innovation-development process. As stated earlier, the launch/implementation methodology or strategy will largely be determined by the type of innovation (among other aspects). This means that the launch or implementation strategy for, say, product or service innovations will vary from those of process, marketing, or customer service innovations. |

to meet the essential requirements for the particular purpose the innovation idea was generated for. The factors or criteria used for testing an innovation depend on a number of aspects, such as the following:
- The purpose of the innovation or the problem/need that the innovation is designed to solve or fulfill
- The type of innovation
- The innovation degree
- Regulatory procedures
- Safety issues

Thus, launch teams should come up with testing guidelines for each innovation. When generating testing guidelines, it is important to include the following aspects:
- The team members involved in testing the innovation should be fully oriented to the problem or need the innovation is designed to solve or fulfill so that they can fully understand the functional purpose the innovation is supposed to serve.

- Testing of an innovation should be done by those who are able to provide valuable feedback on the initial performance of the innovation.
- The duration of the testing period depends on a number of factors, including the criteria for testing mentioned above.
- The innovation-development project teams should use the feedback from testing to make any needed improvements or changes before launch or implementation.
- The feedback could also be used by other teams that are part of the launch project; for example, the sales and marketing team could use the feedback to help with the formulation of sales and marketing strategies.

The other factor that could determine the innovation-launch strategy is the *innovation degree*. That is, the scale or nature of the launch strategy will be affected by the extent of the newness of an innovation. For instance, a *radical innovation* with high risk in terms of investment could influence the need for a robust innovation-launch strategy and a well-thought-out approach to other marketing innovations as compared to a low-risk *incremental innovation*.

The bottom line is that any innovation-launch/implementation strategy started by innovation-launch teams should be fit or effective for the purpose for which it is being initiated or adopted.

## 7. Post-Innovation Launch Evaluation

So far, we've covered three of the components that make up the innovation-idea management framework suggested in this book: innovation-idea preliminary self-assessment, innovation-idea submission process, and innovation-development process. The last component is the *post-innovation launch or implementation evaluation*. This component includes three aspects: (1) definition of post-innovation launch/implementation evaluation, (2) importance, and (3) innovation deliverables index.

1. **Definition**

    The post-innovation launch/implementation evaluation is defined as a process that involves creating a mechanism for determining the efficacy of an innovation in delivering value and expected performance in terms of fixing the problem and achieving the monetary goals set for a particular innovation.

2. **Importance**

    What is the importance of the post-innovation launch or implementation evaluation? This evaluation is important for a number of reasons:

    o First, the development process of an innovation involves a significant amount of resources and time. Chapter 1 defined *innovation* as a process that involves identifying customer needs, generating new ideas not seen on the market before, turning the ideas into solutions to address the identified needs, and then converting the solutions into commercial value for the company in terms of profits, growth, and competitiveness. This means that regardless of the type of innovation—whether it's a product innovation, service innovation, process innovation, marketing strategy innovation, customer service innovation, or any other type of innovation in the context of the organization's business model—the innovation-development process for any innovation idea involves a great deal of resource investment to bring the innovation idea to fruition. Thus, because of the amount of resources and time involved in the development process of an innovation, it is vital that an organization develops a framework for reviewing and evaluating the performance of an innovation after launch or implementation.

    o Second, the post-innovation launch or implementation evaluation affords an opportunity for identifying some weaknesses in the innovation's performance or mistakes in its implementation. Identifying mistakes provides an essential aid for enacting measures aimed at protecting the innovation-development and launch/implementation processes from recurrences of similar mistakes.

    o Third, launching an innovation on the market or implementing an innovation in the organization's system is one thing, but whether the innovation adds value to the organization is another. Thus, once an innovation is launched or implemented, it is good management practice to determine the operational efficacy and monetary value of the innovation.

3. **Post-Innovation Evaluation Technique: The Innovation Deliverables Index**

    Given the importance of the post-innovation performance of an innovation, it is necessary for organizational leaders to develop abilities to create and implement an effective post-innovation evaluation tool that's relevant to the context of the organization's value chain and business model. Such a tool should be embedded with aspects for determining the deliverables of each innovation from the time of launch or implementation to a specified end point. To create such a tool, the top leadership could form an ad hoc committee to formulate guidelines for establishing innovation-evaluation teams across the organization that will be

# An Effective Management System for Innovation Ideas | 191

charged with the responsibility of monitoring the performance of an innovation on an ongoing basis.

*Action Plan*

Once created, the ad hoc committee should come up with an action plan for creating a technique for monitoring the performance of an innovation.

Worksheet 14-7 is a simple example of a worksheet that can be used to develop an action plan for creating a technique for monitoring the performance of an innovation.

Table 14-5. Action plan for creating technique for monitoring an innovation

| **Objective:** *To develop an action plan for creating a technique for monitoring the performance of an innovation* | | | | |
|---|---|---|---|---|
| **Activities:** List of activities to be undertaken to develop a technique for monitoring the performance of an innovation | **Time line:** The actionable time frame within which each listed task shall be completed | **Who:** The individual(s) or subcommittee responsible for undertaking the tasks | **Resources:** The resources needed to undertake each task | **Output:** Completed brochure with the guidelines for establishing innovation-evaluation teams and their responsibilities |
| 1. | | | | |
| 2. | | | | |
| 3. | | | | |
| 4. | | | | |
| 5. | | | | |
| **Evaluation:** Identify the dates for conducting evaluations to determine how the action plan is progressing. | | | | |
| **Date:** | **Date:** | **Date:** | **Date:** | **Date:** |
| State aspects that will be evaluated on this date. | State aspects that will be evaluated on this date. | State aspects that will be evaluated on this date. | State aspects that will be evaluated on this date. | State aspects that will be evaluated on this date. |

*Example*

An example of a tool for monitoring the performance of an innovation is the *innovation deliverables index*. The innovation deliverables index is a simple mechanism designed to monitor and generate data about the performance of an innovation after launch or implementation. In terms of the measures on which the performance of a particular innovation is based, it depends on a number of factors, such as the nature of the industry and organization and the organization's mission and policies. Figure 14-7 shows some of the measures or aspects on which the performance of a particular innovation can be based.

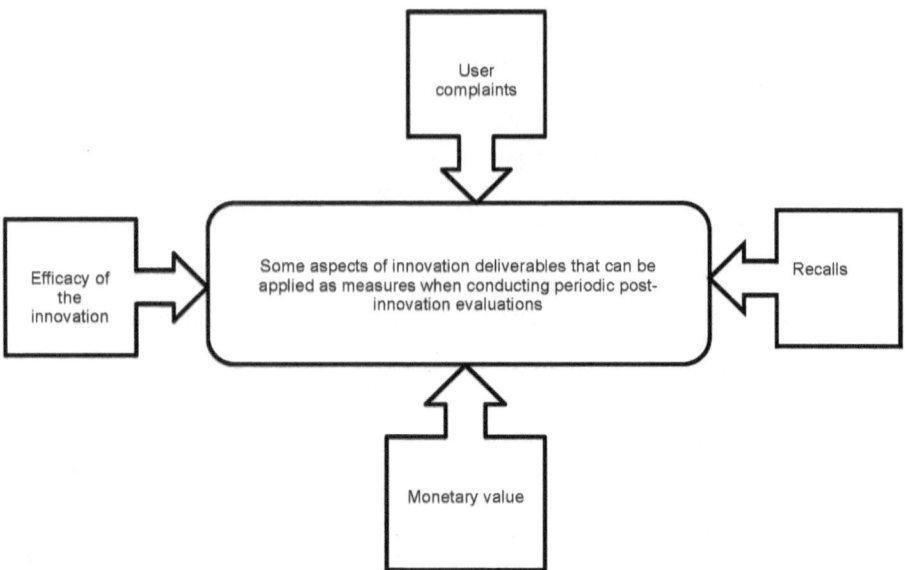

*Figure 14-7. Examples of innovation deliverables*

Based on the deliverable metrics shown in figure 14-7, table 14-6 is an example of a tool for monitoring performance of an innovation, referred to as the innovation deliverables index.

Table 14-6. Innovation deliverables index

| |
|---|
| **Names and position titles of the innovation-evaluation team:** |
| **Name of the innovation being evaluated:** |
| **Date when the evaluation is being conducted:**<br>**Date when the innovation was launched or implemented:** |
| **Financial contribution of the innovation during the period under review** |

| | |
|---|---|
| **Revenue-generation target:** What revenue-generation target was set for the innovation during the period under review?<br>**Revenue contribution:** How much revenue has the innovation contributed during the period under review? | **Cost-saving target:** What cost-saving target was set for the innovation during the period under review?<br>**Cost-saving contribution:** How much savings has the innovation contributed during the period under review? |

| |
|---|
| **Efficacy of the innovation:** What are the comments from users regarding the performance of the innovation in terms of fixing the problem or meeting their needs during the period under review? |
| **Complaints from users:** Are there any complaints from users regarding the performance of the innovation? If yes, give a description. |
| **Recalls:** Were there any recalls of the innovation during the period under review? If so, describe the defects and remedial action taken. |

| |
|---|
| **Checkpoints:** Are there any innovation-evaluation checkpoints that need to be modified to enhance the effectiveness of the innovation-evaluation process? If so, state the checkpoints that need modification and give recommendations. |
| **Indicate the date of the next innovation evaluation:** |
| **Signatures of the innovation evaluators:** |

## CHAPTER 15
## ABILITY TO MEASURE AND REPORT INNOVATION PERFORMANCE

Thus far, we've covered six examples of innovation management skill sets; the seventh example is the ability for organizational leaders to design, implement, and manage, on an ongoing basis, a framework for measuring and reporting innovation performance in the context of an organization's value chain and business model. This book adopts a four-dimensional model for measuring and reporting innovation performance.

When I conduct training on measuring innovation performance, I sometimes ask delegates to indicate by a show of hands if their companies have policies for reporting innovation performance at the functional-unit level, divisional level, or corporate level. I have never gotten more than five hands in the affirmative out of a group of, say, twenty-five to forty. Interestingly, when I ask the delegates to indicate whether innovation is considered a top-three priority in their organizations, 90–95 percent of the delegates raise their hands. A 2009 innovation survey by the Boston Consulting Group, a US-based consulting firm, revealed that although 73 percent of companies surveyed across the globe believe that innovation performance should be tracked as rigorously as other business elements, only 46 percent of the executives said their companies actually track innovation performance. And in a 2011 survey of more than six hundred executives worldwide by the US-based Institute for Corporate Productivity, many respondents indicated that one of the challenges they were wrestling with was how to measure and report the innovation performance of their organizations. Because of the difficulties that many managers face in measuring and reporting the innovation performance of their organizations, chapter 15 covers tools that can be used to build essential skills and knowledge for measuring and reporting innovation performance in organizations.

## Definition
First of all, *What is innovation-performance measurement?* It is a process that involves reviewing and assessing various innovation performance–related activities at the functional-unit and corporate levels of an organization and then determining the extent to which the goals of the various aspects of innovation activities have been achieved.

## Importance
Second, *Why is it important to measure and report innovation performance?* The following are six reasons:

i. First, the information generated is useful for determining the innovation-performance status of an organization in terms of whether the innovation goals, objectives, and targets that were set by various functional units and the organization as a whole have been achieved.

ii. Second, information generated from the cross-functional innovation-performance reporting and communication system is useful for determining, comprehensively, whether the organization's efforts in investing in innovation activities across functional units are yielding results.

iii. Third, the innovation-performance data can be used for making decisions on the way forward regarding the kind of innovation strategies that should be developed and implemented.

iv. Fourth, the information generated helps in analyzing variances in innovation-performance goals and targets. *What does this mean?* In any kind of performance, the positive deviation from set goals and targets indicates better performance. Conversely, negative deviation is generally a matter of concern because it indicates a shortfall in performance. In terms of innovation performance, the information elicited from innovation-performance measurement activities helps in determining the kind of decisions that should be made arising from variances in innovation-performance goals and targets, especially in cases of negative deviations. This section also provides an evaluation tool (referred to as evaluation worksheets) aimed at eliciting information regarding innovation-performance deviations.

v. Fifth, similar to the preceding point, measuring innovation helps in determining the kind of corrective actions that should be undertaken, because once the deviations in innovation-performance goals and targets are identified, the next step is developing plans for taking corrective actions. And if the innovation performance is consistently less than what is desired, then a detailed analysis of the factors responsible for such performance must be undertaken.

vi. Sixth, information collected from measuring innovation performance helps in determining how the company's innovation performance measures up against competitors, and such information is vital for the organization's innovation-strategy development.

## Dimensions of Innovation-Performance Measurement
This book suggests four dimensions of innovation-performance measurement:
1. Innovation input measurement
2. Innovation output measurement
3. Innovation-results measurement
4. Innovation impact measurement

*Evaluation Worksheet*

Before we look at each of the four dimensions of innovation-performance measurement, it is necessary to give a brief description of one of the useful tools aligned with the innovation-performance measurement model adopted in this book, the *evaluation worksheet*. As stated at the beginning of this chapter, the innovation-performance measurement model suggested in this book is aimed at providing tools for determining the innovation performance of an organization in a multidimensional manner. To enhance the effectiveness of the model, an evaluation worksheet is included for each of the four dimensions of innovation-performance measurement.

*Purpose of the Evaluation Worksheets*

It is important to bear in mind that the measurement of innovation performance is not an end in itself. The measurement process merely provides data for determining whether an innovation activity resulted in accomplishing a particular purpose or achieving particular goals. Thus, the worksheets are used to evaluate the data collected through the measurement process.

*Contexts of the Evaluation Worksheets*

As noted, evaluation worksheets can be used for eliciting and deciphering data generated in each of the four dimensions of innovation-performance measurement. Thus, an evaluation worksheet is included for each of the four dimensions. The evaluation worksheet is formulated and phrased in the context of the innovation measurement under consideration. In other words, each evaluation worksheet is designed to fulfill a distinct objective in relation to the particular dimension of innovation-performance measurement, which is to assess the extent to which the goals and targets for each innovation-performance dimension under consideration were realized or achieved over a particular period.

The evaluation worksheets are contextualized in the four dimensions of innovation-performance measurements as follows:
  i. *Innovation Input Evaluation Worksheet:* This is designed to assess how various innovation-support initiatives were implemented and also to determine the extent to which the intended consequences of the initiatives were realized during the period under review.
  ii. *Innovation Output Evaluation Worksheet*: This is designed to assess the degree to which innovation output goals and targets were realized.
  iii. *Innovation-Results Evaluation Worksheet:* This is designed to assess the degree to which the innovations launched or implemented (innovation goals or targets) were realized.

iv. *Innovation Impact Evaluation Worksheet:* This is designed to determine the revenues generated from innovations launched and the savings gained from cost-saving innovations implemented across the functional units of the organization.

## *Checkpoints*

To ensure that each of the evaluation worksheets fulfills its purpose, the following checkpoints should be included in the evaluation worksheets:

i. Determining whether the innovation-support initiatives in various functional units were well implemented during the period under review
ii. Determining the effectiveness of the innovation-support initiatives in terms of realizing the intended consequences
iii. Determining whether the innovation-support initiatives resulted in unintended consequences
iv. Identifying gaps and deviations in the innovation-support initiatives implemented in various functional units and determining corrective measures if necessary
v. Determining whether the targeted number of radical and incremental innovation ideas generated was achieved and providing an explanation for achieving or missing the target
vi. Determining whether the targeted number of radical and incremental innovation ideas undergoing development was achieved and providing an explanation for achieving or missing the target
vii. Determining whether the targeted number of radical and incremental innovations launched or implemented was achieved and providing an explanation for achieving or missing the target
viii. Determining whether the targeted revenue from innovations launched or the targeted savings from cost-saving innovations implemented across functional units was achieved and providing an explanation for achieving or missing the targets

The next sections cover how to apply and present each of the four dimensions of innovation-performance measurement: *innovation input measurement, innovation output measurement, innovation-results measurement,* and *innovation impact measurement.*

## 1. Innovation Input Measurement

The US publication *strategy+business*, published by Strategy& (formerly Booz & Company), has conducted an annual study on the importance of innovation inputs for more than ten years. The studies have, over the years, consistently revealed that innovation success depends on the company's investments in various innovation-related interventions or inputs. Given how vital innovation inputs are to creating a climate for innovation and sustaining innovation-led growth in organizations, it's important that organizational leaders understand various types of innovation inputs and know how to create a presentation format for reporting innovation input metrics in the context of the organization's value chain and business model.

## Definitions

To understand innovation input measurement, it is first necessary to define the terms *innovation inputs* and *innovation inputs measurement.*

## 198 | LEADERSHIP FOR INNOVATION

*Definition of Innovation Inputs*

The basic meaning of the word *inputs*, according to dictionary definitions, varies depending on the context in which the word is being used. According to a number of dictionaries, the term *inputs* means "something that is put in," "to put in," or "an act or process of putting in," with the view of expecting an outcome. Translated in the context of innovation, *innovation inputs* can be defined as various innovation-support systems—such as innovation-related strategies, innovation-related policies and procedures, innovation-enhancing technologies, innovation-skill-development programs, and so forth—that the leadership of an organization implements or invests in across the organization to create a climate for workforce innovation to realize innovation-led growth on an ongoing basis.

*Definition of Innovation Input Measurement*

Therefore, *innovation input measurement* is defined as a process that involves determining and measuring innovation-support systems, such as innovation-support strategies, innovation-support policies and procedures, innovation-skill-development programs, innovation-enhancing technologies, and many other initiatives implemented across functional units during the period under review.

### *Illustration: How to Report Innovation Input Measurements*

This section illustrates how to determine and report innovation input measurements by presenting innovation-support initiatives implemented over a particular period in the core and support functional units of the fictitious company DM Personal Care Products. To demonstrate this, two types of sample worksheets are provided, as follows:

- o Worksheets 15-1 and 15-2 present the innovation-support initiatives implemented by core and support functional units, respectively, across the organization during the period under review.
- o Worksheet 15-3 is the innovation input evaluation worksheet, whose purpose is to assess how the various innovation-support initiatives presented in worksheets 15-1 and 15-2 were implemented and also to determine the extent to which the intended consequences of the initiatives implemented during the period under review were realized.

The worksheets have been applied to the functional units of DM Personal Care Products, which are as follows:

*Core functional units*
- ❖ Product-development unit
- ❖ Manufacturing-processes department
- ❖ Marketing department
- ❖ Customer service department

*Support functional units*
- ❖ Procurement department
- ❖ HR department
- ❖ Finance and accounting department
- ❖ IT department
- ❖ Corporate affairs department

## Innovation Inputs Worksheet

For illustration purposes, two worksheets are provided: worksheet 15-1 describes the innovation inputs or innovation-support initiatives undertaken by core functional units, and worksheet 15-2 describes the innovation inputs undertaken by support functional units. The worksheets are segmented into three categories of innovation-support initiatives, and two columns are used to indicate the innovation-support initiatives implemented in the context of each of the three categories—namely innovative thinking–related initiatives, innovation engagement–related initiatives, and innovation management–related initiatives—and the purpose of each innovation-support initiative.

Worksheet 15-1. Innovation-support initiatives of core functional units undertaken

| **Objective:** *To determine innovation-support initiatives implemented in core functional units during the period under review (e.g., February–May of 2018)* | | |
|---|---|---|
| **Product-development department:** **Period under review:** | | |
| Types of innovation-support initiatives and purposes | | |
| **Type of innovation-support initiative** | State the innovation-support initiative implemented in the context of each of the three categories | State the purpose of each innovation-support initiative |
| Innovative thinking–related initiatives | | |
| Innovation engagement–related initiatives | | |
| Innovation management–related initiatives | | |
| Date when the assessment was conducted: | | |
| Head of department: | | |

Similar worksheets would be created for the other three core functional units of DM Personal Care Products:

❖ Manufacturing-processes department
❖ Marketing department
❖ Customer service department

Worksheet 15-2. Innovation-support initiatives of support functional units undertaken

| **Objective:** *To determine innovation-support initiatives implemented in support functional units during the period under review (e.g., February–May of 2018)* |
|---|
| **Procurement department:** **Period under review:** |
| Types of innovation-support initiatives and purposes |

| Type of innovation-support initiative | State the innovation-support initiative implemented in the context of each of the three categories | State the purpose of each innovation-support initiative |
|---|---|---|
| Innovative thinking–related initiatives | | |
| Innovation engagement–related initiatives | | |
| Innovation management–related initiatives | | |
| Date when the assessment was done: | | |
| Head of department: | | |

Similar worksheets would be created for the other four support functional units of DM Personal Care Products:
- HR department
- Finance and accounting department
- IT department
- Corporate affairs department

*Innovation-Support Initiatives by Committees Appointed by the CEO*

There are cases where some innovation-support initiatives are implemented by a committee or committees created to undertake and implement specific innovation-support initiatives across the organization, and in most cases, such committees are accountable to the CEO. When it comes to reporting these innovation-support initiatives, they could be reported under the office of the CEO with specific evaluation worksheets created for this purpose.

**Innovation Input Evaluation**

As stated earlier, the purpose of the innovation input evaluation is to identify the types of innovation-support initiatives undertaken during the period under review and also to determine the extent to which the intended consequences (the objectives) of the initiatives were realized.

Assuming we are undertaking innovation input evaluation for the core and support (back-office) functional units of DM Personal Care Products, the first step is to outline the core and support functional units, as follows:

*Core functional units*
- Product-development unit
- Manufacturing-processes department
- Marketing department
- Customer service department

## Ability to Measure and Report Innovation Performance | 201

*Support functional units*
- ❖ Procurement department
- ❖ HR department
- ❖ Finance and accounting department
- ❖ IT department
- ❖ Corporate affairs department

The second step is creating simple innovation input evaluation worksheets that are categorized according to the types of innovation-support initiatives undertaken. For this illustration, there are three innovation input evaluation worksheets, as follows:

o Worksheet 15-3: Innovative thinking initiatives
o Worksheet 15-4: Innovation engagement initiatives
o Worksheet 15-5: Innovation management initiatives

Worksheet 15-3. Innovative thinking initiatives

| **Name of department:** Product development **Segment or unit:** | | | | |
|---|---|---|---|---|
| **State the innovative thinking initiatives that were implemented during the period under review** (*example initiatives are given here*) | **Implementation:** State whether the initiative was well implemented and whether the initiative has been well adopted in the organization's systems | **Objectives:** State the objectives of the innovation-support initiatives undertaken during the period under review | **Outcomes:** State the extent to which each initiative has contributed to advancing innovation performance in the organization (i.e., the extent to which the initiative has realized the intended purpose) | **Improvements:** State aspects of the initiative that need to be improved if the program is to be effective |
| Questioning skills program | | | | |
| Observing skills program | | | | |
| Associating skills program | | | | |
| Discovering skills program | | | | |
| Envisioning skills program | | | | |
| Experimenting skills program | | | | |

# 202 | LEADERSHIP FOR INNOVATION

| Networking skills program | | | | |
|---|---|---|---|---|
| Head of department:<br>Date: | | | | |

Worksheet 15-4. Innovation engagement initiatives

| Name of department: Product development<br>Segment or unit: | | | | |
|---|---|---|---|---|
| **State the *innovation engagement initiatives* that were implemented during the period under review** (*example initiatives are given here*) | **Implementation:** State whether the initiative was well implemented and whether the initiative has been well adopted in the organization's systems | **Objectives:** State the objectives of the innovation-support initiatives undertaken during the period under review | **Outcomes:** State the extent to which each initiative has contributed to advancing innovation performance in the organization (i.e., the extent to which the initiative has realized the intended purpose) | **Improvements:** State aspects of the initiative that need to be improved if the program is to be effective |
| Program for educating workforces on the meaning of *innovation* | | | | |
| Program for promoting the significance of innovation | | | | |
| Program for educating workforces on types of innovation | | | | |
| Program for educating workforces on innovation degree | | | | |

## Ability to Measure and Report Innovation Performance | 203

| | | | | |
|---|---|---|---|---|
| Program for promoting the connection between vision and innovation | | | | |
| Head of department:<br>Date: | | | | |

Worksheet 15-5. Innovation management initiatives

| **Name of department:** Product development<br>**Segment or unit:** | | | | |
|---|---|---|---|---|
| **State the *innovation management initiatives* that were implemented during the period under review** (*example initiatives are given here*) | **Implementation:** State whether the initiative was well implemented and whether the initiative has been well adopted in the organization's systems | **Objectives:** State the objectives of the innovation-support initiatives undertaken during the period under review | **Outcomes:** State the extent to which the initiative has contributed to advancing innovation performance in the organization (i.e., the extent to which the initiative has realized the intended purpose) | **Improvements:** State aspects of the initiative that need to be improved if the program is to be more effective |
| Visually illustrated chart showing functional-unit priority areas on which to focus innovation | | | | |
| Innovation-performance job descriptions and job specifications in job positions across functional units | | | | |

| | | | | |
|---|---|---|---|---|
| Innovation-challenge-questions system across functional units | | | | |
| Framework for formulating corporate and functional-unit innovation goals | | | | |
| Innovation-idea-management system | | | | |
| Workforce-diversity framework for advancing innovation across functional units | | | | |
| Framework for identifying and determining innovation talent in job candidates | | | | |
| Framework for evaluating innovation performance of workforces | | | | |
| Innovation-talent-succession planning framework | | | | |
| Functional-unit innovation strategies | | | | |

| Framework for measuring and reporting innovation performance across functional units | | | | |
|---|---|---|---|---|
| Head of department:<br>Date: | | | | |

## 2. Innovation Output Measurement

The second dimension of measuring innovation performance is innovation output measurement.

### Definitions

To understand innovation output measurement, it is first necessary to define the terms *innovation output* and *innovation output measurement*.

*Definition of Innovation Output*

The basic meaning of the word *output*, according to dictionary definitions, varies depending on the context in which the word is being used. According to the *Merriam-Webster* online dictionary, the generic definition of *output* is "the amount of something that is produced depending on the context of what it is."

Contexts of outputs range from basic things like outputs of corn, rice, oranges, and tomatoes in an agricultural context to outputs of gold, copper, and diamonds in a mineral context to the more complex contexts, such as the work output of a machine in engineering terms or the transmission of information in an IT context. In economic terms, output is the amount of goods and services produced, whereas in a telecommunications context, output entails information retrieved from a network. The point is that the term *output* is context specific, and the list of contexts of outputs goes on and on.

In the context of measuring innovation, *innovation output* is defined as the number of innovation ideas generated in the context of the organization's value chain and business segments.

The preceding section noted that innovation input measurement involves assessing various innovation-support initiatives undertaken over a specific period. Therefore, the first evidence to manifest as a consequence of the innovation inputs is the generation of innovation ideas by workforces—hence the characterization of innovation ideas generated as innovation outputs, because they're a result of the specific innovation initiatives undertaken.

*Definition of Innovation Output Measurement*

Given the context of innovation outputs, *innovation output measurement* can be defined as a process that involves determining the number of innovation ideas generated by workforces across functional units as a consequence of the various innovation-support initiatives implemented by the organization over a particular period.

## Two Perspectives

In this book, innovation output is divided into two perspectives: (1) the number of innovation ideas *generated* by workforces over a particular period and (2) the number of innovation ideas *undergoing development*.

i. **Number of Innovation Ideas Generated**

   It's important to understand that determining the number of innovation ideas generated is one of the vital aspects of measuring and reporting innovation performance. This is because if the information on innovation ideas generated is poorly determined and presented, it could potentially negatively affect the quality and accuracy of the data about the number of innovation ideas generated and consequently affect the quality of the innovation-performance report. To avoid this, the teams directly responsible for compiling the organization's innovation-performance report need to do it competently by enacting measures that will contribute to ensuring the quality and accuracy of the data collected on the innovation ideas generated across functional units. Some considerations include the following:

   o *Cross-functional collaboration:* This entails building and sustaining the process and spirit of working together with functional leaders when collecting data on innovation ideas generated across functional units. The earlier discussion of innovation-idea management systems suggested an elaborate approach for establishing various innovation-idea management committees as part of the corporate strategy for sustaining an effective innovation-idea management system. It was further stated that collaboration among functional units is vital in ensuring that an organization has an effective innovation-idea management system. In relation to collecting data on the number of innovation ideas generated over a particular period, it is important that those responsible for writing innovation-performance reports (especially at the corporate level) must ensure that they collaborate with all stakeholders involved—that is, functional units and various innovation-related committees—to, for instance, ascertain the number of ideas generated in each functional unit over a particular period.

   o *Designing the right presentation format:* This means ensuring that the right type of format or technique is used to present the number of innovation ideas generated across functional units. Generally, one of the purposes of reporting innovation performance in organizations is to enable every member of the organization's workforce, from CEO to the most junior, to understand all aspects of the organization's innovation performance. Data presentation therefore plays a critical role in realizing the purpose of reporting innovation performance in the organization. Thus, the data-presentation format or techniques must ensure that data are presented in a simple, creative, and interesting manner, without the audiences across functional units having to work hard to understand the data presented about the number of innovation ideas and other dimensions of innovation-performance measurements.

## Ability to Measure and Report Innovation Performance | 207

*Illustration: How to Present Radical and Incremental Innovation Ideas*

This section demonstrates how to determine and present the number of radical and incremental innovation ideas generated across functional units in the context of the four core functional units and five support functional units of DM Personal Care Products. The steps in the process are presented first.

*Steps*
- First, identify core and support functional units of the company.
- Second, structure the presentation format according to the functional units of the company.
- Third, outline the company's product platforms.

Recall that the core and support functional units of DM Personal Care Products are as follows:

*Core functional units*
- ❖ Product-development unit, with the following segments:
    - Body-lotions segment
    - Skin-cleansing segment
    - Hair-care segment
    - Hand-washing segment
- ❖ Manufacturing-processes department, (the manufacturing-processes department comprises the same segments as the product-development unit)
- ❖ Marketing department, with the following units:
    - Pricing unit
    - Product-promotion unit
    - New-markets unit
    - Product-delivery unit
    - Packaging unit
- ❖ Customer service department

*Support functional units*
- Procurement department
- HR department
- Finance and accounting department
- IT department
- Corporate affairs department

*Presentation Format*

Regarding presentation format, assume that simple charts have been selected for use in presenting the number of radical and incremental innovation ideas generated over a particular period in each of the core and support functional units of DM Personal Care Products. We'll begin with core functional units and then move to the support units. Specifically, we'll start with the product-development unit.

## Product-Development Unit

The first step is to determine the number of product categories and segments in the product-development unit. The following are the product categories of the department under consideration:
- o Body-lotions category
- o Skin-cleansing category
- o Hair-care category
- o Hand-washing category

The second step is to create simple charts for presenting the number of radical and incremental product innovation ideas generated in each of these product categories during the period under review. For purposes of illustration, we'll assume quarterly review in four segments: Q1, Q2, Q3, and Q4. For illustration purposes, innovation ideas in the body-lotions category are referred to as *radical* and *incremental body-lotion innovation ideas*.

The two simple charts in figures 15-1 and 15-2 show radical and incremental body-lotion innovation ideas generated in the body-lotions category in each quarter of 2018. The charts show both the target and actual numbers of innovation ideas generated.

Similar charts would be created to show the number of radical and incremental innovation ideas generated in each of the other three product categories over the same period:
- o Skin-cleansing category
- o Hair-care category
- o Hand-washing category

There are cases where a product category may have a number of product segments. In such cases, the number of radical and incremental innovation ideas generated should be determined per product segment of the particular product category. For instance, under its new corporate structure (with Alphabet as parent company), Google has six product categories: Android, Search, YouTube, Apps, Maps, and Ads. Each of these categories has product segments, and if we were to determine the number of innovation ideas generated, we would determine the number of innovation ideas generated in all product segments of each product category.

## Manufacturing-Processes Department

Recall that the manufacturing department of DM Personal Care Products has four main manufacturing-processes categories in line with the four product categories in the product-development department:
- o Body-lotions manufacturing-processes category
- o Skin-cleansing manufacturing-processes category
- o Hair-care manufacturing-processes category
- o Hand-washing manufacturing-processes category

As with the product-development unit, two simple charts can be used to illustrate the number of radical and incremental innovation ideas generated in these four manufacturing-processes categories in each quarter of 2018. For illustration purposes, figures 15-3 and 15-4 show the radical and incremental innovation ideas generated in the body-lotions manufacturing-processes category in each quarter of 2018.

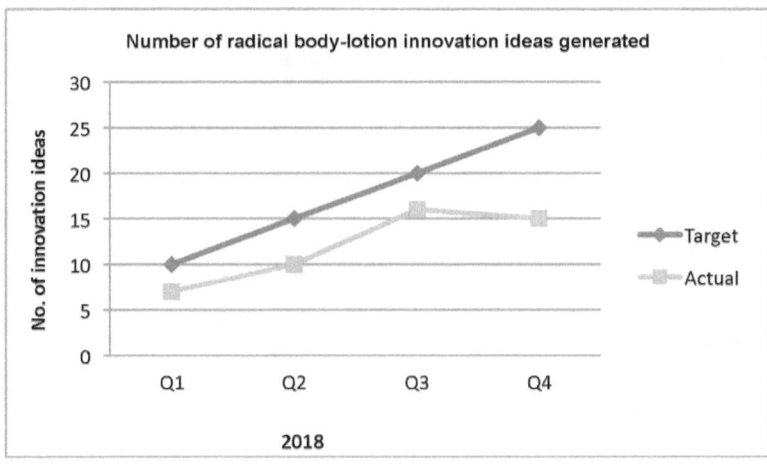

*Figure 15-1*

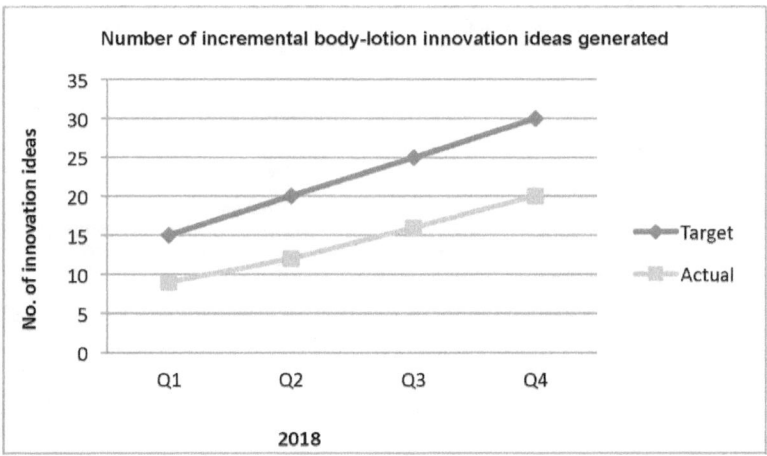

*Figure 15-2*

Similar charts would be created to show the number of radical and incremental innovation ideas generated in each of the other three manufacturing-processes categories over the same period:
- o  Skin-cleansing manufacturing-processes category
- o  Hair-care manufacturing-processes category
- o  Hand-washing manufacturing-processes category

As in the first illustration for the product-development unit, there are instances where a manufacturing-processes category may have a number of product-manufacturing segments. In such cases, the number of radical and incremental innovation ideas generated should be determined per the product-manufacturing segment of the particular manufacturing-processes category.

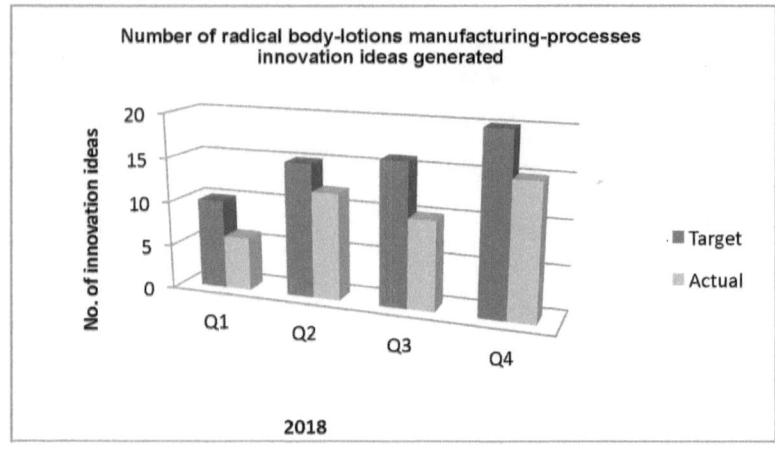

*Figure 15-3*

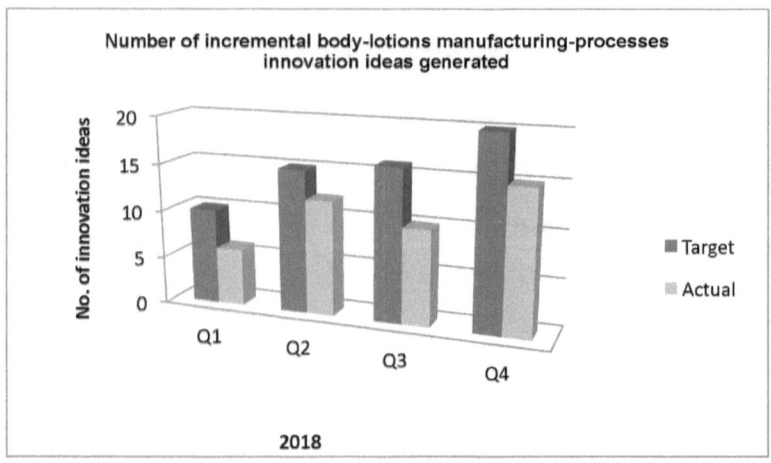

*Figure 15-4*

*Marketing Department*

Recall that this department has five main marketing-related functional subunits, structured as follows:
- Pricing unit
- Product-promotion unit
- Product-delivery unit
- New-markets unit
- Packaging unit

Similar to the presentation format used for the first two functional units, the two simple charts in figures 15-5 and 15-6 present the number of radical and incremental pricing innovation ideas generated for each quarter of 2018.

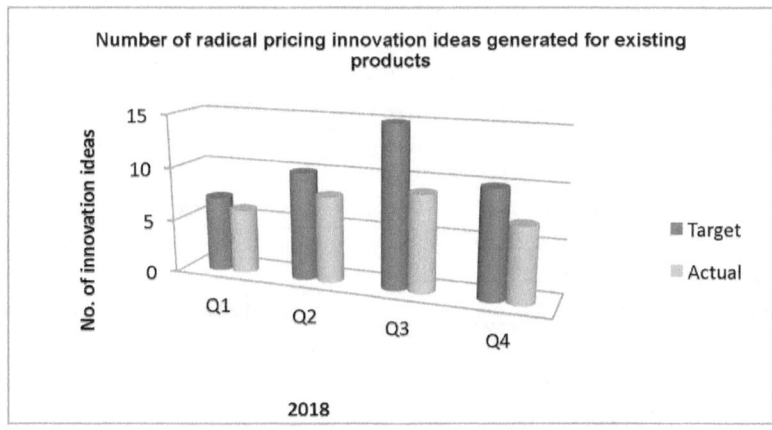

*Figure 15-5*

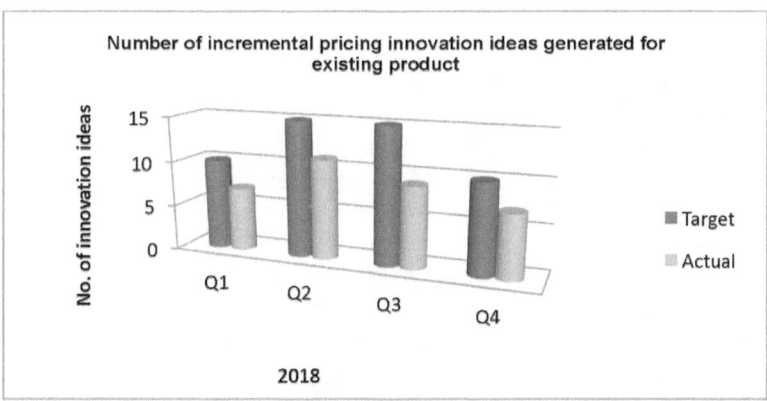

*Figure 15-6*

Similar charts would be created to illustrate the number of radical and incremental marketing innovation ideas generated in each of the other four functional subunits of the marketing department in each quarter of 2018. The other marketing functional subunits and the type of innovation ideas (in parentheses) that would be generated in each unit are as follows:

- o  Product-promotion unit (product-promotion innovation ideas generated for existing products
- o  Product-delivery unit (product-delivery innovation ideas generated for existing products)
- o  New-markets unit (new-market innovation ideas generated for existing products)
- o  Packaging unit (packaging innovation ideas generated for existing products)

## Customer Service Department

Before we look at how to present the number of customer service innovation ideas generated, it's important to reiterate two of the aspects that were described earlier regarding customer service innovations. First, customer service innovations are designed to support the delivery of product offerings at different stages: before purchase, during purchase, and after purchase. Second is that some customer service innovations (usually referred to as *customer experience innovations*) are implemented across all organizational functions and channels and are designed to continually enhance the quality of interaction between the company and its customers at all touchpoints.

The importance of understanding this is that the customer service innovation ideas generated should be presented according to the customer service components. For illustration purposes, the customer service innovation ideas generated could be presented according to the following categories:

- o  Customer service innovation ideas designed to support the delivery of product offerings *before* purchase
- o  Customer service innovation ideas designed to support the delivery of product offerings *during* purchase
- o  Customer service innovation ideas designed to support the delivery of product offerings *after* purchase
- o  Customer service innovation ideas aimed at improving the quality of interaction between the company and its customers at all touchpoints

## Presentation Format

Let's assume we are determining customer service innovation ideas aimed at supporting the delivery of product offerings before purchase. As in the earlier examples, the before-purchase innovation ideas can be organized into two categories: *before-purchase radical customer service innovation ideas* and *before-purchase incremental customer service innovation ideas*.

Figures 15-7 and 15-8 illustrate the number of radical and incremental customer service innovation ideas generated in each quarter of 2018.

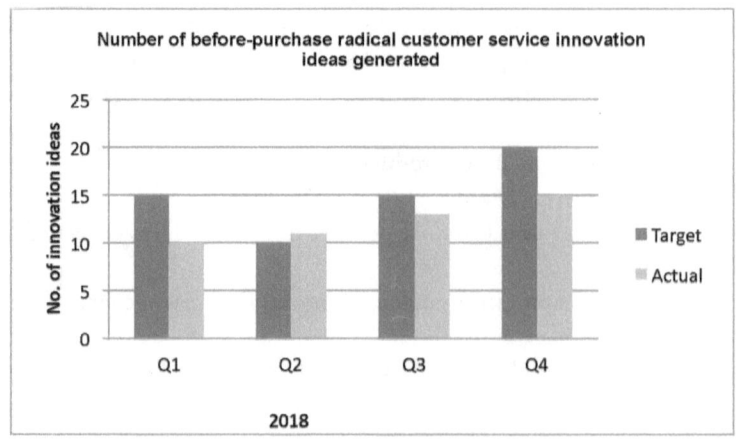

*Figure 15-7*

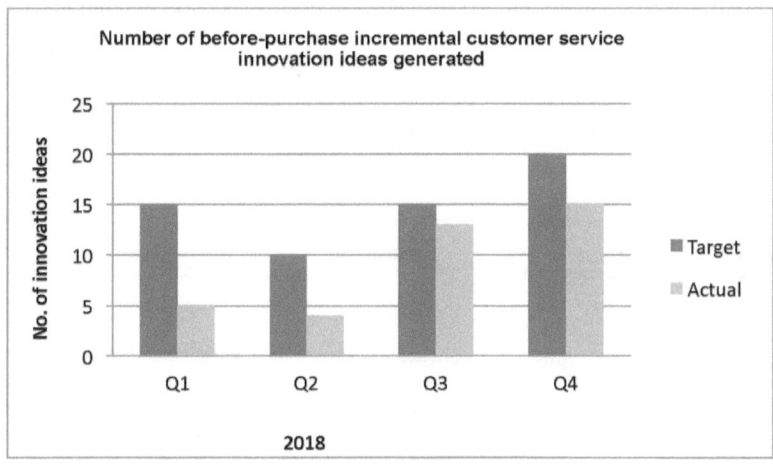

*Figure 15-8*

Similar charts would be created to show the number of radical and incremental customer service innovation ideas generated in each of the other three components during the same period:

- o Customer service innovation ideas designed to support the delivery of product offerings during purchase
- o Customer service innovation ideas designed to support the delivery of product offerings after purchase
- o Customer service innovation ideas aimed at improving the quality of interaction between the company and its customers at all touchpoints

## Presenting Radical and Incremental Innovation Ideas Generated in Support Functional Units

As mentioned, support functional units play a vital role in implementing innovation-support strategies for creating a climate to advance innovation across functional units. Thus, in addition to implementing innovation-support initiatives, organizational leaders should encourage the generation of cost-saving innovation ideas and other efficiency-related innovation ideas in support functional units.

Therefore, this section shows how to present data on the cost-saving innovation ideas generated in the five support functional units of DM Personal Care Products:

- ❖ Procurement department
- ❖ HR department
- ❖ Finance and accounting department
- ❖ IT department
- ❖ Corporate affairs department

Figures 15-9 and 15-10 illustrate how to present the number of radical and incremental cost-saving innovation ideas generated in support functional units over a particular period. For illustration purposes, the procurement department is used as an example to show the

214 | LEADERSHIP FOR INNOVATION

number of radical and incremental procurement innovation ideas generated in each quarter of 2018.

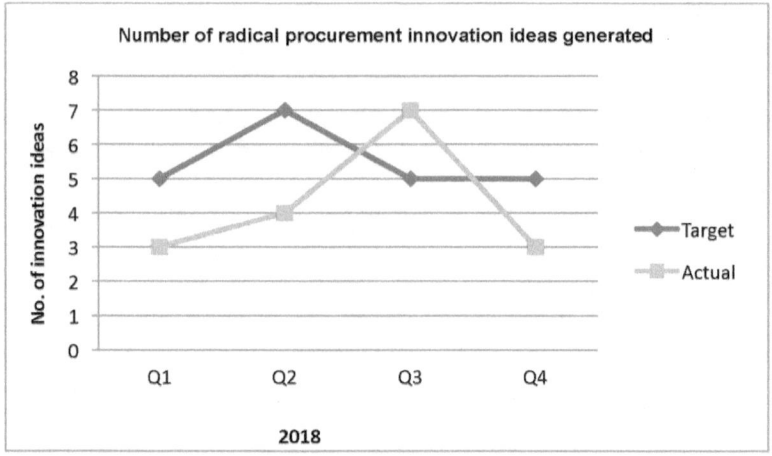

*Figure 15-9*

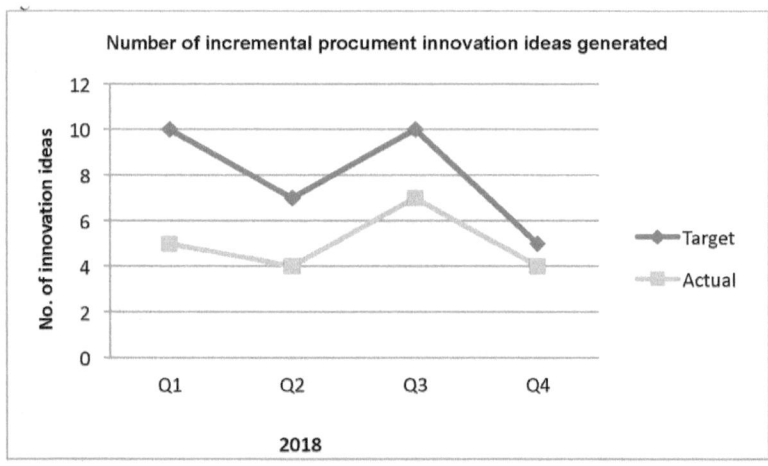

*Figure 15-10*

Similar charts would be created to illustrate the number of radical and incremental cost-saving innovation ideas generated in each of the other four support functional units in each quarter of 2018. The other support functional units and the type of innovation ideas (in parentheses) that would be generated for each support unit are as follows:

❖ HR department (*cost-saving HR innovation ideas*)
❖ Finance and accounting department (*cost-saving accounting innovation ideas*)
❖ IT department (*cost-saving IT innovation ideas*)
❖ Corporate affairs department (*cost-saving corporate affairs innovation ideas*)

Ability to Measure and Report Innovation Performance | 215

ii. **Number of Innovation Ideas Undergoing Development**
Once the information on the number of radical and incremental innovation ideas generated has been presented, the next step is to determine the number, type, and degree of innovation ideas undergoing development during the period under review. Thus, the second context of innovation output measurement involves determining and presenting the number of radical and incremental innovation ideas undergoing development in the innovation-development process over a particular period.

As in previous sections, we'll use the core and support functional units of DM Personal Care Products to illustrate how to present the number of radical and incremental innovation ideas undergoing development. The presentation begins with the core functional units and then covers the support functional units, which are as follows:

*Core functional units*
- Product-development unit, with the following segments:
  o Body-lotions segment
  o Skin-cleansing segment
  o Hair-care segment
  o Hand-washing segment
- Manufacturing-processes department
- Marketing department, with the following units:
  o Pricing unit
  o Product-promotion unit
  o Product-delivery unit
  o New-markets unit
  o Packaging unit
- Customer service department

*Product-Development Department*
Similar to the previous examples of determining and presenting the number of ideas generated, the following charts illustrate how to present the number of radical and incremental innovation ideas undergoing development in each of the following product categories of the product-development unit:
o Body-lotions category
o Skin-cleansing category
o Hair-care category
o Hand-washing category

Figures 15-11 and 15-12 illustrate the number of radical and incremental body-lotion innovation ideas undergoing development in each quarter of 2018 (target and actual).

216 | LEADERSHIP FOR INNOVATION

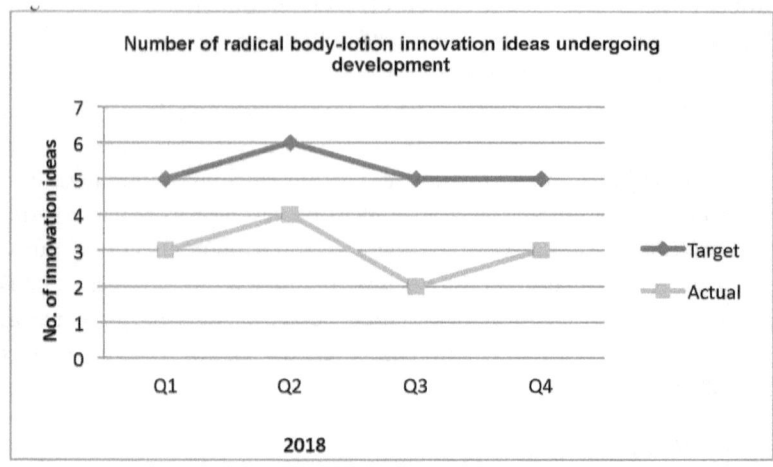

*Figure 15-11*

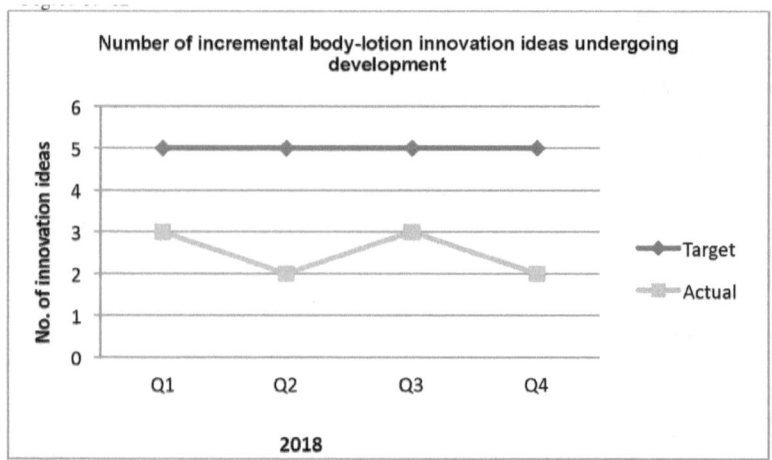

*Figure 15-12*

Similar charts would be created to show the number of radical and incremental innovation ideas undergoing development in each of the other three product categories over the same period:
- o  Skin-cleansing category
- o  Hair-care category
- o  Hand-washing category
- o  Manufacturing Department

Similarly, recall that the manufacturing-processes functional unit has four main manufacturing-processes categories:
- o  Body-lotions manufacturing-processes category
- o  Skin-cleansing manufacturing-processes category
- o  Hair-care manufacturing-processes category
- o  Hand-washing manufacturing-processes category

Ability to Measure and Report Innovation Performance | 217

The simple charts in figures 15-13 and 15-14 illustrate the number of radical and incremental body-lotions innovation ideas undergoing development in each quarter of 2018, (target and actual).

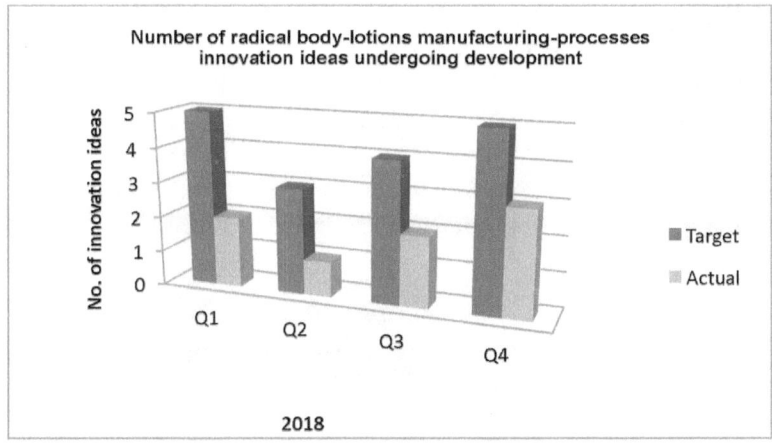

*Figure 15-13*

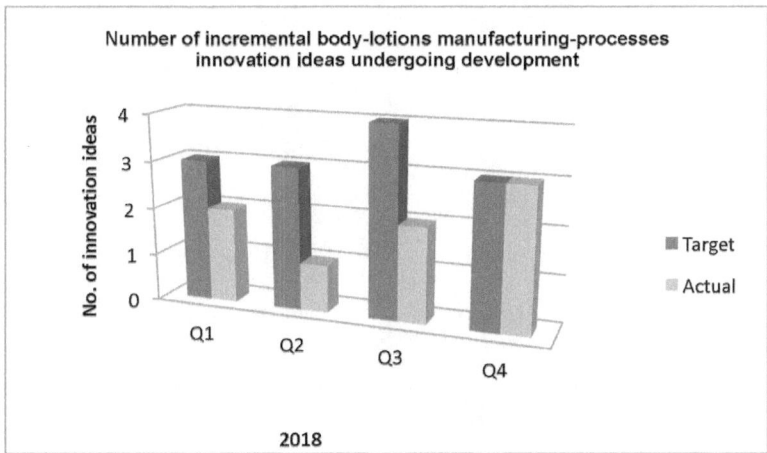

*Figure 15-14*

Similar charts would be created to show the number of radical and incremental innovation ideas undergoing development in each of the other three manufacturing-processes categories over the same period:
- o   Skin-cleansing manufacturing-processes category
- o   Hair-care manufacturing-processes category
- o   Hand-washing manufacturing-processes category

## Marketing Department

The third example shows how to present the number of radical and incremental marketing innovation ideas undergoing development in each of the five marketing-related functional subunits:

o   Pricing unit
o   Product-promotion unit
o   Product-delivery unit
o   New-markets unit
o   Packaging unit

The two charts in figures 15-15 and 15-16 present the number of radical and incremental pricing innovation ideas undergoing development in the four quarters of 2018 (target and actual).

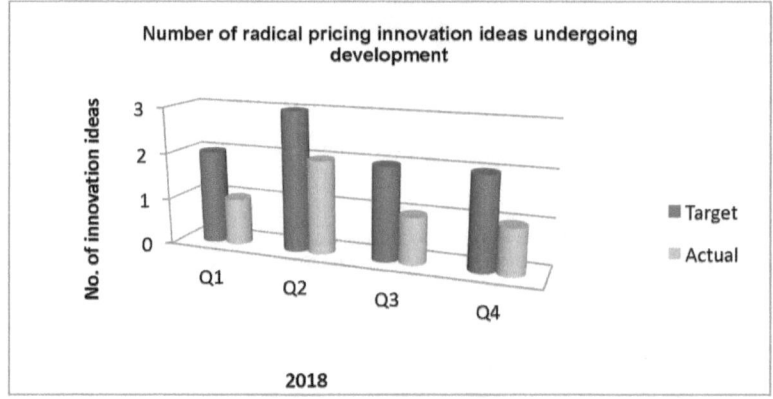

*Figure 15-15*

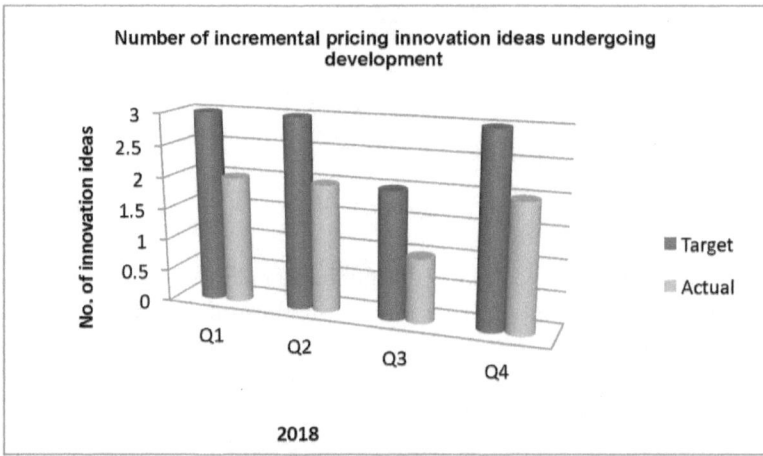

*Figure 15-16*

Similar charts would be created to illustrate the number of radical and incremental marketing innovation ideas undergoing development in each of the other four marketing functional subunits:
- o Product-promotion unit (product-promotion innovation ideas undergoing development for existing products)
- o Product-delivery unit (product-delivery innovation ideas undergoing development for existing products)
- o New-markets unit (new-market innovation ideas undergoing development for existing products)
- o Packaging unit (packaging innovation ideas undergoing development for existing products)

*Customer Service Department*

The earlier discussion of the presentation format for innovation ideas generated in the customer service department outlined four aspects to bear in mind when presenting the number of customer service innovation ideas generated. Similarly, when presenting the number of customer service innovation ideas undergoing development, it's important to bear in mind how the customer service segments of an organization are structured. This will enable you to format the presentation of customer service innovation ideas undergoing development according to the customer service segments.

The customer service innovation ideas undergoing development could be categorized as follows:
- o Customer service innovation ideas undergoing development designed to support the delivery of product offerings *before purchase*
- o Customer service innovation ideas undergoing development designed to support the delivery of product offerings *during purchase*
- o Customer service innovation ideas undergoing development designed to support the delivery of product offerings *after purchase*
- o Customer service innovation ideas undergoing development aimed at improving the quality of interaction between the company and its customers at all touchpoints

*Presentation Format*

Let's assume we are determining the number of customer service innovation ideas undergoing development aimed at supporting the delivery of product offerings before purchase.

The two simple charts in figures 15-17 and 15-18 present the number of before-purchase radical and incremental customer service innovation ideas undergoing development in the four quarters of 2018 (target and actual).

220 | LEADERSHIP FOR INNOVATION

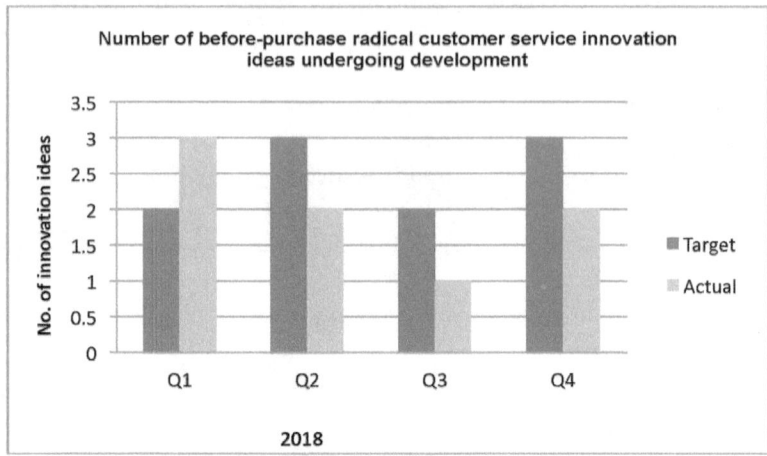

Figure 15-17

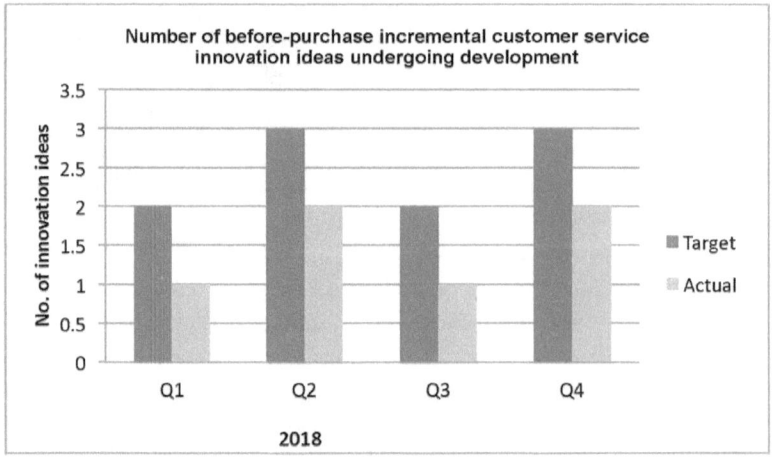

Figure 15-18

Similar charts would be created for each of the other three customer service categories:
- o Customer service innovation ideas undergoing development designed to support the delivery of product offerings during purchase
- o Customer service innovation ideas undergoing development designed to support the delivery of product offerings after purchase
- o Customer service innovation ideas undergoing development aimed at improving the quality of interaction between the company and its customers at all touchpoints

## Determining Radical and Incremental Innovation Ideas Undergoing Development in Support Functional Units

Recall that innovation ideas generated in support functional units are usually focused on cost savings and efficiency. This section looks at how to determine and present cost-saving innovation ideas undergoing development in the support functional units of DM Personal Care Products, which are as follows:

- ❖ Procurement department
- ❖ HR department
- ❖ Finance and accounting department
- ❖ IT department
- ❖ Corporate affairs department

The charts in figures 15-19 and 15-20 show the number of radical and incremental procurement innovation ideas undergoing development in each quarter of 2018 (actual and target).

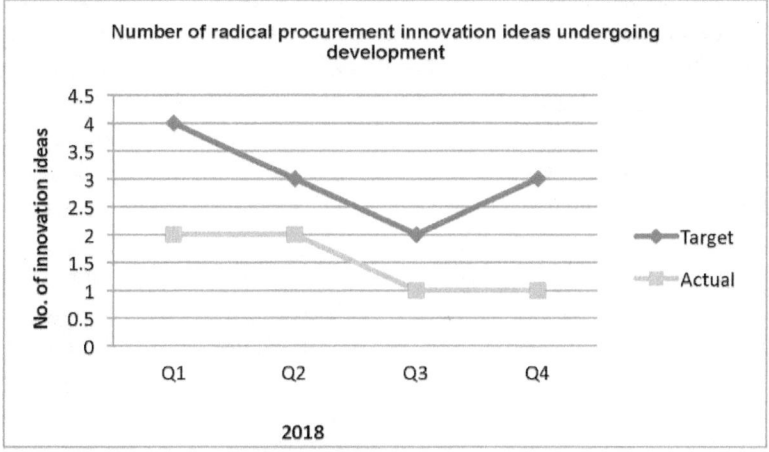

*Figure 15-19*

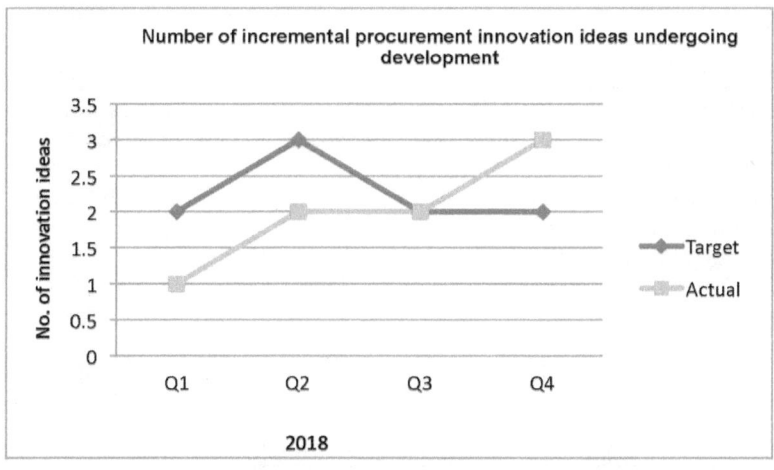

*Figure 15-20*

Similar charts would be created for each of the other four support functional units:
- ❖ HR department (cost-saving HR innovation ideas)
- ❖ Finance and accounting department (cost-saving finance and accounting innovation ideas)
- ❖ IT department (cost-saving IT innovation ideas)
- ❖ Corporate affairs department (cost-saving corporate affairs innovation ideas)

## Innovation Output Evaluation Worksheet

The beginning of chapter 15 noted that each of the four dimensions of innovation-performance measurement has an accompanying evaluation worksheet (e.g., the innovation input evaluation worksheet at the end of the section on innovation input measurement). Thus, once you have determined the number of ideas generated and the number of ideas undergoing development over a particular period, the next activity is to determine whether the *target number of ideas generated* and *target number of ideas undergoing development* over a particular period were achieved. That's where the innovation output evaluation is applied. The example of the innovation output evaluation worksheet in this section is divided into two stand-alone worksheets: an *innovation output evaluation worksheet for ideas generated* and an *innovation output evaluation worksheet for ideas undergoing development*.

*Innovation Output Evaluation for Ideas Generated*

Worksheets 15-6 through 15-8 show examples of the innovation output evaluation worksheet for assessing whether the target number of innovation ideas generated was achieved in both the core and support functional units of DM Personal Care Products over a particular period. For illustration purposes, the evaluation worksheet is applied to three of the functional units: the product-development unit (worksheet 15-6), the marketing department (worksheet 15-7), and the procurement department (worksheet 15-8).

Worksheet 15-6. Example of innovation output evaluation for product innovation ideas

| |
|---|
| **Name of Department:** Product-development unit<br>**Date:** April 30, 2018 |
| **Purpose of evaluation:** *To assess whether the target or goal of generating a particular number of radical and incremental product innovation ideas during the period under review (e.g., January–April of 2018) was achieved*<br>The segments of the product-development unit of DM Personal Care Products are presented in the worksheet as follows:<br>• Part A: Body-lotions segment<br>• Part B: Skin-cleansing segment<br>• Part C: Hair-care segment<br>• Part D: Hand-washing segment |
| Part A<br>Number of *radical* and *incremental* product<br>innovation ideas generated in the body-lotions segment |
| *Radical*: Number of radical innovation ideas generated during the period under review |

| Radical innovation ideas generated in the body-lotions segment: *Was the target for this product category achieved?* (tick "Yes" or "No") | Yes | Comment  If yes, indicate the percentage achieved. **Reasons:** *What factors are responsible for achieving or exceeding the set target?* | No | Comment  If no, by what percentage was the target missed? **Reasons:** *What factors are responsible for not meeting the projected target?* |
|---|---|---|---|---|
| *Incremental*: Number of incremental innovation ideas generated during the period under review |||||
| Incremental innovation ideas generated in the body-lotions segment: *Was the target for this product category achieved?* (tick *"Yes"* or *"No"*) | Yes | Comment  If yes, indicate the percentage achieved. **Reasons:** *What factors are responsible for achieving or exceeding the set target?* | No | Comment  If no, by what percentage was the target missed? **Reasons:** *What factors are responsible for not meeting the projected target?* |
| **Part B**  Number of *radical* and *incremental* product innovation ideas generated in the skin-cleansing segment |||||
| *Radical*: Number of radical innovation ideas generated during the period under review |||||
| **Radical product innovation ideas generated in the skin-cleansing segment:** *Was the target for this product category achieved?* (tick *"Yes"* or *"No"*) | Yes | Comment  If yes, indicate the percentage achieved. **Reasons:** *What factors are responsible for achieving or exceeding the set target?* | No | Comment  If no, by what percentage was the target missed? **Reasons:** *What factors are responsible for not meeting the projected target?* |
| *Incremental*: Number of incremental innovation ideas generated during the period under review |||||
| **Incremental product innovation ideas generated in the skin-cleansing segment:** *Was the target for this product category achieved?* (tick "Yes" or "No") | Yes | Comment  If yes, indicate the percentage achieved. **Reasons:** *What factors are responsible for achieving or exceeding the set target?* | No | Comment  If no, by what percentage was the target missed? **Reasons:** *What factors are responsible for not meeting the projected target?* |
| **Part C**  Number of radical and incremental product innovation ideas generated in the hair-care segment |||||
| *Radical*: Number of radical innovation ideas generated during the period under review |||||

| Radical product innovation ideas generated in the hair-care segment:<br>*Was the target for this product category achieved?* (tick "Yes" or "No") | Yes | Comment | No | Comment |
|---|---|---|---|---|
| | | If yes, indicate the percentage achieved.<br>**Reasons:** *What factors are responsible for achieving or exceeding the set target?* | | If no, by what percentage was the target missed?<br>**Reasons:** *What factors are responsible for not meeting the projected target?* |

*Incremental*: Number of incremental innovation ideas generated during the period under review

| Incremental product innovation ideas generated in the hair-care segment:<br>*Was the target for this product category achieved?* (tick "Yes" or "No") | Yes | Comment | No | Comment |
|---|---|---|---|---|
| | | If yes, indicate the percentage achieved.<br>**Reasons:** *What factors are responsible for achieving or exceeding the set target?* | | If no, by what percentage was the target missed?<br>**Reasons:** *What factors are responsible for not meeting the projected target?* |

**Part D**
**Number of radical and incremental product innovation ideas generated in the hand-washing segment**

*Radical*: Number of radical innovation ideas generated during the period under review

| Radical product innovation ideas generated in the hand-washing segment:<br>*Was the target for this product category achieved?* (tick "Yes" or "No") | Yes | Comment | No | Comment |
|---|---|---|---|---|
| | | If yes, indicate the percentage achieved.<br>**Reasons:** *What factors are responsible for achieving or exceeding the set target?* | | If no, by what percentage was the target missed?<br>**Reasons:** *What factors are responsible for not meeting the projected target?* |

*Incremental*: Number of incremental innovation ideas generated during the period under review

| Incremental product innovation ideas generated in the hand-washing segment:<br>*Was the target for this product category achieved?* (tick "Yes" or "No") | Yes | Comment | No | Comment |
|---|---|---|---|---|
| | | If yes, indicate the percentage achieved.<br>**Reasons:** *What factors are responsible for achieving or exceeding the set target?* | | If no, by what percentage was the target missed?<br>Reasons: *What factors are **responsible** for not meeting the projected target?* |

## Ability to Measure and Report Innovation Performance | 225

Worksheet 15-7. Example of innovation output evaluation for marketing innovation ideas

| |
|---|
| **Name of Department:** Marketing department<br>**Date:** April 30, 2018 |
| **Purpose of evaluation:** *To assess whether the target or goal of generating a particular number of radical and incremental marketing innovation ideas during the period under review* (e.g., January–April of 2018) *was achieved*<br>The worksheet is presented according to the functional components of the marketing department of DM Personal Care Products:<br>• Part A: Product delivery<br>• Part B: Pricing<br>• Part C: Product promotion<br>• Part D: New markets<br>• Part E: Packaging |
| **Part A (i)**<br>Revenue generation–focused product-delivery innovation ideas |
| **Number of *radical* and *incremental* product-delivery innovation ideas generated during the period under review** |
| ***Radical*:** Number of radical product-delivery innovation ideas generated during the period under review |

| Was the target for this category achieved? (tick "Yes" or "No") | Yes | Comment | No | Comment |
|---|---|---|---|---|
| | | If yes, indicate the percentage achieved.<br>**Reasons:** *What factors are responsible for achieving or exceeding the set target?* | | If no, by what percentage was the target missed?<br>**Reasons:** *What factors are responsible for not meeting the projected target?* |

| |
|---|
| ***Incremental*:** Number of incremental product-delivery innovation ideas generated during the period under review |

| Was the target for this category achieved? (tick "Yes" or "No") | Yes | Comment | No | Comment |
|---|---|---|---|---|
| | | If yes, indicate the percentage achieved.<br>Reasons: *What factors are responsible for achieving or exceeding the set target?* | | If no, by what percentage was the target missed?<br>Reasons: *What factors are responsible for not meeting the projected target?* |

| |
|---|
| **Part A (ii)**<br>Cost saving–focused product-delivery innovation ideas |
| **Number of *radical* and *incremental* product-delivery cost-saving innovation ideas generated during the period under review** |
| ***Radical*:** Number of radical product-delivery cost-saving innovation ideas generated during the period under review |

## 226 | LEADERSHIP FOR INNOVATION

| Was the target for this category achieved? (tick "Yes" or "No") | Yes | Comment | No | Comment |
|---|---|---|---|---|
| | | If yes, indicate the percentage achieved. **Reasons**: *What factors are responsible for achieving or exceeding the set target?* | | If no, by what percentage was the target missed? **Reasons**: *What factors are responsible for not meeting the projected target?* |

*Incremental*: **Number of incremental product-delivery cost-saving innovation ideas generated during the period under review**

| Was the target for this category achieved? (tick "Yes" or "No") | Yes | Comment | No | Comment |
|---|---|---|---|---|
| | | If yes, indicate the percentage achieved. **Reasons**: *What factors are responsible for achieving or exceeding the set target?* | | If no, by what percentage was the target missed? **Reasons**: *What factors are responsible for not meeting the projected target?* |

### Part B
### Pricing innovation ideas (for existing products)

**Number of *radical* and *incremental* pricing innovation ideas generated for existing products during the period under review**

*Radical*: **Number of radical pricing innovation ideas generated for existing products during the period under review**

| Was the target for this category achieved? (tick "Yes" or "No") | Yes | Comment | No | Comment |
|---|---|---|---|---|
| | | If yes, indicate the percentage achieved. **Reasons**: *What factors are responsible for achieving or exceeding the set target?* | | If no, by what percentage was the target missed? **Reasons**: *What factors are responsible for not meeting the projected target?* |

*Incremental*: **Number of incremental pricing innovation ideas generated for existing products during the period under review**

| Was the target for this category achieved? (tick "Yes" or "No") | Yes | Comment | No | Comment |
|---|---|---|---|---|
| | | If yes, indicate the percentage achieved. **Reasons**: *What factors are responsible for achieving or exceeding the set target?* | | If no, by what percentage was the target missed? **Reasons**: *What factors are responsible for not meeting the projected target?* |

# Ability to Measure and Report Innovation Performance | 227

| Part C (i) Revenue generation–focused product-promotion innovation ideas |||||
|---|---|---|---|---|
| **Number of *radical* and *incremental* product-promotion innovation ideas generated for existing products during the period under review** |||||
| ***Radical*: Number of radical product-promotion innovation ideas generated for existing products during the period under review** |||||
| *Was the target for this category achieved?* (tick "Yes" or "No") | Yes | Comment | No | Comment |
|  |  | If yes, indicate the percentage achieved. **Reasons:** *What factors are responsible for achieving or exceeding the set target?* |  | If no, by what percentage was the target missed? **Reasons:** *What factors are responsible for not meeting the projected target?* |
| ***Incremental*: Number of incremental product-promotion innovation ideas generated for existing products during the period under review** |||||
| *Was the target for this category achieved?* (tick "Yes" or "No") | Yes | Comment | No | Comment |
|  |  | If yes, indicate the percentage achieved. **Reasons:** *What factors are responsible for achieving or exceeding the set target?* |  | If no, by what percentage was the target missed? **Reasons:** *What factors are responsible for not meeting the projected target?* |
| Part C (ii) Cost saving–focused product-promotion innovation ideas |||||
| **Number of *radical* and *incremental* product-promotion cost-saving innovation ideas generated for existing products during the period under review** |||||
| ***Radical*: Number of radical product-promotion cost-saving innovation ideas generated for existing products during the period under review** |||||
| *Was the target for this category achieved?* (tick "Yes" or "No") | Yes | Comment | No | Comment |
|  |  | If yes, indicate the percentage achieved. **Reasons:** *What factors are responsible for achieving or exceeding the set target?* |  | If no, by what percentage was the target missed? **Reasons:** *What factors are responsible for not meeting the projected target?* |
| ***Incremental*: Number of incremental product-promotion cost-saving innovation ideas generated for existing products during the period under review** |||||

| Was the target for this category achieved? (tick "Yes" or "No") | Yes | Comment | No | Comment |
|---|---|---|---|---|
| | | If yes, indicate the percentage achieved. **Reasons:** *What factors are responsible for achieving or exceeding the set target?* | | If no, by what percentage was the target missed? **Reasons:** *What factors are responsible for not meeting the projected target?* |

**Part D**
**New-market innovation ideas**

Number of *new-unserved-market* and *new-market-segment* innovation ideas generated during the period under review

<u>New-unserved-market ideas:</u> Number of new-unserved-market ideas generated for existing products in geographical locations not served by competitors or the organization during the period under review

| Was the target for this category achieved? (tick "Yes" or "No") | Yes | Comment | No | Comment |
|---|---|---|---|---|
| | | If yes, indicate the percentage achieved. **Reasons:** *What factors are responsible for achieving or exceeding the set target?* | | If no, by what percentage was the target missed? **Reasons:** *What factors are responsible for not meeting the projected target?* |

*New-market-segment ideas:* Number of new-market-segment ideas generated for existing products within existing markets or geographical locations during the period under review

| Was the target for this category achieved? (tick "Yes" or "No") | Yes | Comment | No | Comment |
|---|---|---|---|---|
| | | If yes, indicate the percentage achieved. **Reasons:** *What factors are responsible for achieving or exceeding the set target?* | | If no, by what percentage was the target missed? **Reasons:** *What factors are responsible for not meeting the projected target?* |

**Part E (i)**
**Revenue generation–focused packaging innovation ideas**

Number of *radical* and *incremental* packaging innovation ideas generated during the period under review

*Radical:* Number of radical packaging innovation ideas generated during the period under review

| | | | | |
|---|---|---|---|---|
| *Was the target for this category achieved?* (tick "Yes" or "No") | Yes | Comment | No | Comment |
| | | If yes, indicate the percentage achieved. **Reasons:** *What factors are responsible for achieving or exceeding the set target?* | | If no, by what percentage was the target missed? **Reasons:** *What factors are responsible for not meeting the projected target?* |
| *Incremental*: Number of incremental packaging innovation ideas generated during the period under review ||||| 
| *Was the target for this category achieved?* (tick "Yes" or "No") | Yes | Comment | No | Comment |
| | | If yes, indicate the percentage achieved. **Reasons:** *What factors are responsible for achieving or exceeding the set target?* | | If no, by what percentage was the target missed? **Reasons:** *What factors are responsible for not meeting the projected target?* |
| **Part E (ii)** <br> **Cost-saving packaging innovation ideas** |||||
| Number of *radical* and *incremental* cost-saving packaging innovation ideas generated during the period under review |||||
| *Radical*: Number of radical cost-saving packaging innovation ideas generated during the period under review |||||
| *Was the target for this category achieved?* (tick "Yes" or "No") | Yes | Comment | No | Comment |
| | | If yes, indicate the percentage achieved. **Reasons:** *What factors are responsible for achieving or exceeding the set target?* | | If no, by what percentage was the target missed? **Reasons:** *What factors are responsible for not meeting the projected target?* |
| *Incremental*: Number of incremental cost-saving packaging innovation ideas generated during the period under review |||||
| *Was the target for this category achieved?* (tick "Yes" or "No") | Yes | Comment | No | Comment |
| | | If yes, indicate the percentage achieved. **Reasons:** *What factors are responsible for achieving or exceeding the set target?* | | If no, by what percentage was the target missed? **Reasons:** *What factors are responsible for not meeting the projected target?* |

Worksheets 15-6 and 15-7 show how the evaluation worksheet can be applied to two different core functional units (product development and marketing). Similarly, the evaluation worksheet can be applied to the other core functional units of DM Personal Care Products:

- ❖ Manufacturing-processes department
- ❖ Customer service department

Worksheet 15-8 shows how the evaluation worksheet can be applied to the support functional units of DM Personal Care Products, using the procurement department as an example.

Worksheet 15-8. Example of innovation output evaluation for cost-saving procurement innovation ideas

| **Name of Department:** Procurement<br>**Date:** April 30, 2018 |||||
|---|---|---|---|---|
| **Purpose of evaluation:** *To assess whether the target or goal of generating a particular number of radical and incremental cost-saving procurement innovation ideas during the period under review* (e.g., January–April of 2018) *was achieved*<br>This worksheet is divided into two parts:<br>• Part A: Number of *radical cost-saving procurement* innovation ideas generated during the period under review<br>• Part B: Number of *incremental cost-saving procurement* innovation ideas generated during the period under review |||||
| **Part A**<br>Number of radical cost-saving procurement innovation ideas generated during the period under review |||||
| *Was the target for this category achieved?* (tick "Yes" or "No") | Yes | Comment | No | Comment |
|  |  | If yes, indicate the percentage achieved.<br>**Reasons:** *What factors are responsible for achieving or exceeding the set target?* |  | If no, by what percentage was the target missed?<br>**Reasons:** *What factors are responsible for not meeting the projected target?* |
| **Part B**<br>Number of incremental cost-saving procurement innovation ideas generated during the period under review |||||
| *Was the target for this category achieved?* (tick "Yes" or "No") | Yes | Comment | No | Comment |
|  |  | If yes, indicate the percentage achieved.<br>**Reasons:** *What factors are responsible for achieving or exceeding the set target?* |  | If no, by what percentage was the target missed?<br>**Reasons:** *What factors are responsible for not meeting the projected target?* |

As with the previous two worksheets, worksheet 15-8 can also be applied to the other support functional units of DM Personal Care Products to assess the number of cost-saving innovation ideas generated:
- ❖ HR department
- ❖ Finance and accounting department
- ❖ IT department
- ❖ Corporate affairs department

## Innovation Output Evaluation for Ideas Undergoing Development

The second type of output evaluation is the innovation output evaluation for ideas undergoing development.

Just as it is important to assess the number of ideas generated, it is necessary to assess whether the target or goal of having a particular number of ideas undergoing development in the core and support functional units of DM Personal Care Products over a particular period was achieved. Worksheets 15-9 through 15-11 show how the innovation output evaluation worksheet is applied to assessing the number of innovation ideas undergoing development over a particular period. For illustration purposes, the evaluation worksheet is applied to three functional units: the product-development unit (worksheet 15-9), the marketing department (worksheet 15-10), and the procurement department (worksheet 15-11).

Worksheet 15-9. Example of innovation output evaluation
for product innovation ideas undergoing development

| |
|---|
| **Name of Department:** Product-development unit<br>**Date:** April 30, 2018 |
| **Purpose of evaluation:** *To assess whether the target or goal of having a particular number of radical and incremental product innovation ideas undergoing development during the period under review (e.g., January–April of 2018) was achieved*<br>The worksheet is divided into the four product segments of the product-development unit of DM Personal Care Products:<br>• Part A: Body-lotions segment<br>• Part B: Skin-cleansing segment<br>• Part C: Hair-care segment<br>• Part D: Hand-washing segment |
| Part A<br>Number of *radical* and *incremental* innovation ideas<br>undergoing development in the body-lotions segment |
| *Radical*: Number of radical innovation ideas in the body-lotions segment undergoing development during the period under review |

| Radical innovation ideas undergoing development in the body-lotions segment: *Was the target for this product category achieved?* (tick *"Yes"* or *"No"*) | *Yes* | *Comment* If yes, indicate the percentage achieved. **Reasons:** *What factors are responsible for achieving or exceeding the set target?* | *No* | *Comment* If no, by what percentage was the target missed? **Reasons:** *What factors are responsible for not meeting the projected target?* |
|---|---|---|---|---|

*Incremental:* **Number of incremental innovation ideas in the body-lotions segment undergoing development during the period under review**

| Incremental innovation ideas undergoing development in the body-lotions segment: *Was the target for this product category achieved?* (tick *"Yes"* or *"No"*) | Yes | Comment If yes, indicate the percentage achieved. **Reasons:** *What factors are responsible for achieving or exceeding the set target?* | No | Comment If no, by what percentage was the target missed? **Reasons:** *What factors are responsible for not meeting the projected target?* |
|---|---|---|---|---|

**Part B**
**Number of radical and incremental product innovation ideas undergoing development in the skin-cleansing segment**

*Radical:* **Number of radical innovation ideas undergoing development in the skin-cleansing segment during the period under review**

| Radical product innovation ideas undergoing development in the skin-cleansing segment: *Was the target for this product category achieved?* (tick *"Yes"* or *"No"*) | Yes | Comment If yes, indicate the percentage achieved. **Reasons:** *What factors are responsible for achieving or exceeding the set target?* | No | Comment If no, by what percentage was the target missed? **Reasons:** *What factors are responsible for not meeting the projected target?* |
|---|---|---|---|---|

*Incremental:* **Number of incremental innovation ideas undergoing development in the skin-cleansing segment during the period under review**

| Incremental product innovation ideas undergoing development in the skin-cleansing segment: *Was the target for this product category achieved?* (tick *"Yes"* or *"No"*) | Yes | Comment If yes, indicate the percentage achieved. **Reasons:** *What factors are responsible for achieving or exceeding the set target?* | No | Comment If no, by what percentage was the target missed? **Reasons:** *What factors are responsible for not meeting the projected target?* |
|---|---|---|---|---|

## Ability to Measure and Report Innovation Performance | 233

### Part C
### Number of *radical* and *incremental* product innovation ideas undergoing development in the hair-care segment

*Radical*: Number of radical innovation ideas undergoing development in the hair-care segment during the period under review

| Radical product innovation ideas undergoing development in the hair-care segment: *Was the target for this product category achieved?* (tick "Yes" or "No") | Yes | Comment | No | Comment |
|---|---|---|---|---|
| | | If yes, indicate the percentage achieved. **Reasons**: *What factors are responsible for achieving or exceeding the set target?* | | If no, by what percentage was the target missed? **Reasons**: *What factors are responsible for not meeting the projected target?* |

*Incremental*: Number of incremental innovation ideas undergoing development in the hair-care segment during the period under review

| Incremental product innovation ideas undergoing development in the hair-care segment: *Was the target for this product category achieved?* (tick "Yes" or "No") | Yes | Comment | No | Comment |
|---|---|---|---|---|
| | | If yes, indicate the percentage achieved. **Reasons**: *What factors are responsible for achieving or exceeding the set target?* | | If no, by what percentage was the target missed? **Reasons**: *What factors are responsible for not meeting the projected target?* |

### Part D
### Number of *radical* and *incremental* product innovation ideas undergoing development in the hand-washing segment

*Radical*: Number of radical innovation ideas undergoing development in the hand-washing segment during the period under review

| Radical product innovation ideas undergoing development in the hand-washing segment: *Was the target for this product category achieved?* (tick "Yes" or "No") | Yes | Comment | No | Comment |
|---|---|---|---|---|
| | | If yes, indicate the percentage achieved. **Reasons**: *What factors are responsible for achieving or exceeding the set target?* | | If no, by what percentage was the target missed? **Reasons**: *What factors are responsible for not meeting the projected target?* |

*Incremental*: Number of incremental innovation ideas undergoing development in the hand-washing segment during the period under review

| Incremental product innovation ideas undergoing development in the hand-washing segment: *Was the target for this product category achieved?* (tick "Yes" or "No") | Yes | Comment | No | Comment |
|---|---|---|---|---|
| | | If yes, indicate the percentage achieved. **Reasons**: *What factors are responsible for achieving or exceeding the set target?* | | If no, by what percentage was the target missed? **Reasons**: *What factors are responsible for not meeting the projected target?* |

Worksheet 15-10. Example of innovation output evaluation for marketing innovation ideas undergoing development

| |
|---|
| **Name of Department:** Marketing department<br>**Date:** April 30, 2018 |
| **Purpose of evaluation:** *To assess whether the target or goal of having a particular number of marketing innovation ideas undergoing development during the period under review* (e.g., January–April of 2018) *was achieved*<br>The worksheet is divided into the functional components of the marketing department of DM Personal Care Products:<br>• Part A: Product delivery<br>• Part B: Pricing<br>• Part C: Product promotion<br>• Part D: New markets<br>• Part E: Packaging |
| **Part A (i)**<br>Revenue generation–focused product-delivery innovation ideas |
| Number of *radical* and *incremental* product-delivery innovation ideas undergoing development during the period under review |
| *Radical:* Number of radical product-delivery innovation ideas undergoing development during the period under review |

| Was the target for this category achieved? (tick "Yes" or "No") | Yes | Comment | No | Comment |
|---|---|---|---|---|
| | | If yes, indicate the percentage achieved. **Reasons:** *What factors are responsible for achieving or exceeding the set target?* | | If no, by what percentage was the target missed? **Reasons:** *What factors are responsible for not meeting the projected target?* |

| |
|---|
| *Incremental:* Number of incremental product-delivery innovation ideas undergoing development during the period under review |

| Was the target for this category achieved? (tick "Yes" or "No") | Yes | Comment | No | Comment |
|---|---|---|---|---|
| | | If yes, indicate the percentage achieved. **Reasons:** *What factors are responsible for achieving or exceeding the set target?* | | If no, by what percentage was the target missed? **Reasons:** *What factors are responsible for not meeting the projected target?* |

| |
|---|
| **Part A (ii)**<br>Cost saving–focused product-delivery innovation ideas |
| Number of *radical* and *incremental* product-delivery cost-saving innovation ideas undergoing development during the period under review |
| *Radical:* Number of radical product-delivery cost-saving innovation ideas undergoing development during the period under review |

| Was the target for this category achieved? (tick "Yes" or "No") | Yes | Comment | No | Comment |
|---|---|---|---|---|
| | | If yes, indicate the percentage achieved. **Reasons:** *What factors are responsible for achieving or exceeding the set target?* | | If no, by what percentage was the target missed? **Reasons:** *What factors are responsible for not meeting the projected target?* |

***Incremental:*** **Number of incremental product-delivery cost-saving innovation ideas undergoing development during the period under review**

| Was the target for this category achieved? (tick "Yes" or "No") | Yes | Comment | No | Comment |
|---|---|---|---|---|
| | | If yes, indicate the percentage achieved. **Reasons:** *What factors are responsible for achieving or exceeding the set target?* | | If no, by what percentage was the target missed? **Reasons:** *What factors are responsible for not meeting the projected target?* |

**Part B**
**Pricing innovation ideas** *(for existing products)*

**Number of *radical* and *incremental* pricing innovation ideas undergoing development for existing products during the period under review**

***Radical:*** **Number of radical pricing innovation ideas undergoing development for existing products during the period under review**

| Was the target for this category achieved? (tick "Yes" or "No") | Yes | Comment | No | Comment |
|---|---|---|---|---|
| | | If yes, indicate the percentage achieved. **Reasons:** *What factors are responsible for achieving or exceeding the set target?* | | If no, by what percentage was the target missed? **Reasons:** *What factors are responsible for not meeting the projected target?* |

***Incremental:*** **Number of incremental pricing innovation ideas undergoing development for existing products during the period under review**

| Was the target for this category achieved? (tick "Yes" or "No") | Yes | Comment | No | Comment |
|---|---|---|---|---|
| | | If yes, indicate the percentage achieved. Reasons: *What factors are responsible for achieving or exceeding the set target?* | | If no, by what percentage was the target missed? Reasons: *What factors are responsible for not meeting the projected target?* |

# LEADERSHIP FOR INNOVATION

| Part C (i) Revenue generation–focused product-promotion innovation ideas ||||||
|---|---|---|---|---|---|
| Number of *radical* and *incremental* product-promotion innovation ideas undergoing development for existing products during the period under review ||||||
| *Radical*: Number of radical product-promotion innovation ideas undergoing development for existing products during the period under review ||||||
| Was the target for this category achieved? (tick "Yes" or "No") | Yes | Comment | | No | Comment |
| | | If yes, indicate the percentage achieved. **Reasons:** *What factors are responsible for achieving or exceeding the set target?* | | | If no, by what percentage was the target missed? **Reasons:** *What factors are responsible for not meeting the projected target?* |
| *Incremental*: Number of incremental product-promotion innovation ideas undergoing development for existing products during the period under review ||||||
| Was the target for this category achieved? (tick "Yes" or "No") | Yes | Comment | | No | Comment |
| | | If yes, indicate the percentage achieved. **Reasons:** *What factors are responsible for achieving or exceeding the set target?* | | | If no, by what percentage was the target missed? **Reasons:** *What factors are responsible for not meeting the projected target?* |
| Part C (ii) Cost saving–focused product-promotion innovation ideas ||||||
| Number of *radical* and *incremental* product-promotion cost-saving innovation ideas undergoing development for existing products during the period under review ||||||
| *Radical*: Number of radical product-promotion cost-saving innovation ideas undergoing development for existing products during the period under review ||||||
| Was the target for this category achieved? (tick "Yes" or "No") | Yes | Comment | | No | Comment |
| | | If yes, indicate the percentage achieved. **Reasons:** *What factors are responsible for achieving or exceeding the set target?* | | | If no, by what percentage was the target missed? **Reasons:** *What factors are responsible for not meeting the projected target?* |
| *Incremental*: Number of incremental product-promotion cost-saving innovation ideas undergoing development for existing products during the period under review ||||||

| Was the target for this category achieved? (tick "Yes" or "No") | Yes | Comment | No | Comment |
|---|---|---|---|---|
| | | If yes, indicate the percentage achieved. **Reasons:** *What factors are responsible for achieving or exceeding the set target?* | | If no, by what percentage was the target missed? **Reasons:** *What factors are responsible for not meeting the projected target?* |

<table>
<tr><td colspan="5" align="center">Part D<br>New-market innovation ideas</td></tr>
<tr><td colspan="5">Number of new-unserved-market and new-market-segment innovation ideas undergoing development during the period under review</td></tr>
<tr><td colspan="5">New-unserved-market ideas: Number of new-unserved-market ideas undergoing development for existing products in geographical locations not served by competitors or the organization during the period under review</td></tr>
</table>

| Was the target for this category achieved? (tick "Yes" or "No") | Yes | Comment | No | Comment |
|---|---|---|---|---|
| | | If yes, indicate the percentage achieved. **Reasons:** *What factors are responsible for achieving or exceeding the set target?* | | If no, by what percentage was the target missed? **Reasons:** *What factors are responsible for not meeting the projected target?* |

*New-market-segment ideas:* Number of new-market-segment ideas undergoing development for existing products within existing markets or geographical locations during the period under review

| Was the target for this category achieved? (tick "Yes" or "No") | Yes | Comment | No | Comment |
|---|---|---|---|---|
| | | If yes, indicate the percentage achieved. **Reasons:** *What factors are responsible for achieving or exceeding the set target?* | | If no, by what percentage was the target missed? **Reasons:** *What factors are responsible for not meeting the projected target?* |

<table>
<tr><td align="center">Part E(i)<br>Revenue generation–focused packaging innovation ideas</td></tr>
<tr><td>Number of radical and incremental packaging innovation ideas undergoing development during the period under review</td></tr>
<tr><td>Radical: Number of radical packaging innovation ideas undergoing development during the period under review</td></tr>
</table>

| Was the target for this category achieved? (tick "Yes" or "No") | Yes | Comment | No | Comment |
|---|---|---|---|---|
| | | If yes, indicate the percentage achieved. **Reasons**: *What factors are responsible for achieving or exceeding the set target?* | | If no, by what percentage was the target missed? **Reasons**: *What factors are responsible for not meeting the projected target?* |

*Incremental*: **Number of incremental packaging innovation ideas undergoing development during the period under review**

| Was the target for this category achieved? (tick "Yes" or "No") | Yes | Comment | No | Comment |
|---|---|---|---|---|
| | | If yes, indicate the percentage achieved. **Reasons**: *What factors are responsible for achieving or exceeding the set target?* | | If no, by what percentage was the target missed? **Reasons**: *What factors are responsible for not meeting the projected target?* |

**Part F (ii)**
**Cost-saving packaging innovation ideas**

Number of *radical* and *incremental* cost-saving packaging innovation ideas undergoing development during the period under review

*Radical*: **Number of radical cost-saving packaging innovation ideas undergoing development during the period under review**

| Was the target for this category achieved? (tick "Yes" or "No") | Yes | Comment | No | Comment |
|---|---|---|---|---|
| | | If yes, indicate the percentage achieved. **Reasons**: *What factors are responsible for achieving or exceeding the set target?* | | If no, by what percentage was the target missed? **Reasons**: *What factors are responsible for not meeting the projected target?* |

*Incremental*: **Number of incremental cost-saving packaging innovation ideas undergoing development during the period under review**

| Was the target for this category achieved? (tick "Yes" or "No") | Yes | Comment | No | Comment |
|---|---|---|---|---|
| | | If yes, indicate the percentage achieved. **Reasons**: *What factors are responsible for achieving or exceeding the set target?* | | If no, by what percentage was the target missed? **Reasons**: *What factors are responsible for not meeting the projected target?* |

The evaluation worksheet format shown in worksheets 15-9 and 15-10 can similarly be applied to the other core functional units of DM Personal Care Products:

- ❖ Manufacturing-processes department
- ❖ Customer service department

Worksheet 15-11 shows the format of the evaluation worksheet as applied to one of the support functional units of DM Personal Care Products, the procurement department.

Worksheet 15-11. Example of innovation output evaluation for cost-saving procurement innovation ideas undergoing development

| **Name of Department:** Procurement department <br> **Date:** April 30, 2018 ||||||
|---|---|---|---|---|---|
| **Purpose of Evaluation:** *To assess whether the target or goal of having a particular number of radical and incremental cost-saving procurement innovation ideas undergoing development during the period under review* (e.g., January–April of 2018) *was achieved* <br> The worksheet is divided into two parts: <br> • Part A: Number of *radical cost-saving procurement* innovation ideas undergoing development during the period under review <br> • Part B: Number of *incremental cost-saving procurement* innovation ideas undergoing development during the period under review ||||||
| **Part A** <br> Number of radical cost-saving procurement innovation ideas undergoing development during the period under review ||||||
| Was the target for this category achieved? (tick "Yes" or "No") | Yes | Comment | No | Comment ||
| | | If yes, indicate the percentage achieved. **Reasons:** *What factors are responsible for achieving or exceeding the set target?* | | If no, by what percentage was the target missed? **Reasons:** *What factors are responsible for not meeting the projected target?* ||
| **Part B** <br> Number of incremental cost-saving procurement innovation ideas undergoing development during the period under review ||||||
| Was the target for this category achieved? (tick "Yes" or "No") | Yes | Comment | No | Comment ||
| | | If yes, indicate the percentage achieved. **Reasons:** *What factors are responsible for achieving or exceeding the set target?* | | If no, by what percentage was the target missed? **Reasons:** *What factors are responsible for not meeting the projected target?* ||

As with the previous two worksheets, the evaluation worksheet format shown in worksheet 15-11 can similarly be applied to the other support functional units of DM Personal Care Products to assess the number of cost-saving innovation ideas undergoing development:

- ❖ HR department
- ❖ Finance and accounting department

- IT department
- Corporate affairs department

Having concluded the section on innovation output measurement, we now turn to innovation-results measurement.

## 3. Innovation-Results Measurement

So far, we've looked at two dimensions of measuring innovation performance: innovation input measurement and innovation output measurement. The third dimension of measuring innovation performance is *innovation-results measurement*.

### Definitions

To understand innovation-results measurement, it is first necessary to grasp the meaning of the term. According to the *Merriam-Webster* online dictionary, the word *result* means "a final consequence of a sequence of actions or events expressed qualitatively or quantitatively."

In the context of innovation, the interpretation of *innovation results* is a series of consequences of innovation management–related actions and activities. Recall that chapter 14, in the discussion of innovation-idea management systems, described how innovation ideas go through an assessment process that leads to the conversion of the innovation ideas into innovations. The point is that an innovation is essentially the end product or end result of an innovation idea that has proceeded through a rigorous development process. So what does the term *innovation results* mean?

*Definition of Innovation Results*

This book's definition of *innovation results* is based on two things: first, that innovations are an end product of innovation ideas, and second, that the basic meaning of the word *results* is "a final consequence of a sequence of actions and activities." Thus, this book defines *innovation results* as a resultant end product of the innovation-idea assessment and development processes in the context of a particular type of innovation and innovation degree.

*Definition of Innovation-Results Measurement*

Given the meaning of the term *innovation results*, this book defines *innovation-results measurement* as a process that involves determining whether the intended final resultant end product of the development or conversion process of an innovation idea was realized.

Having covered what innovation results entail, we now turn to the pertinent aspects of innovation-results measurements, which include the following:

o   Aspects to consider when undertaking innovation-results measurement
o   How to present innovation-results measurement
o   Formulating an innovation-results evaluation worksheet

*Aspects to Consider*

The earlier discussion of innovation output measurement stated some important aspects and practices to take into account when compiling an organization's innovation-performance report. Similar considerations apply to innovation-results measurement, although in a different context. The aspects and practices are as follows:

# Ability to Measure and Report Innovation Performance | 241

- o  *Collaboration between various innovation-idea management committees, functional leaders, and teams responsible for compiling innovation-performance reports:* This is helpful in terms of ascertaining the number of innovations developed and, in some cases, patents obtained during the period under review.
- o  *Presentation format:* Generally, one of the purposes of reporting innovation performance in organizations is to enable every person in the organization, from the CEO to the most junior employee, to understand how the organization is faring in all critical elements of its innovation practices. Therefore, using the wrong presentation format will impair the process of reporting innovation performance. For this reason, the leadership should ensure that the presentation format used is simple, creative, and interesting so that audiences across functional units understand every aspect of the data presented on innovations launched or implemented.

***Illustration: How to Present Innovation-Results Measurement***

As in previous sections, this section uses the functional units of DM Personal Care Products to illustrate how to present innovations launched or implemented.

However, before beginning the example, it's important to remember some of the steps mentioned when outlining how to present data on the number of innovation ideas generated. Similar steps should be observed when determining innovations launched or implemented. The three steps are as follows:

- o  Identify the core and support functional units of the company
- o  Select a presentation format for the report that is structured according to the functional units or divisions of the company
- o  In terms of determining the number of product innovations launched, categorize the presentation according to the company's product platforms

An example of how these steps can be applied to present the innovations launched or implemented across the functional units of DM Personal Care Products is presented next.

## *Outline of Functional Units*

Recall that the functional units of DM Personal Care Products are as follows:

### *Core functional units*

- ❖ Product-development unit, with the following segments:
  - o  Body-lotions segment
  - o  Skin-cleansing segment
  - o  Hair-care segment
  - o  Hand-washing segment
- ❖ Manufacturing-processes department
- ❖ Marketing department, with the following units:
  - o  Pricing unit
  - o  Product-promotion unit
  - o  Product-delivery unit
  - o  New-markets unit
  - o  Packaging unit
- ❖ Customer service department

*Support functional units*
- Procurement department
- HR department
- Finance and accounting department
- IT department
- Corporate affairs department

*Presentation Format*

As in previous sections, simple charts are used to show how to present the number of radical and incremental innovations launched or implemented over a particular period in each of the core and support functional units of DM Personal Care Products. As with previous examples, the innovation results of the core functional units are presented first, followed by those for the support units.

*Product-Development Department*

The number of radical and incremental product innovations launched in the product-development functional unit over a particular period is presented for each of the four product categories:
o Body-lotions category
o Skin-cleansing category
o Hair-care category
o Hand-washing category

Figures 15-21 and 15-22 show the number of radical and incremental body-lotion innovations launched in each quarter of 2018 (target and actual).

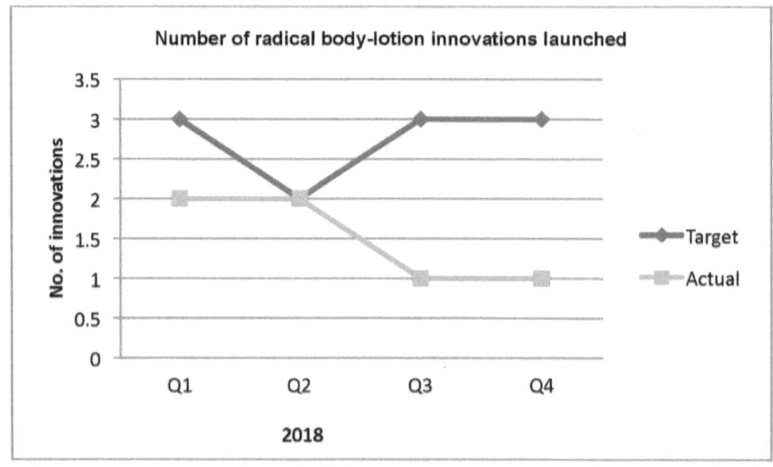

*Figure 15-21*

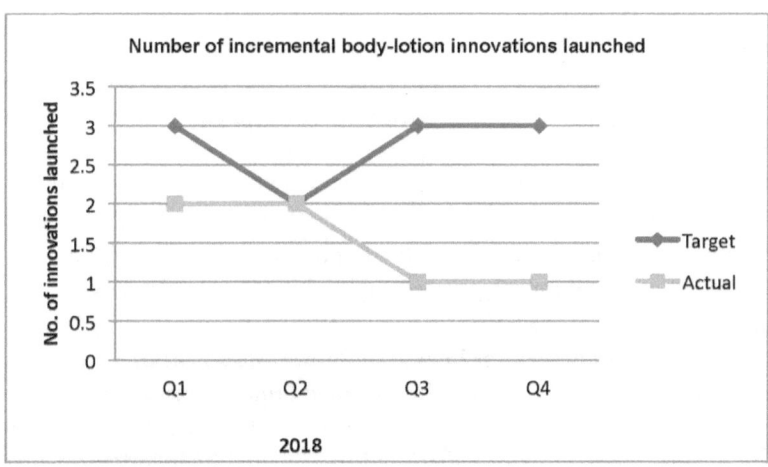

*Figure 15-22*

Similar charts would be created to present the number of radical and incremental innovations launched in each of the other three product categories over the same period:

o   Skin-cleansing category
o   Hair-care category
o   Hand-washing category

As stated in the earlier section on determining innovation ideas, in some instances, a product category may have a number of product segments; in such cases, the number of radical and incremental innovations launched should be determined per each product segment of a particular product category.

*Manufacturing-Processes Department*

The second example shows how to present innovation-results measurement for the manufacturing department. Recall that this functional unit has four main manufacturing-processes categories:

o   Body-lotions manufacturing-processes category
o   Skin-cleansing manufacturing-processes category
o   Hair-care manufacturing-processes category
o   Hand-washing manufacturing-processes category

The chapter 8 discussion of process innovations (under the topic of dimensions of innovation) described processes as a series of behind-the-scenes actions that are usually out of the view of customers and noted that organizations have numerous types and contexts of processes structurally embedded in their core and support functional units depending on the organization's nature and size. Recall that examples of core processes include manufacturing processes, the reservation systems and baggage-tracking methods in airline companies, and the parcel-tracking systems of couriers, among others. Also recall that examples of the contexts of process components in support functional units include procurement processes, accounting processes, HR processes, and so forth. Thus, process activities and components vary from company to company depending on the type and nature of the company and differ across industries.

Manufacturing processes are the behind-the-scenes series of operations or collections of technologies and methods that are used, performed, or applied when making a product in a manufacturing facility. Thus, manufacturing-processes innovations can include things like innovative procedures or technologies aimed at enhancing production processes in terms of the following: quality of the product, time of production, ability to customize the production process within a short time, ability to produce at low cost, ability to produce in large numbers without compromising on quality, and improvements in packaging methods or assembly methods.

That said, the charts in figures 15-23 and 15-24 provide an example of how to present the number of radical and incremental manufacturing-processes innovations in the manufacturing-processes categories of DM Personal Care Products. Specifically, figures 15-23 and 15-24 show the number of radical and incremental body-lotions manufacturing-processes innovations implemented in each quarter of 2018 (target and actual).

Similar charts would be created to show the number of radical and incremental innovations implemented in each of the other three manufacturing-processes categories over the same period:

- o   Skin-cleansing manufacturing-processes category
- o   Hair-care manufacturing-processes category
- o   Hand-washing manufacturing-processes category

In cases where a manufacturing-processes product category has a number of product segments, the number of radical and incremental manufacturing-processes innovations implemented should be determined per each product segment of the particular manufacturing-processes product category.

*Marketing Department*

The discussion of dimensions of innovation in chapter 8 stated that *marketing innovation* is a general term that describes the generation and development of innovative marketing-related ideas. However, marketing is a very wide area, and the structure of the functional components of the marketing department is usually determined by the nature and size of the organization. Similarly, the type of marketing innovation ideas generated usually depends (among other aspects) on (1) the business model of the organization and (2) how the organization characterizes and describes the components that make up its marketing functional unit.

For DM Personal Care Products, recall that the segments or components of the marketing department are categorized as pricing, product promotion, product delivery, new markets, and packaging. Thus, the presentation of types of marketing innovations is organized according to these marketing functional components. For illustration purposes, the continuing example will demonstrate how to present two types of marketing-related innovations: *number of product-promotion innovations launched* and *number of new markets discovered*.

Ability to Measure and Report Innovation Performance | 245

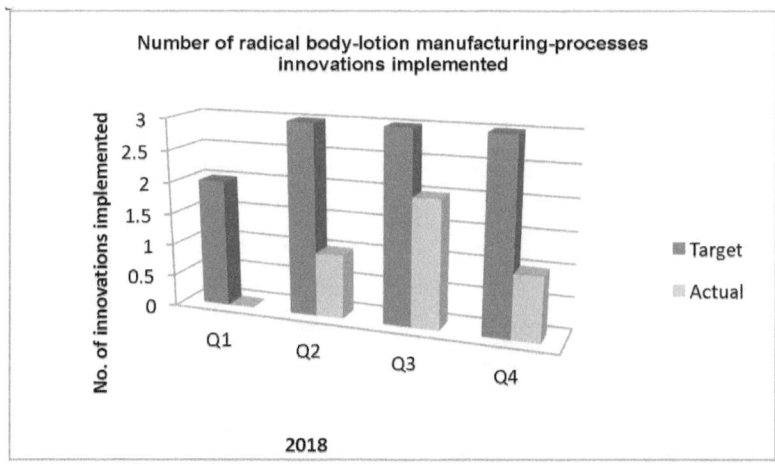

*Figure 15-23*

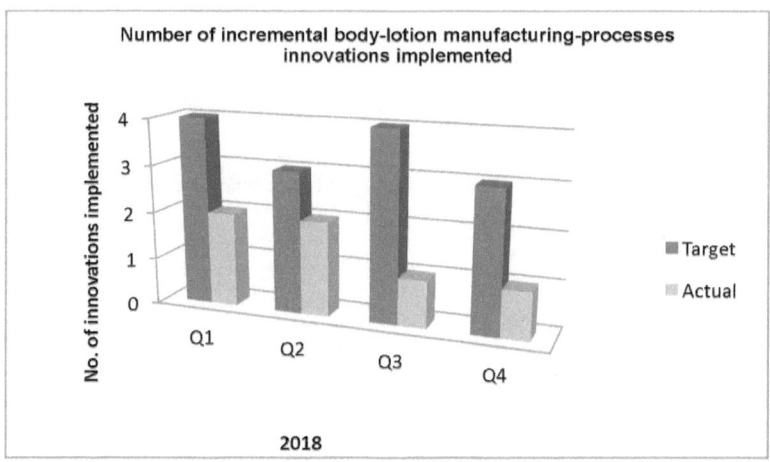

*Figure 15-24*

### Presenting the Number of Radical and Incremental Product-Promotion Innovations Launched

There are two categories of product-promotion innovations. Category 1 is *revenue-focused product-promotion innovations*—that is, product-promotion innovations that result in attracting revenue for the company. Category 2 is *cost saving–focused product-promotion innovations*—that is, product-promotion innovations that are aimed at cutting *product promotion–related costs*.

### Presentation Format

The charts in figures 15-25 through 15-26 show product-promotion innovations launched in categories 1 and 2.

Figures 15-25 and 15-26 show the number of radical and incremental revenue-focused product-promotion innovations (category 1) launched in each quarter of 2018 (target and actual).

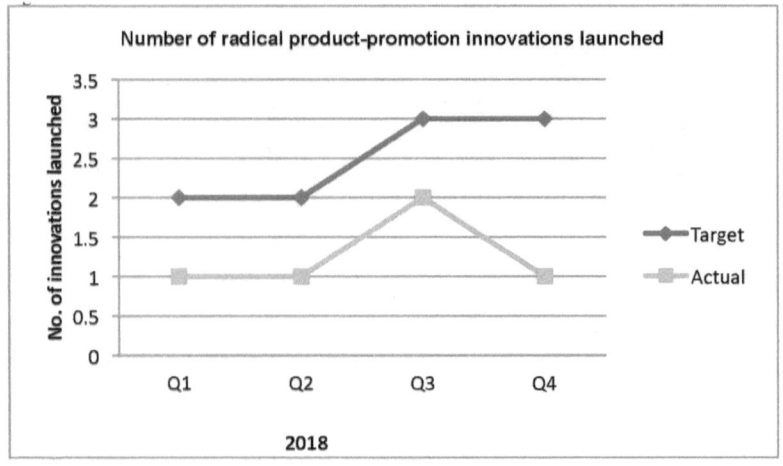

*Figure 15-25*

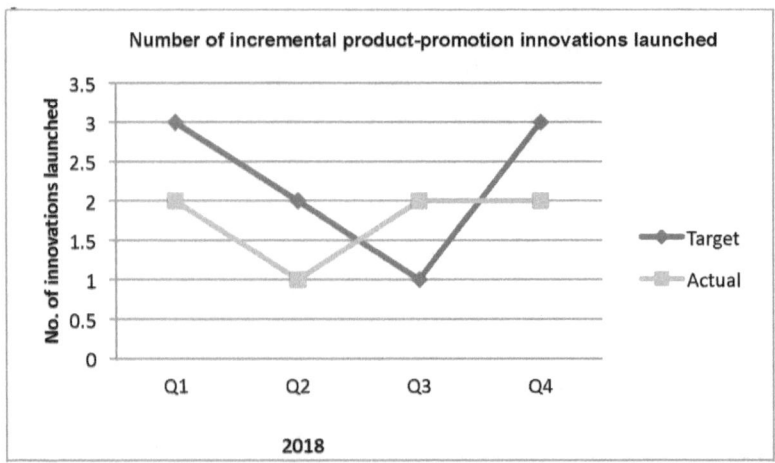

*Figure 15-26*

Figures 15-27 and 15-28 show the number of radical and incremental cost saving–focused product-promotion innovations (category 2) implemented in each quarter of 2018 (target and actual).

Ability to Measure and Report Innovation Performance | 247

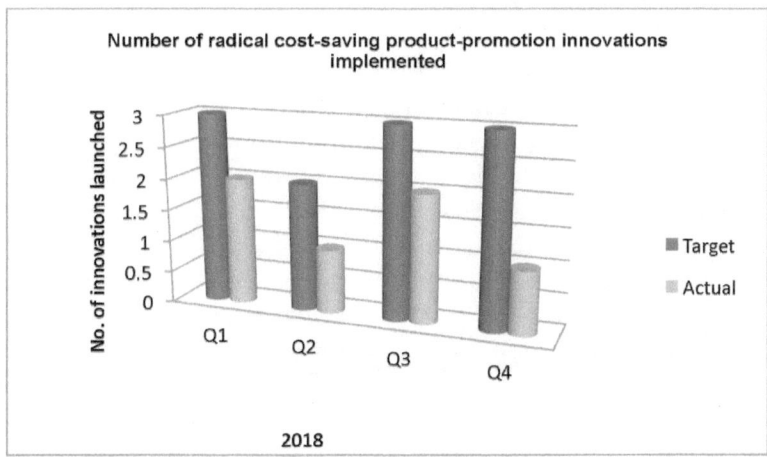

Figure 15-27

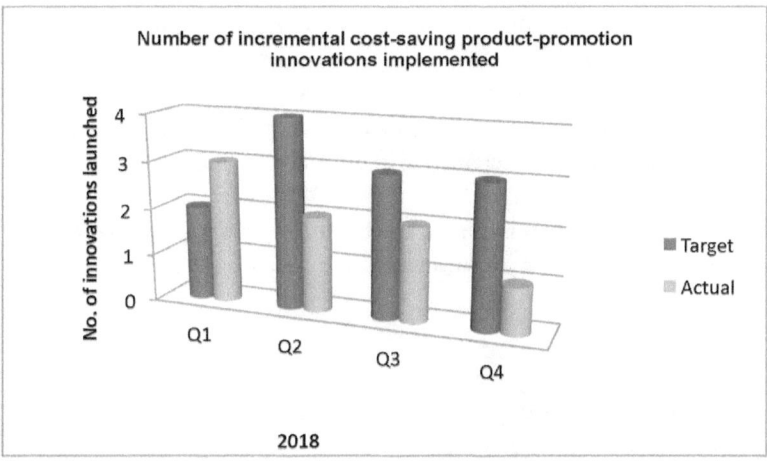

Figure 15-28

Similar charts (for revenue-generation or cost saving–focused innovations) would be created to present the number of radical and incremental marketing innovations implemented over a particular period in three of the other four units of the marketing department:
o   Product-delivery unit
o   Pricing unit
o   Packaging unit

Absent from this list is the new-markets unit; because of the different format used for presenting the results of this unit, it is covered separately in the following subsection.

## New-Markets Unit: *How Is Innovation Characterized in the Context of New Markets?*

Recall that earlier chapters of part III noted that the context of interpreting or expressing the extent of the newness or novelty of an innovation for new markets is different from the contexts of other types of marketing innovations, such as innovations in pricing, product promotion, product delivery, and product packaging. Similarly, when it comes to presenting innovations about new markets discovered, the phrases *new unserved market* and *new-market segment* are again used to characterize the extent of newness or novelty of the new-market ideas generated.

As mentioned previously, *new-market innovation ideas* refers to discovering novel markets not served by the organization or its competitors for existing products and services. In this book, new markets are categorized in the contexts of *new unserved markets* and *new-market segments*, defined as follows:

- *New unserved markets*: This involves discovering customer audiences for the company's existing products and services in a *completely new geographical location* unserved by the company or its competitors.
- *New-market segments*: This involves discovering *new customer segments* for the company's *existing products and services* within an *already-served geographical location*. In other words, it involves the discovery of new-market segments in a larger geographical location already served by both the company and its competitors. This can be thought of as an "incremental" new-market discovery.

The two simple diagrams in figures 15-29 and 15-30 illustrate the context of new markets. Figure 15-29 illustrates a new unserved market in a new geographical area, whereas figure 15-30 illustrates a new-market segment in an already-served geographical area.

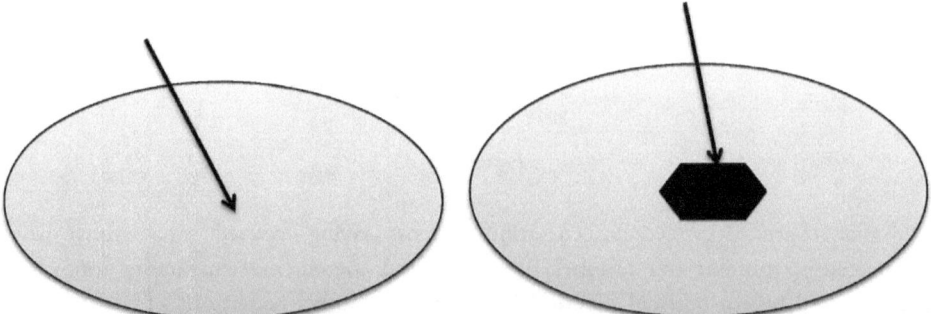

*Figure 15-29. New unserved market in a particular geographical location*

*Figure 15-30. New-market segment in an already-served geographical location*

### Presentation Format

The two simple charts in figures 15-31 and 15-32 show the number of new markets discovered in each of the two categories—new unserved markets (figure 15-31) and new-market segments (figure 15-32)—during the four quarters of 2018 (target and actual).

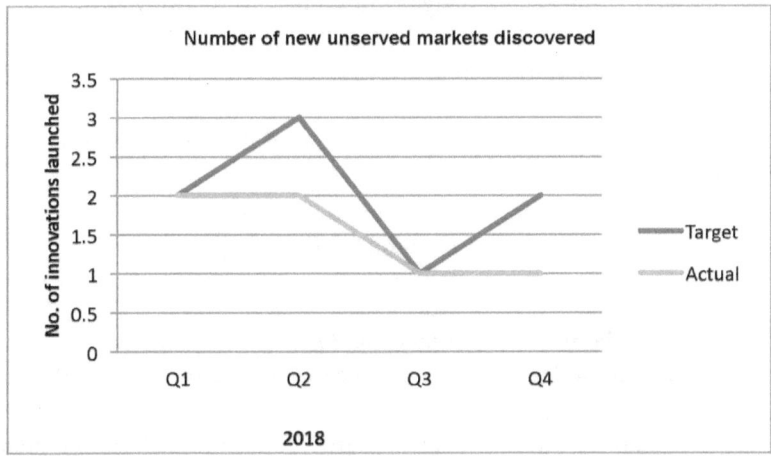

*Figure 15-31*

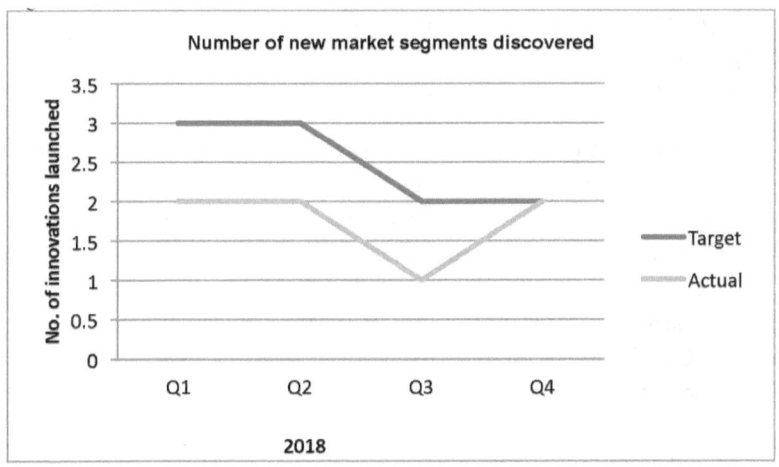

*Figure 15-32*

*Customer Service Department*

The last example of determining innovations launched or implemented by the core functional units of DM Personal Care Products is for the customer service department. The previous section on determining and presenting the number of customer service innovation ideas generated emphasized the importance of bearing in mind how the customer service components of an organization are structured for the purposes of innovation performance. The presentation of the customer service innovations launched or implemented is similar to the approach used earlier to present the number of customer service innovation ideas generated (see the discussion earlier in this chapter under "Innovation Output Measurement"). The presentation approach for customer service innovations launched or implemented is categorized as follows:

- Customer service innovations designed to support the delivery of product offerings *before* purchase
- Customer service innovations designed to support the delivery of product offerings *during* purchase
- Customer service innovations designed to support the delivery of product offerings *after* purchase
- Customer service innovations aimed at improving the quality of interaction between the company and its customers at all touchpoints

*Presentation Format*

Figures 15-33 and 15-34 show the number of *before-purchase* radical and incremental customer service innovations launched or implemented in each quarter of 2018 (target and actual).

Similar charts would be created to present the number of radical and incremental customer service innovations implemented during the same period in each of the other three categories:
- *During-purchase* customer service innovations
- *After-purchase* customer service innovations
- *All-touch-points* customer service innovations

## Presenting Radical and Incremental Innovations in Support Functional Units

The overview section of part III of this book noted that in addition to implementing innovation-support initiatives aimed at advancing the culture of innovation across the functional units of the organization, organizations need to generate innovative ideas for cost-saving and efficiency purposes in support functional units. Thus, this section illustrates how to present cost-saving innovations in the contexts of the five support functional units of DM Personal Care Products:

- ❖ Procurement department
- ❖ HR department
- ❖ Finance and accounting department
- ❖ IT department
- ❖ Corporate affairs department

Figures 15-35 and 15-36 show the number of radical and incremental IT cost-saving innovations implemented during the four quarters of 2018 (target and actual).

Similar charts would be created to present the number of radical and incremental cost-saving innovations implemented over the same period in each of the other four support functional units of DM Personal Care Products.

## Innovation-Results Evaluation

As in the two earlier sections on innovation input measurement and innovation output measurement, the final part of this section provides an example of how to evaluate the innovation results presented in the previous subsections.

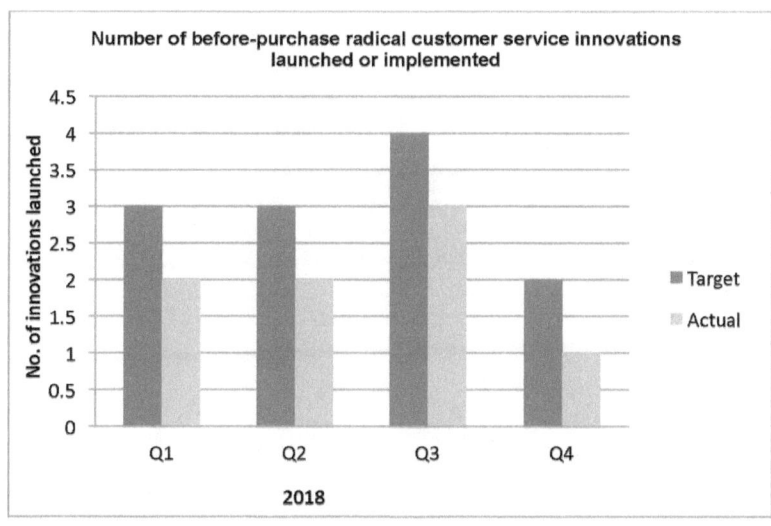

*Figure 15-33*

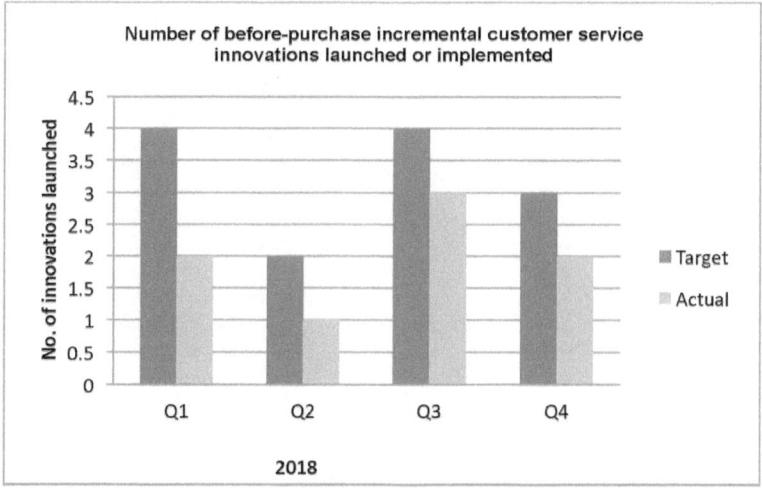

*Figure 15-34*

Once the number of innovations launched or implemented in both core and support functional units over a particular period has been presented, the next step is to assess whether the number of innovations launched or implemented during the period under review met the set goal or targets. Worksheets 15-12 through 15-14 provide examples of how the innovation-results evaluation worksheet can be applied to three of the functional units of DM Personal Care Products: the product-development unit (worksheet 15-12), marketing department (worksheet 15-13), and procurement department (worksheet 15-14).

## 252 | LEADERSHIP FOR INNOVATION

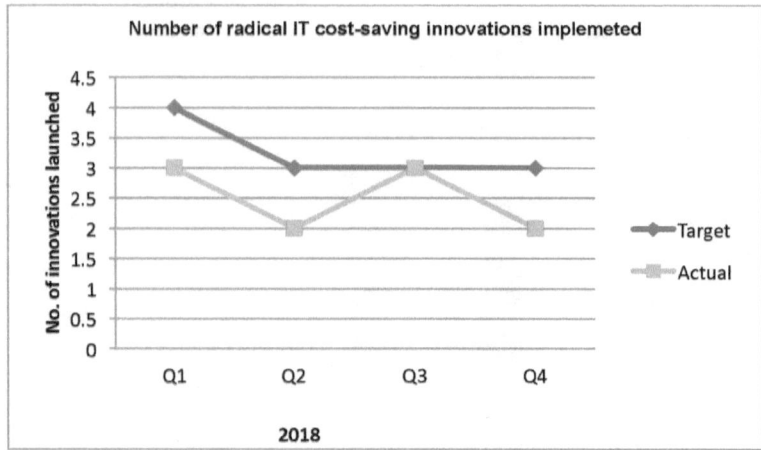

Figure 15-35

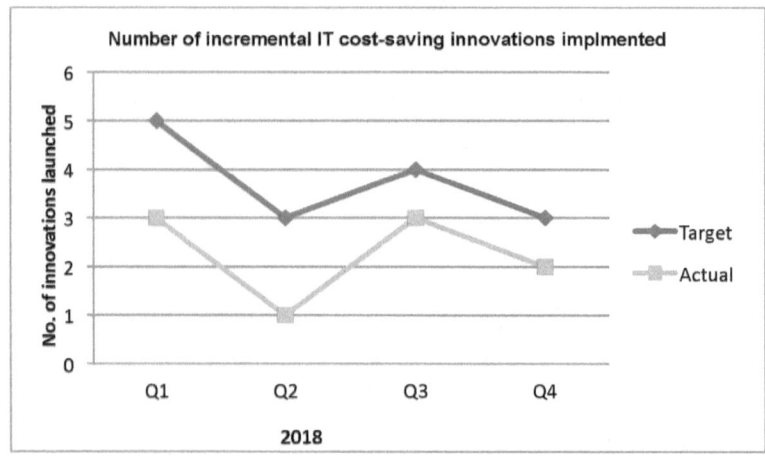

Figure 15-36

Worksheet 15-12. Example of evaluating innovation-results

| |
|---|
| **Name of Department:** Product-development unit<br>**Date:** April 30, 2018 |
| **Purpose of Evaluation:** *To assess whether the goal of launching a particular number of radical and incremental product innovations in this category during the period under review (e.g., January–April of 2018) was achieved*<br>The worksheet is divided into the four product segments of the product-development department of DM Personal Care Products, as follows:<br>• Part A: Body-lotions segment<br>• Part B: Skin-cleansing segment<br>• Part C: Hair-care segment<br>• Part D: Hand-washing segment |

| Part A<br>Number of *radical* and *incremental* product<br>innovations launched in the body-lotions segment ||||||
|---|---|---|---|---|---|
| *Radical*: Number of radical innovations launched during the period under review ||||||
| *Was the target for this product category achieved?* (tick "Yes" or "No") | Yes | Comment | No | Comment |
| | | If yes, indicate the percentage achieved. **Reasons**: *What factors are responsible for achieving or exceeding the set target?* | | If no, by what percentage was the target missed? **Reasons**: *What factors are responsible for not meeting the projected target?* |
| *Incremental*: Number of incremental innovations launched during the period under review ||||||
| *Was the target for this product category achieved?* (tick "Yes" or "No") | Yes | Comment | No | Comment |
| | | If yes, indicate the percentage achieved. **Reasons**: *What factors are responsible for achieving or exceeding the set target?* | | If no, by what percentage was the target missed? **Reasons**: *What factors are responsible for not meeting the projected target?* |
| Part B<br>Number of *radical* and *incremental* product<br>innovations launched in the skin-cleansing segment ||||||
| *Radical*: Number of radical innovations launched during the period under review ||||||
| *Was the target for this product category achieved?* (tick "Yes" or "No") | Yes | Comment | No | Comment |
| | | If yes, indicate the percentage achieved. **Reasons**: *What factors are responsible for achieving or exceeding the set target?* | | If no, by what percentage was the target missed? **Reasons**: *What factors are responsible for not meeting the projected target?* |
| *Incremental*: Number of incremental innovations launched during the period under review ||||||
| *Was the target for this product category achieved?* (tick "Yes" or "No") | Yes | Comment | No | Comment |
| | | If yes, indicate the percentage achieved. Reasons: *What factors are responsible for achieving or exceeding the set target?* | | If no, by what percentage was the target missed? Reasons: *What factors are responsible for not meeting the projected target?* |

# LEADERSHIP FOR INNOVATION

| | | | | |
|---|---|---|---|---|
| \multicolumn{5}{c}{**Part C**<br>Number of *radical* and *incremental* product<br>innovations launched in the hair-care segment} |||||
| *Radical*: Number of radical innovations launched during the period under review |||||
| *Was the target for this product category achieved?* (tick "Yes" or "No") | Yes | Comment | No | Comment |
| | | If yes, indicate the percentage achieved.<br>**Reasons:** *What factors are responsible for achieving or exceeding the set target?* | | If no, by what percentage was the target missed?<br>**Reasons:** *What factors are responsible for not meeting the projected target?* |
| *Incremental*: Number of incremental innovations launched during the period under review |||||
| *Was the target for this product category achieved?* (tick "Yes" or "No") | Yes | Comment | No | Comment |
| | | If yes, indicate the percentage achieved.<br>**Reasons:** *What factors are responsible for achieving or exceeding the set target?* | | If no, by what percentage was the target missed?<br>**Reasons:** *What factors are responsible for not meeting the projected target?* |
| \multicolumn{5}{c}{**Part D**<br>Number of *radical* and *incremental* product<br>innovations launched in the hand-washing segment} |||||
| *Radical*: Number of radical innovations launched during the period under review |||||
| *Was the target for this product category achieved?* (tick "Yes" or "No") | Yes | Comment | No | Comment |
| | | If yes, indicate the percentage achieved.<br>**Reasons:** *What factors are responsible for achieving or exceeding the set target?* | | If no, by what percentage was the target missed?<br>**Reasons:** *What factors are responsible for not meeting the projected target?* |
| *Incremental*: Number of incremental innovations launched during the period under review |||||
| *Was the target for this product category achieved?* (tick "Yes" or "No") | Yes | Comment | No | Comment |
| | | If yes, indicate the percentage achieved.<br>**Reasons:** *What factors are responsible for achieving or exceeding the set target?* | | If no, by what percentage was the target missed?<br>**Reasons:** *What factors are responsible for not meeting the projected target?* |

Ability to Measure and Report Innovation Performance | 255

Worksheet 15-13. Example of evaluating marketing-related innovations

| | |
|---|---|
| **Name of Department:** Marketing department<br>**Date:** April 30, 2018 | |
| **Purpose of evaluation:** *To assess whether the goal of launching a particular number of radical and incremental marketing-related innovations during the period under review* (e.g., January–April of 2018) *was achieved*<br>The worksheet is divided according to the subunits of the marketing department of DM Personal Care Products, as follows:<br>• Part A: Product delivery<br>• Part B: Pricing<br>• Part C: Product promotion<br>• Part D: New markets<br>• Part E: Packaging | |

<table>
<tr><td colspan="5" align="center">Part A<br>Product-delivery innovations</td></tr>
<tr><td colspan="5">Number of radical and incremental product-delivery innovations</td></tr>
<tr><td colspan="5">Radical: Number of radical product-delivery innovations launched or implemented during the period under review</td></tr>
<tr>
<td rowspan="2">Was the target for this category achieved? (tick "Yes" or "No")</td>
<td>Yes</td><td>Comment</td><td>No</td><td>Comment</td>
</tr>
<tr>
<td></td>
<td>If yes, indicate the percentage achieved.<br>Reasons: What factors are responsible for achieving or exceeding the set target?</td>
<td></td>
<td>If no, by what percentage was the target missed?<br>Reasons: What factors are responsible for not meeting the projected target?</td>
</tr>
<tr><td colspan="5">Incremental: Number of incremental product-delivery innovations launched or implemented during the period under review</td></tr>
<tr>
<td rowspan="2">Was the target for this category achieved? (tick "Yes" or "No")</td>
<td>Yes</td><td>Comment</td><td>No</td><td>Comment</td>
</tr>
<tr>
<td></td>
<td>If yes, indicate the percentage achieved.<br>Reasons: What factors are responsible for achieving or exceeding the set target?</td>
<td></td>
<td>If no, by what percentage was the target missed?<br>Reasons: What factors are responsible for not meeting the projected target?</td>
</tr>
<tr><td colspan="5" align="center">Part B<br>Pricing innovations</td></tr>
<tr><td colspan="5">Number of radical and incremental pricing innovations implemented for existing products during the period under review</td></tr>
<tr><td colspan="5">Radical: Number of radical pricing innovations implemented for existing products during the period under review</td></tr>
</table>

# 256 | LEADERSHIP FOR INNOVATION

| Was the target for this category achieved? (tick "Yes" or "No") | Yes | Comment | No | Comment |
|---|---|---|---|---|
| | | If yes, indicate the percentage achieved. **Reasons**: *What factors are responsible for achieving or exceeding the set target?* | | If no, by what percentage was the target missed? **Reasons**: *What factors are responsible for not meeting the projected target?* |

*Incremental*: **Number of incremental pricing innovations implemented for existing products during the period under review**

| Was the target for this category achieved? (tick "Yes" or "No") | Yes | Comment | No | Comment |
|---|---|---|---|---|
| | | If yes, indicate the percentage achieved. **Reasons**: *What factors are responsible for achieving or exceeding the set target?* | | If no, by what percentage was the target missed? **Reasons**: *What factors are responsible for not meeting the projected target?* |

**Part C**
**Product-promotion innovations**

**Number of <u>radical</u> and *incremental* product-promotion innovations implemented for existing products during the period under review**

*Radical*: **Number of radical product-promotion innovations implemented for existing products during the period under review**

| Was the target for this category achieved? (tick "Yes" or "No") | Yes | Comment | No | Comment |
|---|---|---|---|---|
| | | If yes, indicate the percentage achieved. **Reasons**: *What factors are responsible for achieving or exceeding the set target?* | | If no, by what percentage was the target missed? **Reasons**: *What factors are responsible for not meeting the projected target?* |

*Incremental*: **Number of incremental product-promotion innovations implemented for existing products during the period under review**

| Was the target for this category achieved? (tick "Yes" or "No") | Yes | Comment | No | Comment |
|---|---|---|---|---|
| | | If yes, indicate the percentage achieved. **Reasons**: *What factors are responsible for achieving or exceeding the set target?* | | If no, by what percentage was the target missed? **Reasons**: *What factors are responsible for not meeting the projected target?* |

| Part D |
|---|
| New-markets innovations |

| Number of *new unserved markets* discovered and number of *new-market segments* discovered during the period under review |
|---|
| *New unserved markets*: Number of new unserved markets discovered for existing products (i.e., completely new geographical locations not served by the organization or its competitors) during the period under review |

| Was the target for this category achieved? (tick "Yes" or "No") | Yes | Comment | No | Comment |
|---|---|---|---|---|
| | | If yes, indicate the percentage achieved. **Reasons:** *What factors are responsible for achieving or exceeding the set target?* | | If no, by what percentage was the target missed? **Reasons:** *What factors are responsible for not meeting the projected target?* |

| *New-market segments*: Number of new-market segments discovered during the period under review for existing products within existing market or geographical locations |
|---|

| Was the target for this category achieved? (tick "Yes" or "No") | Yes | Comment | No | Comment |
|---|---|---|---|---|
| | | If yes, indicate the percentage achieved. Reasons: *What factors are responsible for achieving or exceeding the set target?* | | If no, by what percentage was the target missed? Reasons: *What factors are responsible for not meeting the projected target?* |

| Part E |
|---|
| Packaging innovations |

| Number of *radical* and *incremental* packaging innovations launched during the period under review |
|---|
| *Radical*: Number of radical packaging innovations launched during the period under review |

| Was the target for this category achieved? (tick "Yes" or "No") | Yes | Comment | No | Comment |
|---|---|---|---|---|
| | | If yes, indicate the percentage achieved. **Reasons:** *What factors are responsible for achieving or exceeding the set target?* | | If no, by what percentage was the target missed? **Reasons:** *What factors are responsible for not meeting the projected target?* |

| *Incremental*: Number of incremental packaging innovations launched during the period under review |
|---|

| Was the target for this category achieved? (tick "Yes" or "No") | Yes | Comment | No | Comment |
|---|---|---|---|---|
| | | If yes, indicate the percentage achieved. **Reasons:** *What factors are responsible for achieving or exceeding the set target?* | | If no, by what percentage was the target missed? **Reasons:** *What factors are responsible for not meeting the projected target?* |

A similar approach to that shown in worksheets 15-12 and 15-13 would be applied to the other core functional units of DM Personal Care Products:

- ❖ Manufacturing-processes department
- ❖ Customer service department

Worksheet 15-14 shows how the innovation-results evaluation worksheet can be applied to the support functional units of DM Personal Care Products, using the procurement department as an example.

Worksheet 15-14. Example of evaluating cost-saving procurement innovations

**Name of Department:** Procurement department
**Date:** April 30, 2018

**Purpose of evaluation:** *To assess whether the goal of implementing a particular number of radical and incremental cost-saving procurement innovations during the period under review (e.g., January–April of 2018) was achieved*

The worksheet is divided into two parts, as follows:
- Part A: Number of radical cost-saving procurement innovations implemented during the period under review
- Part B: Number of incremental cost-saving procurement innovations implemented during the period under review

| Part A<br>Number of radical cost-saving procurement<br>innovations implemented during the period under review ||||||
|---|---|---|---|---|---|
| Was the target for this category achieved? (tick "Yes" or "No") | Yes | Comment | No | Comment ||
| | | If yes, indicate the percentage achieved. **Reasons:** *What factors are responsible for achieving or exceeding the set target?* | | If no, by what percentage was the target missed? **Reasons:** *What factors are responsible for not meeting the projected target?* ||

| Part B<br>Number of incremental cost-saving procurement<br>innovations implemented during the period under review ||
|---|---|

# Ability to Measure and Report Innovation Performance | 259

| Was the target for this category achieved? (tick "Yes" or "No") | Yes | Comment | No | Comment |
|---|---|---|---|---|
| | | If yes, indicate the percentage achieved. **Reasons**: *What factors are responsible for achieving or exceeding the set target?* | | If no, by what percentage was the target missed? **Reasons**: *What factors are responsible for not meeting the projected target?* |

Similar evaluation worksheets would be created to show the number of radical and incremental innovations implemented over the same period in each of the other four support functional units of DM Personal Care Products:

❖ HR department
❖ Finance and accounting department
❖ IT department
❖ Corporate affairs department

### 4. Innovation Impact Measurement

We've now covered three dimensions of measuring innovation performance: innovation input measurement, innovation output measurement, and innovation-results measurement. The fourth and last dimension is *innovation impact measurement*.

### *Definitions*

To understand innovation impact measurement, it is necessary to first interpret the context of the phrase *innovation impact*.

### *Definition of Innovation Impact*

Let's begin by defining the word *impact*. According to the *Merriam-Webster* online dictionary, the word *impact* means "to have an effect" on something. In the context of innovation, *innovation impact* can be defined as an innovation-performance metric that captures the monetary effect of an innovation on the organization.

### *Definition of Innovation Impact Measurement*

Innovation impact measurement can be defined as a dimension of innovation-performance measurement that involves determining the effect of an innovation on the organization's commercial and monetary value in terms of revenue, cost savings, and other aspects, such as market share, stock price, and market value.

### *Data Compilation and Collaboration*

The introduction section of this book noted that leading and managing innovation across functional units involves a combination of various innovation-oriented initiatives and activities across these units. In other words, in order to make innovation a permanent habit across the organization, every functional unit has to play a role. That said, compiling and reporting data on innovation impact is one of the vital aspects of innovation-performance measurement because it is the final determination of the return on investment in innovation initiatives and activities. The question is, *Whose role is it to compile data on innovation impact?* Generally, because finance and accounting teams are traditionally responsible for reporting the financial matters of an organization, it should be their responsibility to determine the content and appropriate reporting format and style for presenting data on various aspects of innovation impact. In terms of collaboration, just as finance teams collaborate or confer with other functional units when creating content for conventional corporate financial reporting, finance teams should collaborate and confer closely with other functional units when putting together content on innovation impact.

*Innovation-Life Time Frame*
The first factor to take into account when determining innovation impact is the innovation-life time frame.

What does *innovation-life time frame* mean? It is a period set by an organization within which an innovation will qualify to be called or characterized as an innovation and after which it will cease to be called or characterized as an innovation.

The innovation-life time frame is vital when it comes to assessing and reporting the innovation impact on monetary value because only innovations that have not elapsed should be included in innovation-performance reports.

Thus, one of the initial tasks to undertake when adopting a framework for innovation-performance reporting is to define the period within which an innovation will carry the *innovation* tag. This would be done by enacting a policy stating the expiration time frame in terms of when an innovation will cease to be referred to as an innovation. Once the period elapses, the innovation—whether a product innovation, process innovation, marketing innovation, or so forth—will no longer carry the *innovation* tag and will be referred to using the same terminology as that used for other existing product offerings, process components, marketing components, customer service components or support functional components. or any . Regarding whether there's a standard time frame in which innovations should carry the *innovation* tag, the time frame varies from company to company depending on the innovation-performance framework of the organization. Thus, the company has to clearly define the innovation-life time period, which should be communicated to all the workforces across functional units. For instance, "Any type and degree of innovation shall be referred to as an innovation for no more than three years. Meaning that after three years, such a product, process, marketing component, or any other type of innovation shall no longer carry the *innovation* tag or be referred to as an innovation." Additionally, the leadership could regularly publicize across the organization innovations that the company has "in stock" as well as those that are due to expire.

*Metrics for Determining Innovation Impact*
How do you determine innovation impact? The following are suggested examples of metrics that can be used to determine the monetary value created by innovations launched or implemented during the period under review:

## Ability to Measure and Report Innovation Performance | 261

- o Percentages of revenue generated from new products or services during the period under review
- o Percentages of revenue from marketing innovations, including the following:
  - Percentages of revenue generated from pricing innovations for existing products and services
  - Percentages of revenue generated or savings gained from promotion innovations for existing products or services
  - Percentages of revenue generated or savings gained from packaging innovations for existing products
  - Percentages of revenue from new markets, including the following:
    - Percentages of revenue generated from existing products or services in new unserved markets in geographical locations not served by either the organization or its competitors
    - Percentages of revenue generated from existing products or services in new-market segments within existing markets or geographical locations
- o Amount of savings gained as a result of cost-saving innovations implemented across functional units of the organization during the period under review

### *Illustration: How to Determine Innovation Impact Measurement*

Let's return to the functional units of DM Personal Care Products, our fictitious example company, to illustrate how to present revenues generated from radical and incremental innovations launched and cost savings gained from radical and incremental cost-saving innovations implemented across functional units during the period under review. As in the previous sections on measuring innovation performance, the first step is to outline the core and support functional units of DM Personal Care Products:

*Core functional units*
- ❖ Product-development unit, with the following segments:
  - o Body-lotions segment
  - o Skin-cleansing segment
  - o Hair-care segment
  - o Hand-washing segment
- ❖ Manufacturing-processes department, (as mentioned earlier, the manufacturing-processes department comprises the same segments as the product-development unit).
- ❖ Marketing department, with the following units:
  - o Pricing
  - o Product promotion
  - o Product delivery
  - o New markets
  - o Packaging
- ❖ Customer service department

## 262 | LEADERSHIP FOR INNOVATION

*Support functional units*
- ❖ Procurement department
- ❖ HR department
- ❖ Finance and accounting department
- ❖ IT department
- ❖ Corporate affairs department

The second step is to show, by use of simple tables, the revenues generated from radical and incremental innovations launched and the cost savings gained from radical and incremental cost-saving innovations implemented. We begin with the product-development department.

*Product-Development Department*

The tables in figures 15-37 and 15-38 show revenues generated from radical and incremental innovations launched in a particular period in all the product segments:
- o Body-lotions segment
- o Skin-cleansing segment
- o Hair-care segment
- o Hand-washing segment

*Radical body-lotion innovations:* Assuming we wish to determine the amount of revenue (by percentage) generated by four *radical body-lotion innovations* launched between January and December of 2018, the simple steps are as follows:
- o First, establish the number (in this case, four) and names of the radical body-lotion innovations launched during the period under review.
- o Second, establish the amount generated by each of the four radical body-lotion innovations launched during the period under review.
- o Third, establish the total amount of revenue generated by all four radical body-lotion innovations during the period under review.
- o Fourth, present data showing the percentage of revenue generated by each of the radical body-lotion innovations launched during the period under review.

The two simple tables in figures 15-37 and 15-38 show the percentages of revenue generated from radical and incremental body-lotion innovations launched between January and December of 2018.

Figure 15-37 shows the percentage of revenue generated from each of the four radical body-lotion innovations launched between January and December of 2018.

For illustration purposes, the four radical body-lotion innovations launched are named as follows:
- Radical body-lotion innovation 1
- Radical body-lotion innovation 2
- Radical body-lotion innovation 3
- Radical body-lotion innovation 4

| | Percentage of revenue generated by radical body-lotion innovations launched during period under review |
|---|---|
| 32% | Radical body-lotion 1 |
| 28% | Radical body-lotion 2 |
| 17% | Radical body-lotion 3 |
| 15% | Radical body-lotion 4 |
| 10% | Radical body-lotion 5 |

*Figure 15-37*

Similarly, figure 15-38 shows the percentages of revenue generated by the five incremental body-lotion innovations launched between January and December of 2018:
- Incremental body-lotion innovation 1
- Incremental body-lotion innovation 2
- Incremental body-lotion innovation 3
- Incremental body-lotion innovation 4
- Incremental body-lotion innovation 5

| | Percentage of revenue generated by radical body-lotion innovations launched during period under review |
|---|---|
| 46% | Incremental body-lotion 1 |
| 27% | Incremental body-lotion 2 |
| 18% | Incremental body-lotion 3 |
| 14% | Incremental body-lotion 4 |

*Figure 15-38*

Similar tables would be created to present the revenue generated from radical and incremental innovations launched in each of the other three product segments during the period under review:
- Skin-cleansing segment
- Hair-care segment
- Hand-washing segment

As stated in the section on presenting innovations launched (i.e., innovation-results measurement), in cases where a product category has a number of product segments, for instance, if the skin-cleansing product segment had four product categories, the revenue generated from the radical and incremental innovations launched would be presented accordingly in each of the four product categories.

### *Manufacturing-Processes Department*

The next example is for the manufacturing-processes department. Recall that this functional unit of DM Personal Care Products has the following manufacturing-processes categories:
- Body-lotions manufacturing-processes category
- Skin-cleansing manufacturing-processes category
- Hair-care manufacturing-processes category

**264** | **LEADERSHIP FOR INNOVATION**

o   Hand-washing manufacturing-processes category

Assuming we wish to determine the amount of savings gained (by percentage) from manufacturing-processes innovations implemented between January and December of 2018, the simple steps are as follows:

o   First, establish the number and names of all radical and incremental manufacturing-processes innovations implemented during the period under review.
o   Second, establish the amount saved from each of the radical and incremental manufacturing-processes innovations implemented during the period under review.
o   Third, establish the total amount of savings gained from the radical and incremental manufacturing-processes innovations during the period under review.
o   Fourth, present data showing the percentage of savings gained from each of the radical and incremental manufacturing-processes innovations implemented during the period under review.

Assume we have savings gained from radical and incremental manufacturing-processes innovations implemented in the following four manufacturing-processes categories:

o   Body-lotions manufacturing-processes innovations
o   Skin-cleansing manufacturing-processes innovations
o   Hair-care manufacturing-processes innovations
o   Hand-washing manufacturing-processes innovations

The percentages of cost savings from these radical and incremental manufacturing innovations would be presented as shown in figure 15-39 for cost savings from radical manufacturing-processes innovations and figure 15-40 for cost savings from incremental manufacturing-processes innovations implemented in 2018.

| | Cost savings from radical manufacturing-processes innovations implemented during period under review |
|---|---|
| 30% | Radical body-lotion manufacturing-processes innovations |
| 25% | Radical skin-cleansing manufacturing-processes innovations |
| 25% | Radical hair-care manufacturing-processes innovations |
| 20% | Radical hand-washing manufacturing-processes |

*Figure 15-39*

| | Cost savings from incremental manufacturing-processes innovations implemented during period under review |
|---|---|
| 32% | Incremental body-lotion manufacturing-processes innovations |
| 28% | Incremental skin-cleansing manufacturing-processes innovations |
| 24% | Incremental hair-care manufacturing-processes innovations |
| 16% | Incremental hand-washing manufacturing-processes |

*Figure 15-40*

## Ability to Measure and Report Innovation Performance | 265

*Marketing Department*

Recall that marketing innovations are types of innovation developed and implemented in various segments of the marketing department and that the type of marketing innovation ideas generated will usually depend on how the organization characterizes or defines the segments that make up the marketing functional unit of the organization. That being said, this section illustrates how to present the monetary impact of marketing innovations based on the marketing functional units of DM Personal Care Products. In this illustration, the monetary impact is segmented into two categories: *revenues generated* and *cost savings*. The contexts of the two categories are outlined as follows:

*Revenues Generated*
- o Percentages of revenue generated from radical and incremental innovative methods of delivering products to customers
- o Percentages of revenue generated from pricing innovations for existing products and services
- o Percentages of revenue generated from promotion innovations for existing products or services
- o Percentages of revenue generated for existing products or services from new markets in geographical locations not served by the organization or its competitors
- o Percentages of revenue generated for existing products or services from new customer segments not served by the organization or its competitors within existing markets or geographical locations
- o Percentages of revenue generated from innovative marketing alliances to deliver products to customers
- o Percentages of revenue generated from radical and incremental packaging innovations launched

*Cost Savings*
- o Percentages of cost savings gained from radical and incremental innovative methods of delivering products to customers for existing products
- o Percentages of cost savings gained from radical and incremental promotion innovations for existing products or services
- o Percentages of cost savings gained from radical and incremental packaging innovations launched for existing products

*Illustration*

Assuming we want to determine the amount of revenue generated and cost savings gained (in percentage terms) from radical and incremental marketing innovations launched or implemented between January and December of 2018, the simple steps are as follows:
- o First, establish the number and names of all radical and incremental marketing innovations launched or implemented during the period under review.
- o Second, establish the amount of revenue generated or cost savings gained from each of the radical and incremental marketing innovations launched or implemented during the period under review.

## 266 | LEADERSHIP FOR INNOVATION

- o   Third, establish the total amount of revenue generated and cost savings gained from radical and incremental marketing innovations during the period under review.
- o   Fourth, present data showing the percentages of revenue generated and cost savings gained from each of the radical and incremental marketing strategy innovations launched or implemented during the period under review.

Let's assume we're determining revenues generated and savings made from the following radical and incremental marketing innovations:

Radical and incremental product-delivery innovations

New unserved markets (i.e., completely new markets and new-market segments for existing products)

Radical and incremental promotion innovations for existing products

Radical and incremental pricing innovations for existing products

Radical and incremental packaging innovations for existing products

The following subsections illustrate how to present this information.

*Revenues Generated*

The percentages of revenue generated from radical and incremental marketing innovations listed previously are presented in two tables: figure 15-41 is for the percentages of revenue generated from various radical marketing innovations launched or implemented for existing products in 2018, and figure 15-42 is for the percentages of revenue generated from various incremental marketing innovations launched or implemented for existing products in 2018.

| | Percentages of revenue generated from radical marketing innovations launched or implemented for existing products during period under review |
|---|---|
| 32% | Radical product-delivery innovations |
| 28% | New markets in new geographical locations |
| 19% | Radical promotion innovations |
| 14% | Radical packaging innovations |
| 7%  | Radical pricing innovations |

*Figure 15-41*

| | Percentages of revenue generated from incremental marketing innovations launched or implemented for existing products during period under review |
|---|---|
| 29% | Radical product-delivery innovations |
| 24% | New market segments in already served geographical locations |
| 19% | Radical promotion innovations |
| 17% | Radical packaging innovations |

*Figure 15-42*

*Cost Savings*

Similarly, savings gained from radical and incremental cost-saving marketing innovations during the period under review are presented in two tables: figure 15-43 is for the percentages of cost savings gained from radical marketing innovations launched or implemented for existing products in 2018, and figure 15-44 is for the percentages of cost savings gained from incremental marketing innovations launched or implemented for existing products in 2018.

| Percentages of cost savings gained from radical marketing innovations launched or implemented for existing products during period under review | |
|---|---|
| 40% | Radical cost-saving product-delivery innovations |
| 34% | Radical cost-saving promotions |
| 26% | Radical packaging innovations |

*Figure 15-43*

| Percentages of cost savings gained from incremental marketing innovations launched or implemented for existing products during period under review | |
|---|---|
| 38% | Incremental cost-saving product-delivery innovations |
| 33% | Incremental cost-saving promotions |
| 29% | Incremental packaging innovations |

*Figure 15-44*

*Customer Service Department*

The last example on how to determine the monetary contributions from innovations in the core functional units of DM Personal Care Products is for the customer service department.

The previous sections on determining customer service innovations—that is, the number of customer service innovation ideas generated, the number of customer service innovation ideas undergoing development, and the number of customer service innovations launched—outlined the importance of understanding perspectives on customer service and how its functional components are structured. Similarly, when presenting the monetary contributions from customer service innovations launched or implemented, it's important to bear in mind how the customer service components of an organization are configured so that the presentation format for the monetary contributions generated from customer service innovations can be aligned with the configuration of the customer service components.

*Illustration*

There are two important aspects to bear in mind when determining and presenting the monetary contributions generated from customer service innovations, as follows:
1. *Types of customer service innovations:* As stated previously, there are four types of customer service innovations:
    o Customer service innovations designed to support the delivery of product offerings *before* purchase
    o Customer service innovations designed to support the delivery of product offerings *during* purchase
    o Customer service innovations designed to support the delivery of product offerings *after* purchase

- Customer service innovations aimed at improving the quality of interactions between the company and its customers at all touchpoints
2. *Contexts of the monetary value generated:* The second important aspect to bear in mind when determining the monetary value generated from radical and incremental customer service innovations is that there are two contexts for the monetary value generated, as follows:
    - Revenue generated from various radical and incremental customer service innovations launched or implemented
    - Cost savings gained from various radical and incremental customer service innovations launched or implemented

Note that whatever format is used, these two contexts should be presented clearly in a manner that can be understood by all worlkforces.

*Presentation Format*

Assume we'd like to determine and present the amount of revenue generated and cost savings gained (in percentage terms) from before-purchase radical and incremental customer service innovations launched or implemented between January and December of 2018. The steps are as follows:
- First, establish the number and names of all radical and incremental before-purchase customer service innovations launched or implemented during the period under review
- Second, establish the amount of revenue generated and cost savings gained from each of the before-purchase radical and incremental customer service innovations launched or implemented during the period under review
- Third, establish the total amount of revenue generated and savings made from all before-purchase radical and incremental customer service innovations during the period under review
- Fourth, present data showing the percentage of revenue generated and savings gained from each of the before-purchase radical and incremental customer service innovations during the period under review

The next step is determining revenue generated and cost savings gained during the period under review, which have the following components:

*Revenue Generated*
- Revenue generated from four before-purchase radical customer service innovations launched or implemented during the period under review
- Revenue generated from four before-purchase incremental customer service innovations launched or implemented during the period under review

*Cost Savings Gained*
- Cost savings gained from four before-purchase radical customer service innovations during the period under review

o   Cost savings gained from four before-purchase incremental customer service innovations during the period under review

Based on these categories of monetary value generated, the presentation will be divided into two categories: category 1 for revenue generation–focused customer service innovations and category 2 for cost savings–focused customer service innovations. For each of the two categories, follow these two steps:

o   First, outline all before-purchase radical and incremental customer service innovations launched or implemented in each particular category during the period under review.

o   Second, use tables to illustrate the monetary value generated by each innovation in both categories (i.e., categories 1 and 2).

For illustration purposes, the radical and incremental revenue generation–centered customer service innovations launched during the period under review (category 1) are identified by the numbers 1–4 for each set (radical and incremental), resulting in the following outline for the first step:

Radical customer service innovations launched or implemented:
- Before-purchase radical customer service innovation 1
- Before-purchase radical customer service innovation 2
- Before-purchase radical customer service innovation 3
- Before-purchase radical customer service innovation 4

Incremental customer service innovations launched or implemented:
- Before-purchase incremental customer service innovation 1
- Before-purchase incremental customer service innovation 2
- Before-purchase incremental customer service innovation 3
- Before-purchase incremental customer service innovation 4

*Presentation of Revenue Generated*

The percentages of revenue generated from the radical and incremental customer service innovations just listed are presented in two tables: figure 15-45 is for the percentages of revenue generated from before-purchase radical customer service innovations launched or implemented during the period under review, and figure 15-46 is for the percentages of revenue generated from before-purchase incremental customer service innovations launched or implemented during the period under review.

| | Percentages of revenue generated from before-purchase radical customer service innovations launched or implemented during period under review |
|---|---|
| 33% | Before-purchase radical customer service innovation 1 |
| 26% | Before-purchase radical customer service innovation 2 |
| 24% | Before-purchase radical customer service innovation 3 |
| 17% | Before-purchase radical customer service innovation 4 |

*Figure 15-45*

| Percentages of revenue generated from before-purchase incremental customer service innovations launched or implemented during period under review ||
|---|---|
| 32% | Before-purchase incremental customer service innovation 1 |
| 27% | Before-purchase incremental customer service innovation 2 |
| 23% | Before-purchase incremental customer service innovation 3 |
| 18% | Before-purchase incremental customer service innovation 4 |

*Figure 15-46*

*Presentation of Cost Savings Gained*
Assuming there are four radical cost-saving customer service innovations and four incremental cost-saving customer service innovations launched or implemented during the period under review, as in the preceding section, the steps are as follows:

o  The first step is to outline radical and incremental cost-saving customer service innovations launched or implemented during the period under review. (For illustration purposes, these are labeled using the numbers 1–4 for each set.)
o  The second step is presentation of the data by use of tables.

The first step results in the following outline:
Radical cost-saving customer service innovations launched or implemented:
- Before-purchase radical cost-saving customer service innovation 1
- Before-purchase radical cost-saving customer service innovation 2
- Before-purchase radical cost-saving customer service innovation 3
- Before-purchase radical cost-saving customer service innovation 4

Incremental cost-saving customer service innovations launched or implemented:
- Before-purchase incremental cost-saving customer service innovation 1
- Before-purchase incremental cost-saving customer service innovation 2
- Before-purchase incremental cost-saving customer service innovation 3
- Before-purchase incremental cost-saving customer service innovation 4

The percentage of savings gained from each of the radical and incremental cost-saving customer service innovations in the previous list is presented in two tables: figure 15-47 is for the percentages of cost savings from radical customer service innovations launched or implemented during the period under review, and figure 15-48 is for the percentages of cost savings from incremental customer service innovations launched or implemented during the period under review.

| Percentages of savings from before-purchase radical cost-saving customer service innovations launched or implemented during period under review ||
|---|---|
| 37% | Before-purchase radical cost-saving customer service innovation 1 |
| 29% | Before-purchase radical cost-saving customer service innovation 2 |
| 19% | Before-purchase radical cost-saving customer service innovation 3 |
| 15% | Before-purchase radical cost-saving customer service innovation 4 |

*Figure 15-47*

| | Percentages of savings from before-purchase incremental cost-saving customer service innovations launched or implemented during period under review |
|---|---|
| 38% | Before-purchase incremental cost-saving customer service innovation 1 |
| 29% | Before-purchase incremental cost-saving customer service innovation 2 |
| 19% | Before-purchase incremental cost-saving customer service innovation 3 |
| 14% | Before-purchase incremental cost-saving customer service innovation 4 |

*Figure 15-48*

## Determining Cost Savings from Innovations Implemented in Support Functional Units

Recall that innovation ideas implemented in support functional units (back-office) are normally radical or incremental cost saving–centered innovations. Thus, this section illustrates how to determine and present cost savings from innovations in support functional units.

*Illustration:*

Assume we'd like to determine the savings gained (in percentage terms) from radical and incremental innovations implemented by the support functional units of DM Personal Care Products between January and December 2018. The five simple steps are as follows:

- o   First, outline the number of support functional units under consideration. Recall that DM Personal Care Products has the following five support functional units:
    - Procurement department
    - HR department
    - Finance and accounting department
    - IT department
    - Corporate affairs department
- o   Second, establish the number and types/names of all radical and incremental cost-saving innovations implemented by support functional units during the period under review.
- o   Third, establish the savings gained from each of the radical and incremental innovations implemented by each support functional unit during the period under review.
- o   Fourth, establish the total amount of savings gained from all radical and incremental innovations implemented by each of the support functional units during the period under review.
- o   Fifth, present data showing the percentage of savings gained from each of the radical and incremental innovations implemented by each support functional unit during the period under review.

For illustration purposes, two tables present the data: figure 15-49 shows the percentage of cost savings gained from radical innovations by each support functional unit during the period under review, and figure 15-50 shows the percentage of cost savings gained from incremental innovations by each support functional unit in the period under review.

| Percentages of cost-savings gained from radical innovations implemented by support functional units during period under review | |
|---|---|
| 26% | Radical cost-saving procurement innovations |
| 23% | Radical cost-saving HR innovations |
| 20% | Radical cost-saving IT innovations |
| 17% | Radical cost-saving accounting innovations |
| 14% | Radical cost-saving corporate affairs innovations |

*Figure 15-49*

| Percentages of cost-savings gained from incremental innovations implemented by support functional units during period under review | |
|---|---|
| 28% | Incremental cost-saving procurement innovations |
| 25% | Incremental cost-saving HR innovations |
| 19% | Incremental cost-saving IT innovations |
| 16% | Incremental cost-saving accounting innovations |

*Figure 15-50*

This concludes the discussion and illustration of what innovation impact measurement entails. Recall that in the sections on the other three dimensions of innovation-performance measurement, an evaluation worksheet in the context of each of the measurement approaches appears at the end of the section. Similarly, the last aspect of this section is the innovation impact evaluation, described next.

**Innovation Impact Evaluation**

As with evaluations of the other three innovation-performance dimensions, the purpose of the innovation impact evaluation is to determine whether the revenue targets or goals from innovations launched or savings gained from cost-saving innovations implemented across functional units were achieved and provide an explanation of why the targets were achieved or missed.

*Illustration*

For our continuing example of DM Personal Care Products, the innovation impact evaluation is based on the following two aspects:
- o  Whether the revenue targets or goals from innovations launched or implemented in the core functional units of DM Personal Care Products during the period under review were achieved
- o  Whether the targets or goals of savings from cost-saving innovations implemented during the period under review were achieved

# Ability to Measure and Report Innovation Performance | 273

For illustration purposes, the *innovation impact evaluation worksheet* is applied to three functional units: the product-development unit (worksheet 15-15), the marketing department (worksheet 15-16), and the procurement department (worksheet 15-17).

Worksheet 15-15. Example of evaluating impact of product innovations

| **Name of Department:** Product-development unit<br>**Date:** April 30, 2018 ||||||
|---|---|---|---|---|---|
| **Purpose of Evaluation:** *To assess whether the target or goal of generating a particular amount of revenue from various radical and incremental product innovations launched during the period under review (e.g., January–December of 2018) was achieved*<br>The worksheet is divided into four product categories according to the product segments of the product-development department of DM Personal Care Products:<br>• Part A: Body-lotions segment<br>• Part B: Skin-cleansing segment<br>• Part C: Hair-care segment<br>• Part D: Hand-washing segment ||||||
| **Part A**<br>Percentage of revenue generated from *radical* and *incremental* product innovations launched in the body-lotions segment during the period under review ||||||
| ***Radical:*** Percentage of revenue generated from radical innovations launched during the period under review ||||||
| *Was the target for this product category achieved?* (tick "Yes" or "No") | Yes | Comment | No | Comment ||
| | | If yes, indicate the percentage achieved.<br>**Reasons:** *What factors are responsible for achieving or exceeding the set target?* | | If no, by what percentage was the target missed?<br>**Reasons:** *What factors are responsible for not meeting the projected target?* ||
| ***Incremental:*** Percentage of revenue generated from incremental innovations launched during the period under review ||||||
| *Was the target for this product category achieved?* (tick "Yes" or "No") | Yes | Comment | No | Comment ||
| | | If yes, indicate the percentage achieved.<br>**Reasons:** *What factors are responsible for achieving or exceeding the set target?* | | If no, by what percentage was the target missed?<br>**Reasons:** *What factors are responsible for not meeting the projected target?* ||
| **Part B**<br>Percentage of revenue generated from *radical* and *incremental* product innovations launched in the skin-cleansing segment ||||||
| ***Radical:*** Percentage of revenue generated from radical innovations launched during the period under review ||||||

# 274 | LEADERSHIP FOR INNOVATION

| Was the target for this product category achieved? (tick "Yes" or "No") | Yes | Comment | No | Comment |
|---|---|---|---|---|
| | | If yes, indicate the percentage achieved. **Reasons**: *What factors are responsible for achieving or exceeding the set target?* | | If no, by what percentage was the target missed? **Reasons**: *What factors are responsible for not meeting the projected target?* |

*Incremental*: Percentage of revenue generated from incremental innovations launched during the period under review

| Was the target for this product category achieved? (tick "Yes" or "No") | Yes | Comment | No | Comment |
|---|---|---|---|---|
| | | If yes, indicate the percentage achieved. **Reasons**: *What factors are responsible for achieving or exceeding the set target?* | | If no, by what percentage was the target missed? **Reasons**: *What factors are responsible for not meeting the projected target?* |

## Part C
### Percentage of revenue generated from *radical* and *incremental* product innovations launched in the hair-care segment

*Radical*: Percentage of revenue generated from radical innovations launched during the period under review

| Was the target for this product category achieved? (tick "Yes" or "No") | Yes | Comment | No | Comment |
|---|---|---|---|---|
| | | If yes, indicate the percentage achieved. **Reasons**: *What factors are responsible for achieving or exceeding the set target?* | | If no, by what percentage was the target missed? **Reasons**: *What factors are responsible for not meeting the projected target?* |

*Incremental*: Percentage of revenue generated from incremental innovations launched during the period under review

| Was the target for this product category achieved? (tick "Yes" or "No") | Yes | Comment | No | Comment |
|---|---|---|---|---|
| | | If yes, indicate the percentage achieved. **Reasons**: *What factors are responsible for achieving or exceeding the set target?* | | If no, by what percentage was the target missed? **Reasons**: *What factors are responsible for not meeting the projected target?* |

# Ability to Measure and Report Innovation Performance | 275

| Part D<br>Percentage of revenue generated from *radical* and *incremental* product innovation ideas generated in the hand-washing segment |||||||
|---|---|---|---|---|---|---|
| *Radical*: Percentage of revenue generated from radical innovations launched during the period under review |||||||
| *Was the target for this product category achieved?* (tick "Yes" or "No") | Yes | Comment | | No | Comment | |
| | | If yes, indicate the percentage achieved. **Reasons**: *What factors are responsible for achieving or exceeding the set target?* | | | If no, by what percentage was the target missed? **Reasons**: *What factors are responsible for not meeting the projected target?* | |
| *Incremental*: Percentage of revenue generated from incremental innovations launched during the period under review |||||||
| *Was the target for this product category achieved?* (tick "Yes" or "No") | Yes | Comment | | No | Comment | |
| | | If yes, indicate the percentage achieved. **Reasons**: *What factors are responsible for achieving or exceeding the set target?* | | | If no, by what percentage was the target missed? **Reasons**: *What factors are responsible for not meeting the projected target?* | |

Worksheet 15-16. Example of evaluating impact of marketing innovations

| |
|---|
| **Name of Department:** Marketing department<br>**Date:** December 30, 2018 |
| **Purpose of evaluation:** *To assess whether the target or goal of generating a particular amount of revenue from various radical and incremental marketing innovations launched during the period under review (e.g., January–December of 2018) was achieved*<br>The worksheet is divided according to the number of subunits or segments of the marketing department of DM Personal Care Products, as follows:<br>• Part A: Product delivery—two parts: part A (i) for determining revenues generated and part A (ii) for determining savings gained<br>• Part B: Pricing<br>• Part C: Product promotion—two parts: part C (i) for determining revenues generated and part C (ii) for determining savings gained<br>• Part D: New markets<br>• Part E: Packaging—two parts: part E (i) for determining revenues generated and part E (ii) for determining savings gained |
| Part A (i)<br>**Product delivery** (*revenues generated*) |
| Percentage of revenues generated from *radical* and *incremental* innovative methods of delivering products to customers |

| | | | | | |
|---|---|---|---|---|---|
| *Radical*: Percentage of revenues generated from radical innovative methods of delivering products to customers during the period under review ||||||
| Was the target for this category achieved? (tick "Yes" or "No") | Yes | Comment | No | Comment ||
| ^ | | If yes, indicate the percentage achieved. **Reasons:** *What factors are responsible for achieving or exceeding the set target?* | | If no, by what percentage was the target missed? **Reasons:** *What factors are responsible for not meeting the projected target?* ||
| *Incremental*: Percentage of revenues generated from incremental innovative methods of delivering products to customers during the period under review ||||||
| Was the target for this category achieved? (tick "Yes" or "No") | Yes | Comment | No | Comment ||
| ^ | | If yes, indicate the percentage achieved. **Reasons:** *What factors are responsible for achieving or exceeding the set target?* | | If no, by what percentage was the target missed? **Reasons:** *What factors are responsible for not meeting the projected target?* ||

**Part A (ii)**
**Product delivery** (*savings gained*)

| | | | | | |
|---|---|---|---|---|---|
| Percentage of cost savings gained from *radical* and *incremental* innovative methods of delivering products to customers during the period under review ||||||
| *Radical*: Percentage of cost savings made from radical innovative methods of delivering products to customers during the period under review ||||||
| Was the target for this category achieved? (tick "Yes" or "No") | Yes | Comment | No | Comment ||
| ^ | | If yes, indicate the percentage achieved. **Reasons:** *What factors are responsible for achieving or exceeding the set target?* | | If no, by what percentage was the target missed? **Reasons:** *What factors are responsible for not meeting the projected target?* ||
| *Incremental*: Percentage of cost savings made from incremental innovative methods of delivering products to customers during the period under review ||||||
| Was the target for this category achieved? (tick "Yes" or "No") | Yes | Comment | No | Comment ||
| ^ | | If yes, indicate the percentage achieved. **Reasons:** *What factors are responsible for achieving or exceeding the set target?* | | If no, by what percentage was the target missed? **Reasons:** *What factors are responsible for not meeting the projected target?* ||

| Part B |
| --- |
| Product pricing |
| Percentage of revenue generated from radical and incremental pricing innovations for existing products during the period under review |
| **Radical:** Percentage of revenue generated from radical pricing innovations on existing products during the period under review |

| Was the target for this category achieved? (tick "Yes" or "No") | Yes | Comment | No | Comment |
| --- | --- | --- | --- | --- |
| | | If yes, indicate the percentage achieved. **Reasons:** *What factors are responsible for achieving or exceeding the set target?* | | If no, by what percentage was the target missed? **Reasons:** *What factors are responsible for not meeting the projected target?* |

*Incremental:* Percentage of revenue generated from incremental pricing innovations for existing products during the period under review

| Was the target for this category achieved? (tick "Yes" or "No") | Yes | Comment | No | Comment |
| --- | --- | --- | --- | --- |
| | | If yes, indicate the percentage achieved. **Reasons:** *What factors are responsible for achieving or exceeding the set target?* | | If no, by what percentage was the target missed? **Reasons:** *What factors are responsible for not meeting the projected target?* |

| Part C (i) |
| --- |
| Product promotion (*revenue generated*) |
| Percentage of revenue generated from *radical* and *incremental* product-promotion innovations for existing products during the period under review |
| *Radical:* Percentage of revenue generated from radical product-promotion innovations for existing products during the period under review |

| Was the target for this category achieved? (tick "Yes" or "No") | Yes | Comment | No | Comment |
| --- | --- | --- | --- | --- |
| | | If yes, indicate the percentage achieved. **Reasons:** *What factors are responsible for achieving or exceeding the set target?* | | If no, by what percentage was the target missed? **Reasons:** *What factors are responsible for not meeting the projected target?* |

*Incremental:* Percentage of revenue generated from incremental product-promotion innovations for existing products during the period under review

# 278 | LEADERSHIP FOR INNOVATION

| Was the target for this category achieved? (tick "Yes" or "No") | Yes | Comment | No | Comment |
|---|---|---|---|---|
| | | If yes, indicate the percentage achieved. **Reasons:** *What factors are responsible for achieving or exceeding the set target?* | | If no, by what percentage was the target missed? **Reasons:** *What factors are responsible for not meeting the projected target?* |

| **Part C (ii)** |
|---|
| **Product promotion** (*savings made*) |
| Percentage of savings made from *radical* and *incremental* product-promotion innovations for existing products during the period under review |
| *Radical*: Percentage of savings made from radical product-promotion innovations for existing products during the period under review |

| Was the target for this category achieved? (tick "Yes" or "No") | Yes | Comment | No | Comment |
|---|---|---|---|---|
| | | If yes, indicate the percentage achieved. **Reasons:** *What factors are responsible for achieving or exceeding the set target?* | | If no, by what percentage was the target missed? **Reasons:** *What factors are responsible for not meeting the projected target?* |

| *Incremental*: Percentage of savings made from incremental product-promotion innovations for existing products during the period under review |
|---|

| Was the target for this category achieved? (tick "Yes" or "No") | Yes | Comment | No | Comment |
|---|---|---|---|---|
| | | If yes, indicate the percentage achieved. **Reasons:** *What factors are responsible for achieving or exceeding the set target?* | | If no, by what percentage was the target missed? **Reasons:** *What factors are responsible for not meeting the projected target?* |

| **Part D** |
|---|
| **New markets** (*new unserved markets and new-market segments*) |
| Revenues from *new unserved markets* and *new-market segments* for existing products during the period under review |
| *New unserved markets:* Percentage of revenues generated from existing products in new unserved markets during the period under review |

## Ability to Measure and Report Innovation Performance | 279

| Was the target for this category achieved? (tick "Yes" or "No") | Yes | Comment | No | Comment |
|---|---|---|---|---|
| | | If yes, indicate the percentage achieved. **Reasons**: *What factors are responsible for achieving or exceeding the set target?* | | If no, by what percentage was the target missed? **Reasons**: *What factors are responsible for not meeting the projected target?* |

**New-market segments:** Percentage of revenues generated from existing products in new-market segments during the period under review

| Was the target for this category achieved? (tick "Yes" or "No") | Yes | Comment | No | Comment |
|---|---|---|---|---|
| | | If yes, indicate the percentage achieved. **Reasons**: *What factors are responsible for achieving or exceeding the set target?* | | If no, by what percentage was the target missed? **Reasons**: *What factors are responsible for not meeting the projected target?* |

### Part E (i)
### Packaging (*revenues generated*)

**Percentage of revenues generated from *radical* and *incremental* packaging innovations launched during the period under review**

*Radical:* Percentage of revenues generated from radical packaging innovations launched during the period under review

| Was the target for this category achieved? (tick "Yes" or "No") | Yes | Comment | No | Comment |
|---|---|---|---|---|
| | | If yes, indicate the percentage achieved. **Reasons**: *What factors are responsible for achieving or exceeding the set target?* | | If no, by what percentage was the target missed? **Reasons**: *What factors are responsible for not meeting the projected target?* |

*Incremental:* Percentage of revenues generated from incremental packaging innovations launched during the period under review

| Was the target for this category achieved? (tick "Yes" or "No") | Yes | Comment | No | Comment |
|---|---|---|---|---|
| | | If yes, indicate the percentage achieved. **Reasons**: *What factors are responsible for achieving or exceeding the set target?* | | If no, by what percentage was the target missed? **Reasons**: *What factors are responsible for not meeting the projected target?* |

# 280 | LEADERSHIP FOR INNOVATION

| Part E (ii) Packaging (*savings made*) |||||
|---|---|---|---|---|
| **Percentage of cost savings gained from *radical* and *incremental* packaging innovations launched during the period under review** |||||
| ***Radical*: Percentage of cost savings gained from radical packaging innovations launched during the period under review** |||||
| Was the target for this category achieved? (tick "Yes" or "No") | Yes | Comment | No | Comment |
|  |  | If yes, indicate the percentage achieved. **Reasons**: *What factors are responsible for achieving or exceeding the set target?* |  | If no, by what percentage was the target missed? **Reasons**: *What factors are responsible for not meeting the projected target?* |
| ***Incremental*: Percentage of cost savings gained from incremental packaging innovations launched during the period under review** |||||
| Was the target for this category achieved? (tick "Yes" or "No") | Yes | Comment | No | Comment |
|  |  | If yes, indicate the percentage achieved. **Reasons**: *What factors are responsible for achieving or exceeding the set target?* |  | If no, by what percentage was the target missed? **Reasons**: *What factors are responsible for not meeting the projected target?* |

Worksheets 15-15 and 15-16 show how the evaluation worksheet can be applied to two different core functional units (product development and marketing). Similarly, the evaluation worksheet can be applied to the other core functional units of DM Personal Care Products:

- ❖ Manufacturing-processes department
- ❖ Customer service department

Worksheet 15-17 shows how the evaluation worksheet can be applied to the support functional units of DM Personal Care Products, using the procurement department as an example.

Worksheet 15-17. Example of evaluating impact of cost-saving procurement innovations

| |
|---|
| **Name of Department:** Procurement department<br>**Date:** December 30, 2018 |
| **Purpose of evaluation:** *To assess whether the target or goal of gaining a particular amount of savings from various radical and incremental procurement innovations implemented during the period under review (e.g., January–December of 2018) was achieved*<br>The worksheet is divided into two parts, as follows:<br>• Part A: Percentage of savings gained from *radical* procurement innovations implemented during the period under review<br>• Part B: Percentage of savings gained from *incremental* procurement innovations implemented during the period under review |

| Part A | | | | | |
|---|---|---|---|---|---|
| Percentage of savings gained from *radical* procurement innovations implemented during the period under review | | | | | |
| *Was the target for this category achieved?* (tick "Yes" or "No") | Yes | Comment | No | Comment | |
| | | If yes, indicate the percentage achieved. **Reasons:** *What factors are responsible for achieving or exceeding the set target?* | | If no, by what percentage was the target missed? **Reasons:** *What factors are responsible for not meeting the projected target?* | |
| Part B | | | | | |
| Percentage of savings gained from *incremental* procurement innovations implemented during the period under review | | | | | |
| *Was the target for this category achieved?* (tick "Yes" or "No") | Yes | Comment | No | Comment | |
| | | If yes, indicate the percentage achieved. **Reasons:** *What factors are responsible for achieving or exceeding the set target?* | | If no, by what percentage was the target missed? **Reasons:** *What factors are responsible for not meeting the projected target?* | |

Similar evaluation worksheets would be created for the other four support functional units of DM Personal Care Products:

❖ HR department
❖ Finance and accounting department
❖ IT department
❖ Corporate affairs department

Worksheets 15-15 through 15-17 show how the evaluation worksheet can be applied to determine whether the goals for target revenue and cost savings from innovations launched or implemented during the period under review were achieved and the reasons why they were met or missed.

*Bottom line*

There are three takeaways from this chapter. First, you cannot create a culture of innovation across the organization using traditional, non-innovation-oriented management tools. Second, in order to make innovation a permanent and ongoing habitual process across functional units, it is vital to implement organization-wide innovation-support systems, and to do this, organizational leaders require innovation management skill sets. Third, the chapter looks at *what* innovation management skill sets entail and *how* to apply them to build and manage the organization-wide innovation-support systems.

# SUMMARY

Let's recap the five main aspects the book has covered:
i. Study after study has observed that in the last ten years or so, company executives across the globe have consistently ranked innovation as one of the top-priority strategies for growth, competitiveness, and survival.
ii. Because of the top-priority perception that many organizational leaders have about innovation, many organizations across the globe have made innovation every employee's responsibility, from the most junior employee to top leadership.
iii. Adopting a culture of innovation does not occur naturally; it happens only if the right organizational climate is created through the application of the right skill sets and tools.
iv. Innovation analysts have observed that traditional management models and tools cannot effectively advance innovation across the organization—hence the need for innovation-oriented management approaches.
v. This book has suggested three categories of innovation skill sets that managers require to lead workforce innovation and create a culture of innovation across the organization: innovative thinking skills (part I), innovation engagement skills (part II), and innovation management skills (part III).

# ABOUT THE AUTHOR

Based in Walnut Creek, California, David is a workforce innovation trainer-consultant and author, with experiences in the USA, Europe, Africa & the Caribbean. An inventor of the upcoming simple kitchen device; the CT Holder, David is the Founder of Innovation Strategy Lab, an innovation training & consulting firm. David has more than 10 years of experience focusing on workforce innovation. He has studied with the University of Manchester, University of Leicester and Swansea University in the UK and all at postgraduate level. David may be reached through email at deemasumba609@yahoo.com info@dmmlab.com.

# SELECTED REFERENCES

A.G. Lafley and Roger L. Martin, *Playing to Win: How Strategy Really Works*, (Boston: Harvard Business School Publishing, 2013)

Dr. Edwin A. Locke, Towards a theory of task motivation and incentives, *Journal of Organizational Behavior and Human Performance, 1968, Volume 3, Issue 2*

Paul R. Niven, *Balanced Scorecard Diagnostics: Maintaining Maximum Performance*, (Hoboken: John Wiley & Sons, 2005)

Robert S. Kaplan and David P. Norton, *The Balanced Scorecard: Translating Strategy into Action* (Boston: Harvard Business School Press, 1996)

# NOTES

- "Innovation Leadership: How to use innovation to lead effectively, work collaboratively, and drive results" 2009, https://www.ccl.org/wpcontent/uploads/2015/04/InnovationLeadership.pdf
- "Executives Fall Short When Leading for Innovation, Global Leadership Study Shows" 2007, https://www.businesswire.com/news/home/20071212005240/en/Executives-Fall-Short-Leading-Innovation-Global-Leadership
- "Leadership: P&G's Bob McDonald on Innovation" 2011 http://rocrockett.com/2011/04/leadership-bob-mcdonald-on-innovation/
- "Human Capital Trends—2012", www.deloitte-touche/human-capital-trends-2012/paperback/product-20009458.html
  "Leadership for Innovation: Summary Report from an AIM Management Research Forum in cooperation with the Chartered Management Institute", 2005, file:///C:/Users/deema/Documents/Leadership%20for%20Innovation%20Smmary%20Report%202005.pdf
- "Learn the Five Secrets of Innovation" 2009, http://www.cnn.com/2009/BUSINESS/11/26/innovation.tips/
- "PwC: 14th Annual Global CEO Survey", 2011 http://www.areadevelopment.com/StudiesResearchPapers/1-28-2011/global-ceo-survey-pwc19393.shtml
- "2016 Innovation Survey Report", https://media-publications.bcg.com/MIC/BCG-The-Most-Innovative-Companies-2016-Jan-2017.pdf
- "2009 Growth, Innovation and Leadership Study" http://www.frost.com/prod/servlet/cpo/166317375

- "Innovation and Commercialization ,2010: McKinsey Global Survey Results", https://www.mckinsey.com/business-functions/strategy-and-corporate-finance/our-insights/innovation-and-commercialization-2010-mckinsey-global-survey-results
- "PwC 20th CEO Survey", 2017, https://www.pwc.com/gx/en/ceo-survey/pdf/20th-global-ceo-survey-us-supplement-executive-dialogues.pdf
- "Association to Advance Collegiate Schools of Business (Compiled by its Task Force on Business Schools and Innovation)" *https://www.aacsb.edu/-/media/AACSB/Publications/research-reports/business-schools-on-an-innovation-mission.ashx*
- "3M CEO: Innovation and International Markets Drive Faster Growth", 2011. *http://news.3m.com/press-release/company/3m-ceo-innovation-and-international-markets-drive-faster-growth*
- "The CFO's Role in Fostering Innovation" *http://deloitte.wsj.com/cfo/2015/08/12/the-cfos-role-in-fostering-innovation/*
- "Measuring Innovation 2009" *https://www.bcg.com/documents/file15484.pdf*
- "Elon Musk Has Raided 150 People From Apple For Tesla" 2015 https://www.forbes.com/sites/timworstall/2015/02/09/elon-musk-has-raided-150-people-from-apple-for-tesla/#1942139b44b8
- "Leadership and Innovation: 2008" https://www.mckinsey.com/business-functions/strategy-and-corporate-finance/our-insights/leadership-and-innovation

# INDEX

**A**
Alphabet Inc., 24
Amazon, 26, 78–79
Apple, Inc., xiii, 23–24, 78, 79, 80, 119
ArcelorMittal, 61
association skills, 12–13
Association to Advance Collegiate Schools of Business report, 86

**B**
Benioff, Marc, 30
Bezos, Jeffrey, 26
Boston Consulting Group survey, 194
Brin, Sergey, 24
Buckley, George, 29–30, 119
business models
    and dimensions of innovation, 69–76; and innovation-challenge questions, 119

**C**
Center for Creative Leadership reports, xii
Chartered Management Institute reports, xiii, xiv
Clinton, Bill, 39–40
CNN study, 12, 13, 14
communications
    action plan example, 102–103; informative vs. inspirational, 39–41; for workforce engagement, 22, 43–45, 46–51
companies and innovation, xiii–xiv, 22–23, 57–62
Confederation of British Industry (CBI) survey, 58
Cooper, Robert, 170
cost savings presentations, 271–272
customer service innovations
    characteristics, 74–75; goal-setting examples, 143–145; innovation-challenge questions, 131–132; innovation context, 68; measurement examples, 212–213, 219–220, 249–250, 251, 267–271; skills examples, 9, 93

**D**
Dell, Michael, 15, 25–26
Deloitte LLP reports, 5
Deschamps, Jean-Philippe, 5, 33
dimensions of innovation, 69–76
diversity, 16, 52
DM Personal Care Products examples
    goal-setting, 137–155; idea-innovation management committees, 159–162; innovation-challenge questions, 117–119, 125–133; innovation contexts, 63–69; innovation-idea

Index | 289

process, 180–181; innovation management, 87–100; innovation measurement, 198–205, 207–222, 222–240, 241–259, 261–281; innovation priority worksheets, 104–110; innovation types, 76–78; innovative thinking skills, 6–10

**E**
Elop, Stephen, 60
employees *see* workforce
Environmental Solutions example, 122–124
evaluation worksheets, 196–197
experimentation, 14–15

**F**
Facebook, 30–31, 60
Freda, Fabrizio, 30
Frost & Sullivan studies, 58
functional units, xix, xx–xxi

**G**
Gates, Bill, 27–28
goal setting, 80–81, 134–136

**H**
Harris Interactive studies, 58
Harvard Business School innovation conference, xv, 85
Hastings, Reed, 31

**I**
IBM, 24–25, 59
ICQC *see* innovation-challenge-questions committees (ICQC)
idea-progression valves, 175–176, 178–179
innovation
aspects overview, xi; context examples, 63–69; definitions, 4, 62–63; incremental and radical, 78–79, 80; messages about, 44–45, 53, 56–58; myths, 76; responsibility for, 42; systemic, xx–xxi; types of, 71–76, 77–78
innovation-challenge questions
characteristics, 119–120; committees (ICQC), 116–119, 121; definition and goals, 114–115; worksheets, 121–133
innovation degrees, 78–81
innovation deliverables index, 190–193
innovation development
process overview, 169–170; stages, 186–188
innovation drivers, 57, 59–62, 120–121
innovation engagement
committees (IECs), 52–54; initiatives, 46–51, 202–203; in job descriptions, xix, 112–113; principles, 33–34; skills, xvii, xxii, 37–39, 42–43; styles, 39–41; and vision, 55–56
Innovation Excellence survey, 20
innovation goals
definition and guidelines, 134–137; functional unit examples, 137–155
innovation-idea assessment process
committees, 173–175; criteria, 175–179; overview, 173; planning and implementation, 179–183
innovation-idea database, 171–173
innovation-idea management systems
assessment and submission, 164–169; committees, 158–163; definition and importance, 156–158; framework overview, 163–164
innovation-idea reception committees (IIRC), 170–171
innovation impact measurement
definitions, 259–261; examples, 261–281
innovation inputs, xvii–xviii, 196, 197–205
innovation launch and evaluation, 188–193

innovation leadership perspectives, xii–xiii
innovation management
    functional unit examples, 86–100; initiatives worksheet, 203–205; in job descriptions, xix, xx, 112–113; skills, xvii, xxii, 83–86
innovation-oriented planning, 101–103
innovation outputs
    definition, xvii, xviii; evaluation worksheets, 222–240; measurement, 205–222
innovation performance
    job specifications, 113; measurement, xvii, 194–195
innovation prioritization, 104–110
innovation project teams, 183–186
innovation quotient, 177–178
innovation results
    evaluation, 250–259; measurement, 240–250
innovation skill sets, xvi–xviii, xxi
innovation-support systems, 84, 199–200
innovative performance, 4
innovative thinking
initiatives worksheet, 201–202; in job descriptions, xix, 112–113; skill development, 11–17; skills, xviii, 4, 5–10
Institute for Corporate Productivity surveys, xiv, 5, 194

**J**

job descriptions and specifications, xviii–xx, 111–113
Jobs, Steve, 16, 23–24

**K**

Kaplan, Robert S., 43
Kuczmarski & Associates survey, 20

**L**

Lafley, Alan George, 26–27, 43
leadership
    Clinton vs. Obama, 39–40; and goal-setting, 134–136; vs. management, 84; as role models, 18–20; skills, xv, 12, 31–32, 81; top performers, 23–31; and workforce engagement, xiv–xv
leadership for innovation, xv–xvi
Levis, John, 158
Locke, Edwin, 135

**M**

McKinsey & Company surveys, xv, 58
management models, xi, xv, 85–86
mantras, 21–22
manufacturing process innovation
    goal-setting examples, 140–141; innovation-challenge-questions example, 127–128; innovation context, 66; measurement examples, 208–210, 243–244, 263–264; skills examples, 7, 89
market segments, 129, 142, 248–249
marketing innovation
    characteristics, 74; goal-setting examples, 141–143; innovation-challenge-questions example, 128–131; innovation context, 67–68; measurement examples, 210–211, 218–219, 225–229, 234–238, 244–249, 255–258, 265–267, 275–280; skills examples, 7–8, 90–92
MassDevice.com report, 31
Microsoft, 27–29
motivation, 21–22, 135
Musk, Elon, 29

**N**

Nadella, Satya, 28–29
Netflix, 31
networking, 16
Nike, 79
Niven, Paul, 43
Nokia, 60, 119, 120
Norton, David P., 43
Novartis, 59

## O

Obama, Barack, 39–40, 61–62
observation skills, 13–14
Oliver Wyman study, xiv

## P

Page, Larry, 24
Palmisano, Samuel, 24–25
Panasonic, 61
Pfizer, 60
planning, 101–103
post-innovation launch evaluation, 189–193
PriceWaterhouseCoopers (PwC) studies, xv, 57–58, 60
problem identification, 4, 62–63
process innovation examples, 72–73
Procter & Gamble (P&G), xiv, 26–27
product development innovation
    challenge-question example, 118, 125–127; goal-setting examples, 138–139; innovation context, 64–65; measurement examples, 201–205, 208, 209, 215–217; skills examples, 7, 88
product innovations
    examples, 71–72; measurement, 222–224, 231–233, 242–243, 252–254, 262–263, 273–275
Purat, Ruth, 20–21

## Q

questioning skills, 13
    *see also* innovation-challenge questions

## R

regulation, 169
risk, 168–169
Rometty, Ginni, 25, 59

## S

Salesforce, 30
Schultz, Howard, 26
Schweitzer, Albert, 19–20
service innovation examples, 72
slogans, 21–22, 23, 39, 40, 41, 47–49
stage-gate model, 170
strategy, xi, xiv, 43, 55–56
*strategy+business* study, 197
support unit innovations
    challenge question examples, 118–119, 132–133; characteristics, 75–76; goal-setting examples, 145–155; innovation context, 69; measurement examples, 213–214, 220–222, 230–231, 239–240, 250, 252, 258–259, 271–272, 280–281; skills examples, 9–10, 93–99

## T

talent retention, xiii–xiv, 20–21
Tesla, Inc., 21, 29, 61
3M Company, 29–30, 119
Thulin, Inge, 30
training programs, 13

## V

Vagn Jensen, Anna Rose, 156
vision, 16–17, 55–56
visual illustrations, 49–51

## W

Walkers potato chip plant, 73
workforce engagement
    communications for, 39–41, 76, 81; initiatives, 46–51; leadership, xiv–xv
workforce innovation
    idea generation, 135, 158; perspectives, xi, xii–xiii; and skills, xxii, 37–39; systemic, xv, xx
workforces
    expectations, xiii–xiv, 42; motivations, 58–59

## Z

Zuckerberg, Mark, 30–31, 60

www.ingramcontent.com/pod-product-compliance
Lightning Source LLC
Chambersburg PA
CBHW020855180526
45163CB00007B/2507